Baking School

King Arthur Baking Company

ESTD 1790

BAKING COMPANY

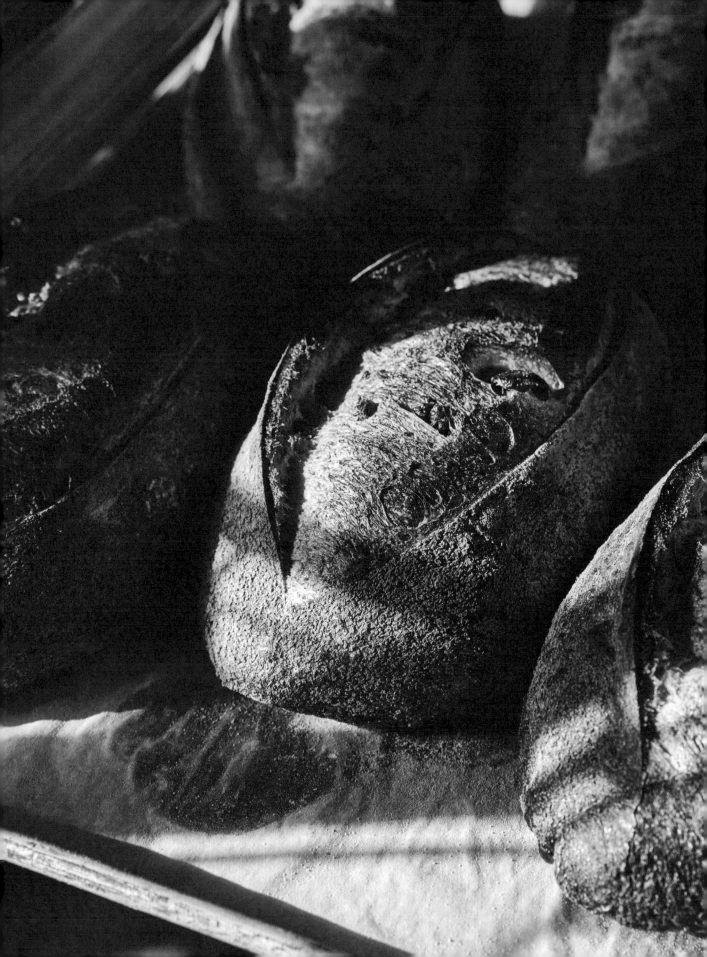

Baking School

LESSONS AND RECIPES FOR EVERY BAKER

Countryman Press

An Imprint of W. W. Norton & Company
Independent Publishers Since 1923

For information about permission to reproduce selections from this book, write to
Permissions, Countryman Press, 500 Fifth Avenue, New York, NY 10110

For information about special discounts for bulk purchases, please contact
W. W. Norton Special Sales at specialsales@wwnorton.com or 800-233-4830

Manufacturing by Toppan Leefung Pte. Ltd.
Book design by Michelle Chen and Ruth Perkins
Photographer: Mark Weinberg
Art director: Allison Chi
Prepress production director: Joe Lops
Production editor: Jess Murphy
Production manager: Devon Zahn

Countryman Press
www.countrymanpress.com

An imprint of W. W. Norton & Company, Inc.
500 Fifth Avenue, New York, NY 10110
www.wwnorton.com

978-1-68268-615-7

10 9 8 7 6 5 4 3 2 1

CONTENTS

WELCOME TO THE

Baking School

In 2000, the King Arthur Baking School opened its doors on our campus in Norwich, Vermont. The school was the longtime vision of Brinna Sands, who was the co-owner of King Arthur along with her husband, Frank. Over the decades since the school opened, we've taught thousands upon thousands of students. We've expanded to the West Coast, opening a campus in Washington State, and held countless private classes in addition to our regular schedule. We've traveled around the country to teach, done classes at conferences and schools, and developed a free baking class program where all the baked goods are donated to local food pantries. In recent years, we've added interactive virtual baking classes to our roster, expanding our baking community even further. We now teach well over 10,000 students each year—reaching all skill levels and covering every baking topic.

We could fill an entire book with the incredible stories and adventures from the people we've met and the communities we've visited over the years! We've had people meet in class and become baking partners, returning together for multiple classes over the years. We even had one couple who met in class and returned a year later to announce (in another class) that they were getting married! That's the power of combining baking and community.

In these pages, we're harnessing that power by passing on the lessons and recipes we've taught for over 20 years. For former students, this book will be a refresher of what they've learned; for future students, it's a primer. But this book is also for all of the people who may never get the chance to attend a King Arthur class in person—with this book in hand, you're one of our students now, too. Welcome. We can't wait to bake together.

Our teaching philosophy

A book can only tell you so much. Baking is a craft—there's a reason recipes are often passed down through generations, as younger people stand and watch experienced bakers work a dough with their hands or mix a batter.

Our philosophy in the classroom mirrors this; baking is a living, breathing thing. So much of the magic of baking is in understanding how ingredients interact, seeing how a dough changes as you knead it or let it sit to allow the yeast to ferment.

Baking is at once both precise and intuitive. So many variables, from your kitchen temperature to the types of ingredients you buy, will affect your results. We aim to empower students with the knowledge and confidence to make baking their own. Often, recipes or cookbooks or classes tell you "what" to do to bake. They treat baking as a set of fixed instructions to follow. We focus instead on the "how" and "why," because by understanding what's occurring as each ingredient goes into the mix, you're better equipped to achieve success. It also allows you to gain a comfort level with baking—you know what's happening! You can tweak as needed! You can troubleshoot problems, customize recipes, and more.

We feel beyond lucky to spend our days spreading the joy of baking to students everywhere. Watching bakers' faces light up when they touch a finger to perfectly risen bread dough or pull a golden pie crust from the oven is a privilege that we never take for granted. So we're thrilled to be able to bring the experience of the classroom into your kitchen through these pages, and we hope this book brings you confidence and true delight in your baking journey, just as the school has for generations of students before you.

How to use this book

When the classroom doors open each day in the Baking School and the students stream in, we know there will be a wide range of knowledge, skill levels, and goals in every class. For this reason, we try to keep the recipes themselves relatively spare so that each student can take the notes that are most pertinent to them, filling in the space around the recipes with the information they hear in class. Beginning bakers may take notes on how to measure and what kind of butter to use, while more advanced bakers jot down tips about shaping or technique. We've structured this book the same way: The recipes are leaner and more streamlined than what you might find in other cookbooks, and explanations about *why* and *how* are written in sidebars so that readers can pick out what they need to know to execute a given recipe. So, if you feel an instruction or additional detail is missing from the recipe, look around and you'll find it nearby. In this way, the book mimics the experience of the classroom: The printed recipes each student receives are bare bones; the bulk of the instruction and guidance comes from

the instructor and the wonderful back-and-forth with students—exactly the information you'll find captured in and around the actual recipes.

The voice of our students informs all of our classes. We listen to requests and focus our education on what students want, choosing recipes that best illustrate techniques they're interested in learning. We don't select a recipe because we think it's the "best" of any particular type (we believe "best" is a pretty subjective judgment). Instead, we select solid, reliable recipes that serve as a lens to illustrate the lessons we teach: We want to teach you what you need to know to make what *you* think is the best! We recognize that will vary enormously from person to person (in fact, we hear that daily in the classroom when we ask people to describe their ideal pie or bread or croissant).

In writing this book, we've stayed true to the recipes chosen for the classroom. When we start to build a new class, there are a number of practical constraints to take into consideration. Timing parameters, oven capacity, ingredient availability,

and the range of skill level in the room are just a few. For instance, we don't teach banana bread. This isn't because we don't love banana bread—we do!—but because it's extremely challenging to get an entire classroom's worth of bananas to ripen to the proper stage at precisely the same time. Another example: We may like the idea of making tuiles in class, but tuiles spread a *lot* on a pan. That means that all 17 students in a class would need their own full sheet pan, and our oven only fits 14 pans at a time, so it would take us twice as long to bake everyone's cookies. We've developed strategies to deal with all of these challenges: The selection, as well as the style and format of our recipes, is the result of those strategies.

In general, our recipes tend to yield smaller quantities than you're apt to find in most cookbooks. This isn't because we're trying to save on ingredients or limit your appetite, but because time is our biggest constraint in the classroom. Keeping the quantities smaller allows us to bake in a shorter time frame so we can fit more recipes in a given class and spend more time engaged

in teaching. If you want to make more, you can double the recipe.

We've sequenced the chapters in the book to flow best through lessons and techniques. We start with **Yeast Breads** because of all the information it offers on how ingredients function in baking and follow it with a chapter on **Sourdough Baking**. Next up, we offer **Laminated Pastries**, some of which use yeasted doughs as part of the process. From lamination, it seemed a simple transition to **Pies and Tarts**, since pies are a form of pastry and there are many commonalities between the two genres. Then, of course, pie crusts are connected to **Cookies** in both technique and texture, so that seemed the logical next step. After cookies, we move into **Quick Breads**, going from biscuits and scones, which share technique and ingredients with pie and cookies, and moving into the sweet quick breads that begin to approach simple cakes. Last but not least, we complete the book with **Cakes**, probably our most technically challenging topic—but one of the most celebratory, too.

Weight or volume?

You'll notice that our recipes are written by weight first, with volume in parentheses. We always weigh ingredients in the classroom unless the quantity is so small that the scales might not measure accurately. For example, ⅛ teaspoon of a spice is difficult to weigh precisely on most standard scales. While we have microgram scales, we recognize that not everyone does, so amounts smaller than 5 grams are listed with volume rather than weights.

Grams are so much more precise than volume measurements and students tend to find weighing ingredients much easier than measuring with cups and teaspoons. Many of our students become avowed fans of the scale after taking our classes. (The promise of less time and fewer dishes is enough to win over most anyone!) A good digital scale can be found for under $50, and you'll swear it's your best baking investment.

In the classroom, we often start our beginner classes by asking all the students to measure a cup of flour and weigh it on the scales at their bench. They call out their weights from around the room and are so surprised to hear that the amounts can vary between fewer than 100 grams to over 160 grams! That's a swing of up to 60%, which can make an enormous difference in a recipe. We tell our students that often people who think they're unsuccessful bakers are actually imprecise measurers. Scales take the measurement variable out of the equation, leaving you to do your best work.

Because our recipes are written by weight, the volume measures are approximations. For instance, gram weights of flour from 110 to 130 grams will all be translated as 1 cup—a scant cup for 110 grams, a generous cup for 130 grams. This can be confusing if you're used to measuring by volume; it's another reason why we strongly urge you to use a scale, as it'll ensure precision and set you up for success.

The bench

One moment that every student remembers vividly is stepping into the classroom and seeing the setup. We refer to the workstation in front of each student as "the bench"—here students will find the ingredients and equipment that they'll need for the class ahead. Pastry classes might have pastry blenders and whisks; bread classes might have loaf pans and proofing baskets; cake classes might have mixers and cake flour. We'll cover some important information about our general approach to ingredients and equipment in this introduction, but you'll find more specific information on both in each chapter's introduction: Each chapter covers the key ingredients and equipment that we use most during that particular class.

Our ingredient philosophy

Buy the highest-quality ingredients you can. In the classroom, we source our ingredients locally whenever possible, including seasonal fruits and vegetables, as well as local dairy products. When you're putting in the time and effort to bake something, it's worth using the best: real vanilla extract, real maple syrup, fresh butter, high-quality chocolate, and of course, good flour. What follows is a list of the ingredients you'll likely find at your bench when attending a class at the Baking School.

BUTTER

We always use **unsalted butter**. Students often ask why we don't just use salted butter if we're adding salt anyway, which is an excellent question. The main reason is that the amount of salt added to **salted butter** can vary considerably by brand, and there's no way to know how much salt you're really adding. Using unsalted butter and adding salt separately allows us to regulate with more precision how much salt we're adding to a recipe. In addition, salted butter generally has a higher water content than unsalted butter, which can affect your final product. Some of our recipes, particularly those in the laminated chapter, call for **European-style butter**, which has a higher fat content, making it somewhat more pliable and easier to work with when laminating.

EGGS

For our recipes, eggs are always large. If the recipe calls for room-temperature eggs and yours are cold from the fridge, place them in a bowl of hot tap water for 10 minutes before using.

FLOUR

Our recipes are formulated to work with King Arthur flours. That's what we use in the classroom, of course, and we know our recipes will

work with our flour. Most of our recipes are developed to use King Arthur's unbleached all-purpose flour because we know its specs are consistent. (By "spec," we mean "specification," which here refers to the guidelines our mills have to follow when milling our flour. King Arthur has some of the strictest specs in the industry—when you buy a bag of King Arthur flour, it will always have a protein content that falls in a very, very tight range, which means the flour will perform consistently. Other brands have a much wider allowable range, so they can yield variable results even if you do the exact same thing.)

Another reason we call for all-purpose flour is accessibility. It's easy to find in stores across the country. We understand that there's not always universal access to all our specialty flours, so we strive to offer suggestions for alternatives where appropriate. If you can't find King Arthur all-purpose flour, please make sure to use unbleached all-purpose flour, particularly in any bread recipe. Bleached flours have had the carotenoids removed, removing the potential for flavor in the process, so your bread simply won't taste the same. Many of our artisan bread recipes encourage gentle mixing to baby the carotenoids, giving your loaves a creamy color and full flavor.

King Arthur sells two types of whole wheat flour—**white whole wheat** and **traditional whole wheat**—and that's often a source of confusion. The flours are virtually interchangeable. They're just two different types of wheat—red (traditional) and white (lighter in color and flavor). The white whole wheat is not a partially white flour or a GMO flour—it's simply a naturally occurring type of wheat with a lower amount of phenolic acid than you find in red wheat, giving it a lighter color and flavor. It's a nice "entry-level" whole wheat flour, as it tastes more like all-purpose than traditional whole wheat.

In this book, as in our classrooms, you'll encounter a few other types of flour: **bread flour**, which is higher in protein content, giving it the potential to form a stronger gluten network; this is ideal for creating high-rising loaves with an even crumb. Our **high-gluten flour** (also called Lancelot when sold in 50-pound bags) is even higher in protein and is wonderful for achieving a pronounced chew, as in bagels (page 40). A few of our cake recipes call for **unbleached cake flour**, but we offer suggestions for alternatives, as cake flour is still most commonly found in bleached form. If you have questions about any of our flours or about flour education in general, visit www.kingarthurbaking.com for more information.

SALT

Some of the most common questions we hear from students are "Which salt do I use?" and "Can I leave out the salt?" We use table salt for our recipes, which is what we recommend for success since it disperses and dissolves quickly and easily. We occasionally call for a larger-flake sea salt as a garnish in recipes where its flavor will stand out. You can remove the salt from most recipes (with the exception of yeast breads) without affecting the structure or texture, but salt is the key to flavor, allowing other flavors to shine, and you'll notice a very obvious difference without it. Baked goods will taste "flat" without salt. Salt acts as a functional ingredient in yeast breads: It's often around 2% of the flour weight, so we don't recommend omitting salt in bread recipes, as it will affect structure and performance.

SUGAR

Most often our recipes call for **granulated sugar**—it's widely available and serves an important function in the creaming step. The **brown sugar** we use in the classroom is almost always light brown sugar: If the recipe doesn't specify, that's what we're using. You can exchange light and dark brown sugar in most recipes with only a slight change in flavor and texture. Dark brown sugar contains more molasses, so it will add a more pronounced molasses flavor and a slightly denser texture. On occasion we use **confectioners' sugar**, also referred to as powdered sugar. Most confectioners' sugar has some sort of starch added to it to limit clumping. We also love our **sparkling sugar**, which maintains its glitter and crunch under the heat of the oven, making it a beautiful garnish that adds texture to things like scones and muffins. Sugar binds with liquid in recipes and thereby keeps the products to which it's added moist and tender.

VANILLA

We use King Arthur's blend of Tahitian and Madagascar vanilla in the classroom. There are many varieties of vanilla extract, which have slightly different flavor notes (Tahitian tends to be more floral, Mexican more earthy, and so on). The variety you use is less important; what matters is that you use the real thing! Again, you're putting in the time and effort to make something from scratch—don't shortchange the outcome with your ingredient choice. Vanilla, though called for in very small quantities, is a noticeable addition. This is especially true in recipes where vanilla is *the* prominent flavor but it also gives a boost to other flavors, so is a wonderful addition to many "non-vanilla" recipes.

Our equipment

We try to keep the equipment lists for our classes as lean as possible. This is partly a space issue, which is definitely a constraint that's also applicable to most home bakers' kitchens! Working at a baking supply company is a dangerous proposition for dedicated bakers—many of us joke about the degree to which our paychecks are recycled back into the company. Over time, though, we realize we simply don't have the space at home for yet another set of measuring cups or one more shape of Bundt pan, enticing as they may be! There's a sense of accomplishment that comes from baking efficiently without an excess of equipment.

Those guidelines translate directly to our classrooms and our recipes. In some situations, we call for a very specific tool or pan—but it's rare that no other substitute will suffice. We try to offer alternatives, particularly with pan shapes and sizes, so that you can make do with what you have. Our goal is to make baking as accessible as possible to as many people as possible. Making it simple to do helps us reach more of you. With that in mind, there are a few items we include at every station to make it easy for students to have the tool they need at hand.

In every class, you'll see a **dough scraper** and a **bench knife**. We use the dough scrapers to mix and turn out most doughs and scrape batter out of bowls. The bench knives have multiple applications, too—they help with folding and dividing doughs, with keeping your bench clean while you work, and even serve as a handy guide for measuring on the fly.

We provide a set of **measuring spoons** for those ingredients that are added in smaller increments, such as yeast and spices. A good, flexible **rubber spatula** is so helpful for most recipes, along with a sturdy metal **balloon whisk** for mixing both wet and dry ingredients. We use **heat-resistant spoons** in the school for stirring ingredients as we heat them.

Our classrooms are equipped with heavy **full-size sheet pans**, and we line them with **parchment paper** because it makes our baking lives so much simpler. We think you'll find it saves you time and effort, too.

We also have so many other more specialized pieces of equipment, from **stand mixers** to **biscuit cutters**, **linen couches** to **pastry bags**, but we list those in the chapters in which they're most applicable so you can evaluate your need for them based on the baking you do. When using a stand mixer, always use the paddle (flat beater) attachment unless the recipe specifically states otherwise.

As we've pivoted into offering more online classes, we've become particularly adept at "making it work" with whatever home bakers have on hand. We try to avoid teaching recipes that require a very niche utensil because we don't ever want that to be a true obstacle for bakers at home.

Perhaps the one exception to this philosophy—and the *single* piece of equipment we'd most recommend—is a good **digital scale** (see page xvi).

WHAT'S A

"Master Class"?

From the very first days of the school, guest instructors have played an enormous role. Most of our classes are taught by our wonderful in-house roster of King Arthur teachers, but we also regularly hold classes taught by exceptionally talented guest instructors—most often professional pastry chefs or bakery owners—on a range of topics. Their classes offer our students the opportunity to stretch themselves by learning from the best in the world, and we've included a few recipes from these guest instructors in this book. These "Master Classes" build upon each chapter's skills, allowing you to apply what you've just learned to a new idea or baked good. These instructors are bona fide experts in their field and very particular about how they approach their craft. Each guest instructor brings their own individual voice and perspective, and you'll notice that variation in the wording and approach of the Master Class recipes—that's part of the magic of having them visit the school, and we've deliberately chosen to preserve that here, offering you a chance to learn from their diverse teaching styles just as our students do.

Acknowledgments

Every King Arthur book is a team effort and that's probably most true with this book, which reflects the work of King Arthur teams through the more than 20 years since the school began. Over those years the company has changed dramatically: we've grown tremendously, signed up as a founding B Corp, and become 100% employee owned. We even changed our name to reflect the shifting culture of our company and our commitment to baking and education.

The Baking School personifies that commitment. We're fortunate to have had instructors who brought their passion for teaching to our curriculum development: Judy Ulinski, Wendi Krishock, Rosemary Hubbard, Richard Miscovich, Robyn Sargent, and Melanie Wanders to name just a few. The many instructors we've had over the years, both internal and external, have each left their imprint on what we do in the classroom, as collaboration has always been central to the school's operation.

For this project, in particular, we're incredibly grateful to the Baking School instructors—especially Melanie Wanders, Becca Regier, and Jessica Meyers—and to Amber Eisler, the school's director, all of whom took time out of very busy lives to offer their expertise in building and reviewing the book. The chapters couldn't have taken shape without the careful eyes of our readers, including Rossi Anastopoulo and Leah Starr, who offered feedback to keep us on track. PJ Hamel and Susan Reid lent their invaluable wisdom and experience in testing and editing recipes.

Ruth Perkins, Michelle Chen, and Mark Weinberg are responsible for the stunning photography and design of this book, and the talented Lydia Fournier was our food stylist. We were so lucky to have the experience of Ann Treistman and Allison Chi, our capable, forward-thinking editor and designer, respectively, at Countryman Press. Chris McLeod and David Tamarkin guided this project with steady hands and thoughtful oversight. Posie Brien, the lead writer for the book, deliberated over each word that appears in its pages.

The Baking School owes its existence to Frank and Brinna Sands and to Jeffrey Hamelman, who had the vision and perseverance to bring it to life.

Last and most important, we're profoundly grateful to all our students—every one of you who walked through the classroom doors has taught us so much.

—THE KING ARTHUR BAKING SCHOOL

chapter 1.

YEAST BREADS

The Classroom

Welcome! We're so pleased you've chosen to embark on the journey of baking bread with us. Along with most students in our yeast bread classes, you're likely eager to understand what it takes to make great bread and how to demystify the process. The beauty of yeast breads lies in their simplicity: The humble combination of flour, water, yeast, and salt yields so many different—and exceptional—results. Whether you're a newcomer flouring your hands for the first time or a seasoned expert, we hope you'll find a useful takeaway to help you become a better bread baker.

We cover a wide range of yeast breads in our classes, but we recommend starting with our Basic Bread class because it contains so much information about the function of ingredients. For this same reason, we begin our chapter with Basic Bread, a sandwich bread made with the straight dough method where all the ingredients are mixed together at once. We then move through a variety of straight dough breads to illustrate principles such as enrichments, flour substitution, and the effects of shaping. From these simpler breads, we proceed to pre-fermented loaves, where part of the flour is fermented ahead of time to add flavor to the bread (see page 42).

We end our chapter with a Master Class on Unkneaded Six-Fold French Bread (Baguette) from Jeffrey Hamelman, the former director of our bakery. Our "Beauty and the Baguette" class is the most popular of our yeast bread classes because bakers leave with a profound respect for the skill and time it takes to master such a seemingly simple bread. Jeffrey's recipe offers a straightforward technique you can practice repeatedly to develop your skill in baking this challenging bread.

In this chapter, as in our classes, we emphasize the underlying *how* and *why*. Understanding the function of each ingredient is essential for success. Baking yeast bread requires precision, but it also requires you to use your senses to develop a baker's intuition. Factors such as humidity, temperature, kneading time, and how much flour you use for dusting will each affect your dough. Seeing the connection between the characteristics of the dough and the finished bread will help you develop your baking instincts. These recipes are guidelines; our aim as teachers is to provide you with the knowledge you need to follow those guidelines confidently and to help you develop the skills you need to bake exactly the breads you envision.

The Lessons

The curriculum in our yeast bread classes emphasizes concept and technique through the following lessons. Each recipe is an opportunity to see these lessons in action. In this chapter, as in bread class, our goals are for you to:

- Understand the function of ingredients and the role of gluten in yeast breads

- Mix and knead dough by hand and mixer, using both traditional and wet-dough kneading methods

- Shape breads using pan and free-form methods

- Practice scoring loaves

- Identify when dough has reached each stage: developed, risen, proofed, and baked

- Assess the baked bread—crust, crumb, aroma, flavor, and texture—and observe the connections between technique/ingredients and the baked loaf

KEY INGREDIENTS

The ingredient list for yeast breads tends to be quite short, often as few as four ingredients (flour, water, yeast, and salt), though enriched breads will include such fats as butter and eggs, dairy, and often sugar. As with all baking, but especially here, we strongly encourage you to weigh your ingredients—particularly your flour, as too much or too little is often the culprit when problems arise.

FLOUR

Perhaps more than *anywhere* else in this book, it's essential to understand the impact of your choice of flour. Wheat flour has two different types of proteins, glutenin and gliadin, which contribute to the dough's elasticity and strength. These proteins are activated by liquid. Once you add water to flour, the proteins combine and begin forming a gluten network. The resulting grid traps the carbon dioxide bubbles given off during yeast fermentation. Mixing your dough by kneading, stirring, or folding will speed the formation of those gluten networks. The more you mix your dough, the stronger the gluten structure becomes.

We primarily use all-purpose flour, but some of our recipes call for bread flour or high-gluten flour. These flours have a higher protein content, meaning more potential for gluten to form; this adds structure to doughs and can help offset the addition of non-gluten-producing ingredients. These higher-protein flours often require a mixer to fully develop the gluten. Another notable characteristic of higher-protein flours is that they are "thirstier": They absorb more water; thus, recipes using bread flour will have higher hydration levels. If you swap in bread flour for all-purpose flour in a recipe that calls for the latter, you'll likely need to compensate by adding a bit more liquid.

Introducing whole grains affects your dough, too. Whole-grain flours include the nutritious germ and the bran (the tough outer covering of the wheat berry). Those sharp pieces of bran can cut the gluten strands as they form, causing the dough to lose structure. This is one reason whole-grain breads can be dense. That doesn't mean you can't use whole grains and still have a high-rising, nicely textured bread; often whole-grain recipes rely on increased hydration and a resting period to soften the bran, and the addition of higher protein flours to stabilize the gluten structure and maintain the rise.

These are the functional ingredients we focus on as teaching points during our yeast bread classes—and what students find waiting at the bench. For more on our ingredient philosophy, please see page xix.

LIQUID

Liquid is essential in bread dough. When we talk about a dough's hydration level, we mean the ratio of liquid to flour: A dough with 100% hydration has equal parts by weight, not volume, of flour and liquid. Adding liquid to flour is what creates a dough and triggers gluten formation. It also serves as a dispersing agent for salt, sugar, and yeast. Wetter doughs ferment more quickly than dry ones. Wetter doughs are also softer, stickier, and more difficult to work with. Adding extra liquid opens up the gluten structure, creating more space for the carbon dioxide bubbles, so you can end up with airier breads like ciabatta with its large pockets and open crumb.

SALT

If you've ever left the salt out of your bread dough accidentally, you know firsthand what a critical component it is (see page 102 for a different method of adding salt). Salt is essential to taste, as in all baking, but in yeast bread it also performs the following critical functions:

- Tightens the gluten structure, allowing the dough to efficiently hold carbon dioxide given off as the yeast ferments. If you don't add salt, the dough will be slack, sticky, and hard to handle, and the bread won't have as much volume.

- Regulates fermentation: Salt is hygroscopic, meaning it attracts moisture. When salt is added to yeast dough, the yeast reacts by releasing some of its water. This slows the yeast's fermentation since yeast needs water to function. Slowing down the yeast might seem like a bad thing, but if you don't keep the fermentation in check, the dough won't have much rise left to give by the time your bread makes it to the oven. In the absence of salt, the yeast also consumes too much of

the sugars, leaving a loaf that's flatter, paler, and less flavorful as a result of the overly fast fermentation.

YEAST

Yeast is a living organism, and just like all living things, it requires proper conditions to thrive and promote fermentation in dough. If you provide the right moisture, food, and temperature, then the yeast can do its job of converting sugars into carbon dioxide, organic acids, and alcohol.

Our recipes call for instant yeast, which can be used interchangeably with active dry yeast. To extend its shelf life, store it in the freezer. Recipes used to require you to "proof" your yeast to check that it was active and to disperse it evenly in your dough. Yeast is now formulated such that you can skip that step, though you'll want to remember to include any liquid that was part of that step.

ENRICHING INGREDIENTS

For enriched doughs, such as sweet breads and brioche, you'll see the addition of fats (typically butter or sometimes olive oil), sweeteners, dairy, and eggs. Fats add tenderness and flavor. Sweeteners promote browning and tenderness and add some keeping quality—the most common are sugar, honey, and maple syrup. For the purposes of substitutions, we consider sugar to be a liquid ingredient, so you can swap it 1:1 by weight for honey or maple syrup in breads. When it comes to dairy, we use whole milk in the school, but you can use whatever you have, including dairy-free alternatives. If your recipe calls for eggs, know that they'll make your dough feel stickier: It's not a bad thing, but something to keep in mind as you handle it.

THE EQUIPMENT

Bread is one of the most elemental of all categories of baking—just your hands and a baking surface are all you need to make a simple loaf. As you move beyond the basics, we recommend a few pieces of equipment to help you bake your best.

BAKING SURFACES

There are many shaping options beyond a pan loaf, most of which need to be placed on a surface for baking. Baking stones or steels work well here: They hold and transfer heat efficiently, helping achieve a well-baked crust without overbaking the interior. If you don't have either, a Dutch oven or a baking sheet will work well. For hearth breads, you'll find that a baking peel and high-quality parchment paper are very useful to have on hand.

BENCH KNIFE

A good, sturdy bench knife is a boon when working with sticky dough. The sharp edge is useful for scraping down counters and dividing dough.

BOWL SCRAPERS

These flexible tools are soft enough to follow the contours of your bowl to scrape out dough but stiff enough to mix doughs together, scrape off dried dough on countertops, divide doughs, and more.

BOWLS

Start with a bigger bowl than you think you'll need since your dough will rise. We use lightweight metal bowls in the school, which is a practical choice we recommend to everyone.

COUCHE

A couche is a piece of unbleached linen canvas used to support freeform loaves as they proof. They help the dough hold its shape as it rises and absorb a bit of moisture from the dough surface. Since a drier surface is easier to cut than a tacky one, this helps provide a more defined score for the finished loaf. If you don't have a couche, use a lightly floured tea towel instead.

COVERS

While your dough is rising and proofing, you'll need to cover it to protect it from drying out. You can use plastic wrap, a reusable bowl cover, or even a large bowl flipped upside down: anything to cover the dough loosely and keep it protected.

PANS

For yeast breads baked in a loaf pan rather than directly on a a baking stone or standard baking sheet, we use standard-size (8½″ × 4½″) metal pans. For rolls, 8″ or 9″ metal pans are ideal.

PROOFING BASKETS

Called bannetons or brotforms, these baskets (usually made from cane or wicker) support your dough during the final proof as the gluten relaxes and spreads a bit. A bowl lined with a lightly floured flat-weave cloth also works well.

SCALE

All of our recipes are written by weight first, which is how we urge students to bake, so a good digital scale is essential. This is true in all our classes, but we emphasize it for bread bakers. Bread has very few ingredients, so getting the amounts right makes all the difference in yielding a dough with the right texture and feel. You'll need to rely on tactile and visual cues to adjust for your own environment, but starting with the precise amount of ingredients called for will set you on the right path to success, allowing you to tweak as needed.

Commonly Asked Questions

HOW LONG SHOULD MY DOUGH RISE?

Timing depends on the conditions in your kitchen and how warm your dough is. The timings in recipes are guidelines: If your kitchen is warmer or cooler, that will speed or slow the process, so time is less reliable than your own observations of the dough. When checking whether your bread has risen enough, gently press on it with the pad of a floured finger. It should feel very light but not fragile. We say it should feel "marshmallow-y." The indentation from your finger will slowly rebound but may not rebound all the way. If it feels quite bouncy, and the indentation rebounds immediately, give it more time to rise. See page 16 for more about visual and tactile cues.

WHAT IF I UNDERPROOF OR OVERPROOF MY DOUGH?

If you press gently on your shaped dough and it *does* feel quite fragile, it may be slightly overrisen. There's no way to reverse this, but don't despair entirely. If it's at the point of collapse, you can reshape it and proof it again before baking. This will yield a less than perfect loaf but can salvage a batch that might otherwise be inedible. If it still has some life to it but feels overrisen, bake it right away and treat it as a lesson. Every batch of bread teaches you something! Assessing the baked loaf can inform the rise the next time around. If you have a smaller loaf with an area that ripped open on the sides or top, it was likely underrisen and kept expanding after the crust set. If it comes out flat, a bit collapsed, or if your sandwich loaf has a very large bubble just beneath the top crust, these are signs that it was a little overrisen. Make a note for next time. Training your hands to feel the differences in under- and overrisen dough can take practice but is well worth the effort, and you'll usually still have tasty bread to eat between practices.

CAN I USE A MIXER?

Absolutely! We teach making dough by hand as it trains your hands to feel the stages of dough development, and we find it enjoyable. That said, using a mixer will do the job nicely if it's what you need or want. Take care not to mix your dough on high speeds, as most home mixers aren't built for that, and you'll lose flavor and texture by overoxygenating your dough.

DID I KNEAD MY DOUGH TOO MUCH?

In general, overkneading is less of a danger than underkneading. The purpose of kneading is to develop the gluten in the dough, and if you're kneading by hand, it would take a lot of elbow grease to overdevelop the gluten. The bigger risk is that the longer you knead the more flour you add, resulting in a dry dough that won't rise well in the oven.

CAN I CUSTOMIZE THESE RECIPES?

There's not much that can beat the flavor of homemade yeast bread pulled fresh from the oven! It's understandable, though, that as your skill grows, you'll be interested in trying your hand at some variations, and as long as you observe a few practical considerations, it's fun to experiment. You could start by rolling your basic bread dough around a swirl of cinnamon and raisins, or mixing caraway seeds and cheese into your soft pretzel dough, or adding orange zest and cardamom to your tender sweet bread. Just keep in mind that if you're adding such ingredients as nuts or dried fruit or seeds, you're adding an item that the gluten network has to support, so you might not get quite the same amount of rise. If you do want more rise, you can try substituting bread flour for some of the all-purpose to compensate for the additional ingredients, but remember you'll also need a bit more liquid because bread flour is higher in protein, so it requires higher hydration. There are also a few ingredients that inhibit fermentation when added directly to the dough: cinnamon and other tree bark spices (hence the swirl in cinnamon breads) and garlic (one reason why garlic is used on the already baked bread), among others.

HOW DO I PROOF MY BREAD?

We get lots of questions about proofing at home. The ideal location is somewhere that is 75° to 80°F, where your dough is protected. Strategies include anything from gently covering the dough with a tea towel, to putting a cup of hot water in the microwave with your rising loaf (don't turn it on!), to using a baking sheet filled with hot water and a cooling rack to set your bread on, then inverting a box or plastic tub over the top. If you can't figure out how to make a spot that warm, don't worry—your bread will just rise a bit more slowly.

TIME

People think of baking bread as very time consuming, but much of that time is inactive for you. That's one of the secrets of baking: You can weave the baking around your life and your life around the baking. Even if you don't have to be busy *with* it, the dough is busy! The actual hands-on time is interspersed with longer periods of rest while the dough rises. Most yeast breads have at least two periods of rising, when nothing is required from you. Bakers refer to the *first rise* or *bulk fermentation*: This is when the dough has been mixed but not yet shaped (still in "bulk" form as one big mass). Once the dough has been shaped, it has a second—usually shorter—rise called *proofing* (not to be confused with proofing the yeast; see page 7).

You might be tempted to adjust the recipe's timetable to fit into your schedule by sticking your dough in the refrigerator overnight. This will work if the recipe already calls for a longer rise (2 hours or more); if it calls for a shorter and faster rise, you likely have a higher amount of yeast in your dough, and letting it sit overnight will yield a very yeasty flavor. If you *do* want to let it rise overnight, dial back the yeast a bit.

Cool It!

It's so tempting to slice immediately into warm bread, just as you slide it out of the oven. Resist this urge! It's important to let your bread cool fully before slicing: As the bread cools, moisture continues to leave the loaf. Why? As bread bakes, the starch molecules swell and become waterlogged. After you remove it from the oven, the molecules reform as that moisture evaporates, becoming firmer. In the long run, this process is what causes bread to go hard and stale. But in the short term, it's a good thing: It sets the interior crumb. If you cut into your bread too soon, you risk finding a gummy interior that's easily compressed by the knife. Always allow your bread to cool fully on a rack; if your bread was baked in a pan, turn the bread out of the pan immediately after baking.

Basic Bread

Yield: 2 loaves

Mixing, kneading, rising, shaping, proofing: These are basic steps you'll want to master to bake almost every kind of yeast bread. This simple recipe, which we've used to teach thousands of students to bake bread, makes a pair of lovely, golden loaves with medium grain—perfect for slicing when baked as a pan loaf. It's the starting point for bread baking and one of the most important foundational recipes in our classroom. We use it to demonstrate the feel of kneading by hand so you can see how the dough changes from a rough and shaggy mass to a smooth and silky developed dough as you work with it. *(See photo on page 13.)*

---

624 to 680 grams (5¼ to 5⅔ cups) unbleached all-purpose flour

35 grams (¼ cup) dry milk powder

12 grams (1 tablespoon) granulated sugar

7 grams (2¼ teaspoons) instant yeast

12 grams (2 teaspoons) salt

28 grams (2 tablespoons) unsalted butter, room temperature

472 grams (2 cups) water

Tip: In place of dry milk powder, you may replace 1 cup of the water with milk. Scalded and cooled milk will yield the best final volume; nonscalded milk will still be fine.

1. In a medium to large bowl, combine 624 grams (5¼ cups) of the flour with the milk powder, sugar, yeast, and salt.

2. Cut the butter into small pieces and stir into the dry ingredients.

3. Pour the water into the mixture and stir to make a cohesive mass.

4. Lightly flour your work surface with some of the remaining flour, then turn the dough out of the bowl onto the floured surface. Make sure you keep your hands well floured.

5. Knead the dough by picking up the far edge and folding it in half toward you. Press the dough with the palms of your hands and push lightly, down and away from you. Rotate the dough 90 degrees. Start off more gently than you think you should.

6. Continue this process (fold, push, turn) until the dough is smooth and springy, about 5 minutes. It will still feel slightly tacky. Handle the dough very gently at first, and as it increases in strength, increase the pressure. Keep your work surface scraped clean (a bench knife works well here), and if the dough sticks, sprinkle the surface lightly with flour. You want the outside to feel tacky while the inside remains sticky.

7. Allow the dough to rise in a covered bowl (no need to grease it) until it's doubled in bulk, about 1 hour.

Tip: See page 52 for temperature guidance.

8. After the dough has risen, turn it out onto a lightly floured surface and pat it down gently to deflate (de-gas) it. Divide the dough in half and form into your desired shapes (see page 56).

9. Cover the loaves and allow them to rise until puffy and not quite doubled in volume, about 45 to 90 minutes depending on room temperature.

10. Bake the bread in a preheated 375°F oven for 30 to 35 minutes, until the crust is golden brown.

VISUAL CUES

The best way to learn to bake bread is to observe: Visual and tactile cues are the most important way to know when your dough is ready at each stage. The time it takes to properly knead, rise, and proof your dough will depend on your specific environment, so rather than give you an exact time for each step, learn to use your senses to identify each stage. This can be challenging at first, but the more you bake, the more you'll understand how the dough progresses through these stages.

KNEADING: Most recipes will instruct you to knead until "properly developed" or "fully developed" and occasionally "moderately developed." That's because as you knead, you're developing the gluten in the dough. Here's why and what to look for:

- As you fold and work it, the dough will start to form a ball. The dough begins to feel *alive*; as you push it, it moves and expands. It's dynamic: The dough will be relatively smooth and should feel elastic. As you work it into a ball, push into it with the side of your hand and it should spring back at you. If your hands get sticky as you knead, resist the temptation to wash your hands—that will just make the dough stickier. Instead, give them a light dusting of flour, rub them together to get rid of the sticky bits, and carry on. (We call this a "flour wash.")

- What you're looking for in a fully or properly developed dough is one that has some muscle to it. You'll feel the dough go from rough and marbly to very smooth. If you grab a handful (a real handful!), it shouldn't tear immediately but should pull back. Use the "doorbell test": Press the dough lightly with a floured fingertip, and it should bounce back quickly.

RISING AND PROOFING: Rather than time—which varies a *lot* based on temperature— the best gauges of readiness for both the rising and proofing stages are look and feel. Again, you can use the "doorbell test": Press the dough lightly with a floured fingertip. The dough should leave an indent and then spring back slowly (see photo on opposite page). If it springs back quickly, it needs more time. If the indentation remains without springing back, it's gone too far.

  The dough should look and feel light, gassy, and full of air; it shouldn't be collapsed but should feel "marshmallow-y." You're aiming for fluffy but not fragile. The dough at both stages should have increased considerably in volume, but it won't always double in size, so we urge you to rely more heavily on the tactile cues. If the dough is fragile, the gluten network is close to collapsing, which will yield dense, heavy bread.

  If your kitchen is cold, and you're concerned about the time it'll take to proof properly, try to create a warm, moist environment (see page 11) to ensure the dough is at the optimal temperature.

HOW TO KNOW WHEN BREAD IS DONE

There are a few instances where we may use a digital thermometer to assess doneness, but many breads will reach the technical "finished" internal temperature well before they have achieved the bake we would like. Bakers have been using their senses to determine doneness for centuries, and that's our method, too. Your sense of smell is the first indicator: Your kitchen starts to smell delicious!

Color is another important indication. Pay attention to the area of the bread that is taking on color last, whether that's along a mark you've scored on the crust or where the strands of a braid meet. Some color variation is normal, but you want that lovely golden brown "finished" color to extend well into that final area.

Don't be afraid of color: Allowing your bread to bake fully is important for both the interior and exterior. You want the interior crumb nicely baked for its own sake, but also because excess moisture in the interior damages the crust as it leaves the loaf, making it tough and gummy.

As bread bakes, the natural sugars in the dough are caramelizing and creating that beautiful baked color. Some breads contain added sugar and will caramelize more. Breads with pre-ferments often have a richer color: The enzymes activated during fermentation convert starches into sugar, so there's more available for caramelization.

Touch is another key. Gently squeeze the sides of the bread. Breads baked in pans should have good structure and well-established sides, and crusty artisan bread should feel very hard and crisp. Don't be concerned if it feels *too* hard—it should: Breads will soften some as they cool, as the moisture continues to leave the loaf.

Pick up the loaf to gauge the weight. It will feel lighter than it looks. Some bakers who bake hundreds of loaves a day like to use their hearing to check for a hollow sound, and while thumping on the bottom of a loaf of bread is pretty fun, the difference can be extremely subtle, and it's hard to train your ears on one or two loaves at a time.

We can't overstate how much practice helps here, too: The more bread you bake, the better attuned your senses will be to when it's ready.

ASSESSMENT

Once you've determined that your bread is done, it's time to taste and assess. This is a crucial step in your baking education and a fundamental step in our classes to understand how each piece of the recipe process affects the final loaf. This is why it can be very helpful to take notes as you're baking, so you can make the connection between your method and the final result and can make adjustments on your next batch.

SMELL: Your bread should smell amazing! If it smells very yeasty, that can be a sign that it overproofed or wasn't fully baked.

RISE: Look at the height of your bread. Did it rise as expected, or too high, or not enough? This is connected with the oven spring, which is the initial burst of growth of your dough when it hits the oven, before the crust sets. If your dough has overproofed, there won't be much spring left when it goes in the oven. If it's shredded along the sides, that can be an indication it went into the oven before it was fully proofed.

CRUMB: Assessing the crumb structure will tell you whether the dough was properly kneaded, properly hydrated, and properly risen and proofed. Is it dense? Maybe it didn't get enough water or wasn't kneaded sufficiently. Open and airy? This is wonderful in an artisan loaf but may not be what you're after in a sandwich loaf. You might cut back on liquid if you're looking for a finer crumb. Tender or tough? This can be an indication of the volume or type of flour used, or whether or not the dough was properly kneaded.

FLAVOR: Taste it! Notice the flavor and see how you like it. Does it have a pleasant flavor of fermentation? How's the salt? You can adjust up or down next time you bake.

HOW TO STORE BREAD

If you don't eat your freshly baked bread immediately, you'll want to try to keep it from going stale. Here's why staling happens: As the bread bakes, the starch granules in the flour swell with moisture, gelatinizing and losing their rigid structure. This makes the bread soft. Over time, those starch granules undergo a process called retrogradation: The starches begin to firm up and become rigid again, causing breads to get hard and lose flavor. To keep your bread fresh for as long as possible, never store it in the refrigerator, which speeds up that starch retrogradation. Bread is best kept wrapped tightly at room temperature or in the freezer for longer storage. If you like, you may slice your bread beforehand if freezing it.

Tender Sweet Bread

Yield: 2 loaves

We've taught this bread since the school opened in 2000 because we love its versatility. We move from a basic bread to an enriched bread by adding more sugar, butter, and milk, as well as eggs. These additions make for a wonderfully tender dough that's easily transformed into a variety of shapes. We start by showing you how to make two braids with the dough, but the shaping possibilities are endless, from cinnamon rolls to a spectacular six-strand braid. Two of our more popular shaping variations follow this recipe.

DOUGH

690 to 720 grams (5¾ to 6 cups) unbleached all-purpose flour

100 grams (½ cup) granulated sugar

35 grams (¼ cup) dry milk powder

9 grams (1 tablespoon) instant yeast

14 grams (2¼ teaspoons) salt

56 grams (4 tablespoons) unsalted butter, room temperature

2 large eggs

315 grams (1⅓ cups) water

10 grams (2 teaspoons) vanilla extract

EGG WASH

1 large egg

15 grams (1 tablespoon) water

⅛ teaspoon salt

DOUGH

1. In a large bowl, combine 690 grams (5¾ cups) of the flour with the sugar, milk powder, yeast, and salt. Mix well.

2. Work the butter into the flour mixture until it's evenly dispersed, then stir in the eggs, water, and vanilla.

3. Sprinkle your work surface with some of the remaining flour and turn the dough out onto it, scraping out the bowl thoroughly.

4. Knead the dough, using only enough flour to keep it from sticking. The dough should be soft, pliable, and tacky but not wet or sticky.

5. When the dough is springy and begins to smooth out, place it back in the bowl, cover, and set in a warm place (75° to 78°F) until nearly doubled in size, about 60 to 90 minutes.

Tip: If you press it with a floured fingertip and it leaves residue on your finger, that's sticky. If you press on it, and it feels sticky but doesn't leave residue, that's tacky.

(Continued) →

6. Turn the risen dough out onto a lightly floured surface. Divide and preshape lightly into six equal cylinders (see page 25), then cover and let rest for 15 to 30 minutes.

7. Roll three of the cylinders into 18-inch-long strands and braid (see opposite page). Repeat for the other loaf. Place the braids on parchment-lined or lightly greased baking sheets, cover, and proof until puffy, about 30 to 40 minutes.

EGG WASH AND BAKING

1. In a small bowl whisk together the egg, water, and salt until well combined. Brush over the braids and bake in a preheated 375°F oven for 25 to 30 minutes, until they're a rich golden brown.

> ### VARIATION: RASPBERRY MOCK BRAID

Place one half of the risen dough on a lightly floured surface, and, using a lightly floured rolling pin, roll it into a rectangle approximately 16″ × 9″. Spread 170 grams (½ cup) raspberry jam in a 3″-wide ribbon down the length of the dough, leaving 1″ of clear space at both shorter ends. On each long side, cut the same number of 1″-wide strips from the edge of the filling to the outer edge of the dough. Fold the two short ends of the dough over, and starting at one end, bring the strips across the filling on a diagonal, alternating from side to side like a two-stranded braid. Transfer to a parchment-lined baking sheet. Cover and let rise in a warm place until puffy, about 30 to 40 minutes. Brush the braid with egg wash and bake as directed above.

> ### VARIATION: POPPY TWIST (PICTURED ON PAGE 20)

Stir together 177 grams (a generous ½ cup) canned poppy seed filling, 15 grams (1 table-spoon) egg white, and the zest of ½ lemon or orange (or ⅛ teaspoon lemon or orange oil). Set aside. Place one half of the risen dough on a lightly floured work surface. Using a lightly floured rolling pin, roll the dough into a rectangle approximately 12″ × 16″. Spread with the filling, leaving 1″ clear on one long side. Starting with the opposite long side, roll with your hands into a log jelly-roll style and pinch the seam tightly closed. Transfer to a parchment-lined baking sheet. Starting 1″ from one end, slice down and completely through the rolled dough lengthwise. Turn the two resulting strands so the filling faces up and cross them over each until you reach the end of the strands. Tuck the ends of the strands together neatly. Cover and let rise in a warm place until nearly doubled in bulk. Bake in a preheated 375°F oven for 30 to 35 minutes, until golden brown. *(See photo on page 20.)*

HOW TO SHAPE A THREE-STRAND BRAID

1. Lightly dust three dough strands and line them up in front of you vertically. To get the most symmetrical braid, start in the middle of the strands, rather than from one end.

2. Take the strand on the right and cross it over the center strand, so it becomes the new center strand.

3. Next, take the strand on the left and cross it over the center strand.

4. Continue with this pattern until you reach the ends of the strands. Pinch them together.

5. Now you need to flip the braid, end over end, so you can braid the rest of the strands in the other direction.

6. Check the section in the center to determine which outer strand has been crossed over the center last. Take the opposite outer strand and cross it over the center strand. Resume the above pattern.

7. Once you reach the ends, pinch them together and tuck the pinched ends under the loaf.

How to Fold

Folding dough builds strength with minimal effort. It's as simple as it sounds: Fold from four imaginary corners of your dough. Pick up one corner of the dough with lightly floured hands and stretch it up, folding it about two-thirds of the way across to the opposite corner and press down gently to de-gas the dough a bit. Repeat with the remaining three corners. This quick step is especially helpful in developing the structure of wet doughs. You can perform the folds in the bowl or on a lightly floured surface.

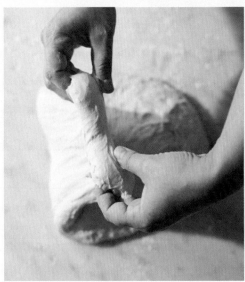

PRESHAPING

Think of preshaping as the bridge between one big mass of dough and your final, beautiful shapes. There are *many* different ways to preshape, but they all have the same goal: to give some structure to the dough, making it easier to create the final shape. The gluten in your dough tightens up when you handle it, so preshaping your dough, then letting it rest before shaping will give the gluten time to relax, making it easier to achieve the final shape.

To preshape, divide your dough into as many portions as you plan to shape. When you divide the dough, you're agitating the gluten, so handle it gently but confidently (think of yourself as a bread therapist here!). Working with one piece at a time on a lightly floured surface, pull the edges of the dough up and into the center, pressing down lightly and pinching the edges together to create a loose round. A round is a universal preshape, although some bakers opt to preshape differently if they're making a nonround final shape, such as a baguette.

Perfectly Pillowy Cinnamon Rolls

Yield: 8 large rolls

Who doesn't love cinnamon rolls? There's a good reason this fragrant recipe was chosen as our Recipe of the Year in 2021. It's a great illustration of the benefits of the *tangzhong* method, resulting in the most tender rolls you can make, with a shelf life that keeps them delectable for days. Used more commonly in enriched doughs, this technique—which has origins in Japan's *yukone* (or *yudane*)—cooks a small percentage of the flour and liquid very briefly before combining the resulting thick slurry with the remaining ingredients. We use bread flour instead of all-purpose flour because of its higher protein content, which allows it to absorb more liquid without diluting the structure of the gluten strands. The more liquid in your dough, the softer it will stay for longer, which you'll notice in these incredibly pillowy rolls that won't go stale quickly like regular ones.

TANGZHONG

119 grams (½ cup) whole milk

23 grams (3 tablespoons) unbleached bread flour

DOUGH

159 grams (⅔ cup) whole milk

300 grams (2½ cups) unbleached bread flour, plus more for dusting

25 grams (2 tablespoons) granulated sugar

6 grams (1 teaspoon) salt

6 grams (2 teaspoons) instant yeast

57 grams (4 tablespoons) unsalted butter, softened

TANGZHONG

1. Combine the milk and flour in a small saucepan, and whisk until no lumps remain.

2. Place the saucepan over medium heat and cook the mixture, stirring frequently, until thickened and pastelike; the whisk should leave lines on the bottom of the pan. This will take 1 to 3 minutes, depending on the strength of your burner.

3. Remove from the heat and transfer to the bowl of a mixer.

DOUGH

1. Immediately add the dough ingredients to the mixer bowl in the order listed. The heat from the tangzhong will help warm the cold milk.

2. Using the dough hook, mix on low speed to bring the dough together, then increase the speed to medium-low and continue to mix until the dough is smooth and elastic. This should take about 10 to 12 minutes.

3. Shape the dough into a ball, place it back in the bowl, and cover.

4. Let the dough rise until puffy but not necessarily doubled in bulk—about 60 to 90 minutes, depending on the warmth of your kitchen.

(Continued) ⟶

FILLING

14 grams (1 tablespoon) unsalted butter, melted, plus **21 grams (1½ tablespoons)** for brushing

107 grams (½ cup) brown sugar

15 grams (2 tablespoons) unbleached bread flour

8 to 10 grams (3 to 4 teaspoons) cinnamon

pinch of salt

ICING

21 grams (1½ tablespoons) melted unsalted butter, divided

½ teaspoon vanilla extract

170 grams (1½ cups) confectioners' sugar

pinch of salt

14 to 28 grams (1 to 2 tablespoons) milk, enough to thin to desired consistency

FILLING

1. While the dough is rising, combine the melted butter with the remaining filling ingredients, stirring until the mixture is the texture of damp sand. Set aside.

2. Lightly grease a baking sheet or line it with parchment.

ASSEMBLY AND BAKING

1. Transfer the dough to a lightly floured work surface and press it into a 10″ × 12″ rectangle about ½″ thick.

2. Sprinkle the filling over the dough, covering all but a ½″ strip along one long side.

3. Starting with the filling-covered long side, roll the dough into a log. Pinch the seam together to seal.

4. Using a serrated knife or dental floss, cut the dough into eight rolls, about 1½″ to 2″ each.

5. Place the rolls onto the prepared baking sheet, spacing them at least 2″ apart; a 3-2-3 arrangement works well. To prevent them from unraveling while they rise and bake, tuck the ends of the spirals underneath the rolls to hold them in place.

6. Cover the rolls with lightly greased plastic wrap and let them rise for 30 to 60 minutes. The rolls should be puffy and the dough shouldn't bounce back immediately when gently pressed.

7. Preheat the oven to 375°F with a rack in the top third.

8. Uncover the rolls and bake them for 14 to 18 minutes, until they're a very light golden brown.

9. Remove from the oven and brush the hot rolls with the remaining 21 grams (1½ tablespoons) of melted butter. Let cool for 10 to 15 minutes before icing.

ICING

1. In a medium bowl, combine the icing ingredients, mixing until smooth.

2. Ice the rolls and serve immediately. If you're planning to serve the rolls later, wait to ice them until just before serving. Store icing at room temperature, tightly covered, until ready to use.

3. Let the rolls cool completely before wrapping tightly in plastic wrap or placing in an airtight container.

Add any of the following to the filling: ½ teaspoon orange zest; 85 grams (½ cup) mini chocolate chips; 75 grams (½ cup) dried cranberries or raisins; or 57 grams (½ cup) chopped pecans, walnuts, or nut of your choice. You can also substitute other ground spices for the cinnamon in the filling. We recommend reducing strongly flavored spices, such as nutmeg or ginger, to ½ teaspoon.

Advance Prep

Students often ask whether they can shape these rolls the night before, then bake them the next morning. Because of the tangzhong method, we recommend making and baking the rolls in advance, since they'll stay wonderfully soft for at least 3 days (you can bake them up to several days in advance, then store tightly wrapped and uniced at room temperature). When ready to serve, lightly cover the rolls with foil and warm them in a 300°F oven for 5 to 10 minutes, until warmed through. Ice and enjoy. We guarantee they'll be just as delicious as those that were freshly baked.

Cream Cheese Icing

Omit the milk and use 57 to 90 grams (4 to 6 tablespoons) softened cream cheese. The softer the cream cheese, the easier it will be to incorporate. If the icing is too thick to spread easily, add milk (1 teaspoon at a time) to get the consistency you want.

Whole Wheat Sandwich Bread

Yield: 2 loaves

Here you'll find a partially whole grain version of our basic sandwich bread, illustrating the shift away from 100% white flour. You can use either traditional or white whole wheat flour in the recipe, depending on your preference. In the classroom, we use half of the dough for a pan loaf and the other half for a braid or dinner rolls that will disappear as soon as you pull them from the oven.

600 grams (5¼ cups) whole wheat flour

14 grams (2¼ teaspoons) salt

6 grams (2 teaspoons) instant yeast

28 grams (¼ cup) dry milk powder

554 grams (2⅓ cups) water

35 grams (1½ tablespoons) honey

28 grams (2 tablespoons) unsalted butter, room temperature

100 grams (⅞ cup) unbleached all-purpose flour, plus more for dusting

Tip: Store your whole-grain flours in the freezer, as the oil in the germ can go rancid at room temperature.

Tip: Use a light dusting of flour. We like to describe it as a "whisper" or thin veil of flour.

1. Stir together all the dry ingredients, except the all-purpose flour, in a large bowl.

2. Add the water, honey, and butter and stir to mix into a wet dough.

3. Cover the dough and set it aside to rest for about 15 minutes to soften the bran.

4. After resting, stir in only enough of the all-purpose flour to create a soft, shaggy dough.

5. Knead on a lightly floured surface until the dough is smooth and elastic.

6. Allow the dough to rise in a covered bowl until puffy though not necessarily doubled in bulk, about 1 hour.

7. Turn the dough out onto a lightly floured surface. De-gas it and divide it in half. Shape it into two pan loaves (see page 57). Place the loaves in two greased 8½″ × 4½″ loaf pans, cover, and allow to rise until the loaves have increased in volume and feel soft and airy to the touch, about 1 hour. They should crown over the tops of the pan by about 1″.

8. Bake the loaves in a preheated 375°F oven for about 35 minutes; the crust should be golden brown on the tops and sides.

9. Remove the breads from the oven and turn the loaves out of the pans onto a rack. The bottoms of the loaves should sound hollow when tapped, and the sides should feel firm, not wobbly.

10. Allow the breads to cool completely before slicing; the crust will soften a bit.

What's the Impact of Whole Grains?

Feel free to swap in whole-grain flours in other bread recipes by using the the lessons demonstrated in this recipe: more liquid and a longer rest period. Start small at first by changing 25% of the flour and add an extra bit of liquid, as whole grains absorb more water. They also absorb liquid more slowly than white flour, so while the dough might feel a little too wet at first, give it a rest period. Bring the ingredients together, then let sit for 15 minutes before kneading. This aids in the absorption of liquid *and* softens the bran, which might otherwise cut the gluten strands and inhibit rising.

When working with a recipe that calls for more than 30% whole grains, it never hurts to swap the same weight of bread flour for the listed weight of all-purpose flour as added insurance for dough strength—bread flour will give you a little more structure to carry the weight of the grains.

SCORING

Scoring dough allows bread to achieve maximum volume and an open internal structure. When you place dough in a hot oven, there's a frenzy of yeast activity and a burst of gases called "oven spring." Without scoring, those gases will find the weakest point in the crust and rip through. Scoring replaces those ruptures with intentional cuts to help define the bread's final shape. Skilled scoring makes for an even internal structure and allows the loaf to attain its maximum volume.

You can score in many different patterns, from a single straight slash to decorative designs. To score your loaf, use a bread lame (pronounced "lahm") or very sharp blade. Straight blades are ideal for straight cuts; curved blades are best for slashing to produce an ear.

Don't press down on the dough. If using a straight blade, hold it perpendicular to the surface of the dough and slash quickly and decisively. If using a curved blade, hold the blade at a 30-degree angle to the surface of the dough and make a cut using the corner of the blade. Aim for a cut about ¼″ to ½″ deep.

If you want to score a dough with lots of add-ins, such as grains, seeds, or fruit, it can be easier to use a pair of scissors to make cuts in the surface of the dough.

You can score pan loaves, but it's not critical. The pan itself provides structure, allowing the bread to rise in a more controlled way, reducing the risk of the crust rupturing.

CURVED SCORE

STRAIGHT SCORE

Multigrain Bread

Yield: 2 loaves

We add grains whole here, rather than ground into flour, for added texture. Making the soaker ahead softens the grains and ensures a high-rising bread. The higher protein content of bread flour helps offset any loss of structure from the grains. As with most of our bread recipes, you can make this dough in whatever shape you prefer. In class, we make boules (rounds) with this recipe and brush them with an egg white wash for added rise in the oven. Feel free to use your favorite grain blend, or make your own, keeping in mind that the ratio of seeds to grains should be somewhat even.

SOAKER

85 grams (½ cup) multigrain and seed blend

236 grams (1 cup) water

DOUGH

680 grams (5⅔ cups) unbleached bread flour, plus more for dusting

15 grams (2½ teaspoons) salt

7 grams (2½ teaspoons) instant yeast

340 grams (1½ cups) water

SOAKER

1. Combine the grain blend and the water in a large bowl. Cover and leave at room temperature for 8 to 16 hours.

DOUGH AND BAKING

1. Add the dough ingredients to the soaked grains. Mix to form a shaggy mass, using additional water as needed to achieve a rough but not too dry consistency.

2. Knead the dough, using a minimal amount of bench flour, until it's smooth and elastic.

3. Place the dough in a bowl, cover, and allow to rise until visibly puffy, 60 to 90 minutes.

4. Turn the dough out onto a very lightly floured surface, divide it in half, preshape (see page 25), and let rest 15 minutes.

5. Shape each piece into a boule (see page 59) and place on a parchment-lined baking sheet.

6. Cover lightly and allow to rise until the loaves almost double in size, about 45 to 60 minutes. Just before baking, score the top of each loaf (see page 32).

7. Bake the loaves in the center of a preheated 400°F oven for 28 to 32 minutes, until golden in color and firm on the sides.

Soft Pretzels

Yield: 12 pretzels

Salty or sweet, pretzels are a fun, relatively fast project. They're good for bakers of all ages and skills; we love seeing how proud kids are to pick up the shaping, often outpacing the adults. Pretzels also lend themselves to so many options—sweet, savory, stuffed, rolls, or bites. Whatever your taste, you'll be sure to find a version you love. Chilling the risen pretzels just before baking firms up the dough and makes them easier to handle as you dunk them in the water bath; this step is particularly helpful to ensure success if you're not as practiced with the shaping. *(See photo on page 35).*

DOUGH

600 grams (5 cups) unbleached bread flour

354 grams (1½ cups) water

28 grams (2 tablespoons) unsalted butter, room temperature

12 grams (2 teaspoons) salt

5 grams (1½ teaspoons) instant yeast

¼ teaspoon diastatic malt powder

WATER BATH

3,785 grams (16 cups) water

130 grams (½ cup) baking soda

TOPPING

6 grams (2 tablespoons) coarse pretzel salt

71 grams (5 tablespoons) unsalted butter, melted

DOUGH

1. Combine all the dough ingredients in the bowl of a stand mixer.

2. Mix for about 3 minutes on low speed, then increase the speed to medium and mix for 5 to 6 minutes. Alternatively, mix and knead by hand for 10 minutes.

3. Cover the bowl and allow the dough to rest for 30 to 40 minutes.

4. Divide the dough into 12 pieces, about 80 grams each. Lightly preshape each piece into a short cylinder (see page 25).

5. Roll each cylinder into a log about 24˝ long, with the center thicker than the ends. You may need to let the dough pieces rest between rolling to reach the full length.

6. To shape the pretzels, pick each piece of dough up by the ends and twist twice. Bring the ends over the loop and press onto the bottom edge, one on each side, to make a pretzel shape (see photos on opposite page).

7. Place the pretzels on two parchment-lined baking sheets, cover, and let rest at room temperature for 30 minutes.

8. Chill the risen pretzels, still covered, for 15 to 30 minutes.

WATER BATH, BAKING, AND TOPPING

1. Preheat the oven to 400°F.

2. While the pretzels are chilling, make the water bath by combining the water and baking soda in a large pot. Bring the mixture to a gentle boil over high heat.

3. Poach the pretzels in the water bath for 10 seconds per side. Work with just a few pretzels at a time so they don't crowd one another.

4. Using a skimmer or a strainer, remove them from the water and place the poached pretzels back on the baking sheet, then sprinkle lightly with coarse pretzel salt.

5. Bake the pretzels for 14 to 18 minutes, until deep golden brown.

6. While still warm, brush the pretzels with melted butter.

> **VARIATION: CINNAMON SUGAR PRETZELS**

Combine 99 grams (½ cup) granulated sugar and 15 grams (2 tablespoons) cinnamon in a small bowl. Don't sprinkle the pretzels with salt before baking. After baking, brush the pretzels with melted butter and sprinkle liberally with cinnamon sugar. Alternatively, dip the buttered pretzels in a shallow bowl of cinnamon sugar to coat.

Simits

Yield: 12 simits

If you've never tried this cousin of the bagel before, you're in for a treat. We use a mixer here, instead of mixing by hand, since this is a drier and stiffer dough and needs to be mixed pretty intensively to develop enough gluten to create great chew in the simits. As you mix, you'll add chunks of cold butter; incorporating them fully into a stiff dough is difficult to do properly by hand. That intensive mix yields a chewy interior, and the crispy exterior is achieved with a quick dunk in a molasses bath before coating the dough with sesame seeds. The result is an exceptionally delicious combination of textures and flavors.

DOUGH

560 grams (4⅔ cups) unbleached bread flour

340 grams (1½ cups) water

12 grams (2 teaspoons) salt

1 teaspoon instant yeast

113 grams (8 tablespoons) unsalted butter, cold

WATER DIP

sesame seeds

43 grams (2 tablespoons) molasses

100 grams (7 tablespoons) water

DOUGH

1. In the bowl of a mixer fitted with the dough hook, combine all the dough ingredients, except the butter, and mix on low speed for 3 minutes.

2. Increase the speed to medium and continue to mix for 5 to 6 minutes, until the dough is well developed.

3. Remove the cold butter from the fridge and pound it with a rolling pin a few times until pliable. This step makes it easier to incorporate the butter without warming it up.

4. Add the butter gradually in chunks. Continue to knead on medium speed until the dough is well developed, scraping the sides of the bowl as needed. The dough will seem loose at first as you add the butter but will eventually come together and smooth out.

5. Cover the bowl and allow the dough to rise for 1½ hours, folding it once after 45 minutes (see page 24).

6. Divide the dough into 24 pieces, about 42 grams each.

7. Roll two pieces into ropes about 15″ to 18″ in length. Place them next to each other and place a hand over each end. Twist the two strands together by rolling one hand away from you and one toward you. Wrap the twisted ropes around the broad part of your hand with the ends underneath. Create a ring by joining the ends of the ropes under your palm and rolling them against your work surface to seal. Repeat with the remaining pairs of ropes.

WATER DIP AND BAKING

1. Place the sesame seeds in a thin layer on a baking sheet. Whisk together the water and molasses in a bowl and dip each ring in the liquid, then roll to coat in the seeds.

2. Space the simits on a baking sheet. Cover and proof until puffy, about 30 minutes.

3. Uncover the simits and bake them in a preheated 450°F oven for 20 to 22 minutes, until golden and crispy.

Bagels

Yield: 8 bagels

Bagels are one of the most gratifying breads to make, as your efforts are likely to outmatch anything you can buy—unless you're lucky enough to have a bagel bakery in your neighborhood. Here we introduce the use of high-gluten flour, which is a step above bread flour in protein content (14% compared to 12.7% for King Arthur flours), ensuring that iconic chewiness we love about great bagels. Like the simits, we use a mixer to work the dough and a simple shaping technique. The water bath is the key to getting the best texture, and making them up to step 7 the day before gives the opportunity for the most flavorful fresh bagels for breakfast.

DOUGH

510 grams (4¼ cups) high-gluten flour

12 grams (2 teaspoons) salt

12 grams (1 tablespoon) non-diastatic malt powder

5 grams (1½ teaspoons) instant yeast

295 grams (1¼ cups) water

WATER BATH

2,000 grams (about 2 quarts) water

24 grams (2 tablespoons) non-diastatic malt powder (optional)

13 grams (1 tablespoon) granulated sugar (optional)

TOPPINGS

sesame seeds, poppy seeds, coarse salt, everything bagel topping, or your favorite

DOUGH

1. Combine all the dough ingredients and knead vigorously by hand for 10 to 15 minutes, or in a stand mixer equipped with the dough hook at medium-low speed for about 10 minutes.

2. Place the dough in a covered bowl and let rise until noticeably puffy though not necessarily doubled in bulk, 30 to 60 minutes.

3. While the dough is rising, prepare the water bath by heating the water, malt powder, and sugar to a very gentle boil in a large, wide-diameter pan.

4. Transfer the dough to an unfloured work surface and divide it into eight pieces.

5. De-gas each piece of dough and preshape each into a tight cylinder (see page 25). Cover lightly and give a 15-minute rest.

6. Starting with the first cylinder you rolled and keeping the others covered, roll each cylinder into an 8˝ to 9˝ rope. Wrap the dough around the broad part of your hand with the ends underneath. Connect the ends of the dough under your palm and roll the dough against your work surface to seal.

Tip: The dough is relatively dry, so you may have to press firmly to seal.

7. Place each bagel on a parchment-lined baking sheet and repeat with the remaining pieces of dough. Give the shaped bagels a 15-minute rest.

WATER BATH, TOPPING, AND BAKING

1. Carefully transfer the bagels to the simmering water, using your hands or a skimmer. Cook as many bagels at a time as fit comfortably in the pot without crowding. Simmer the bagels for 20 seconds, flip them over (a pair of tongs works well here), and cook for 20 seconds more.

2. Place your selected topping in a shallow dish. Using a skimmer or strainer, individually remove the bagels from the water and, while still moist, place them face down in the topping to coat their top crust. Place topping side up on a parchment-lined pan and repeat with the remaining bagels.

3. Bake the bagels in a preheated 425°F oven for 20 to 25 minutes, until a deep golden brown.

Overnight Rest

Bagels benefit from an overnight rest in the refrigerator after shaping but before boiling; this rest develops flavor and helps promote a shiny, blistered crust. To accomplish this:

1. Shape the bagels and place them on a parchment-lined baking sheet.
2. Tightly cover the baking sheet and refrigerate for 6 to 24 hours.
3. When ready to bake, remove the bagels from the refrigerator and boil them as directed in the recipe. There's no need to bring them to room temperature first.

Why Malt?

Most white flours are malted (check the ingredient list to find out for sure). Why? Malt contains active enzymes that speed up yeast fermentation by converting starch into sugar. When used in small amounts, malt gives better texture, enhanced crust color, and improved shelf life. When we use nonmalted flours, such as high-gluten, we sometimes add diastatic malt powder (an all-natural, barley-based powder made from sprouted grain) to get those benefits. Even if your recipe doesn't call for it, you can try adding ¼ teaspoon per 340 grams (3 cups) of flour—you only want a pinch because the enzymes in it are so active. Don't confuse it with nondiastatic malt powder, which is not enzymatically active. Nondiastatic malt is essentially a sweetener and adds a subtly sweet, roasted flavor as well as some shine on the crust of breads and bagels: Try your water bath with and without to see the difference it makes.

Pre-ferments

As we move into lean dough hearth breads, we turn to pre-ferments to add a depth of flavor from long fermentation and a degree of increased extensibility to the dough. A pre-ferment is a small portion of dough that's fermented ahead of the final dough.

A pre-ferment is simple to make. Mix a pinch of yeast with some water and flour, cover, and let it ferment until it's at its peak of flavor, at which point you use it to mix the final dough. It develops flavor and power, which you then add to your final dough.

Varying the proportion of water to flour is what differentiates the styles of pre-ferments, but you can also vary your pre-ferment by using a different flour altogether.

There are a dizzying number of pre-ferments—some are quite specific, some are very general. The following are those we use most frequently in the school.

BIGA: A pre-ferment of Italian origin, usually stiff, made with a small amount of commercial yeast (the yeast can be as little as 0.1% of the biga flour weight) and *no* salt. Ferments for a few hours, at minimum, and up to 16 hours.

PÂTE FERMENTÉE: A French term that means fermented dough, or as it is occasionally called, old dough. Since pâte fermentée is a piece of fully mixed dough, it contains all the ingredients of finished dough; that is, flour, water, salt, and yeast.

POOLISH: A loose pre-ferment with Polish origins; originally used in pastry production. It's made with equal weights of flour and water (meaning 100% hydration), a small portion of commercial yeast, and *no* salt.

SOURDOUGH: Because they're always made ahead, all sourdoughs are considered pre-ferments.

SPONGE: A high-hydration, warm pre-ferment that uses a high proportion or all of a recipe's yeast, so has a shorter fermentation time, usually ranging from 15 minutes to 4 hours. It's intended as a jump start for the yeast, rather than a way to slowly build flavor and structure.

When Is It Ready?

How do you know when your pre-ferment has matured sufficiently and is ripe and ready to use? If the pre-ferment is dense and seems not to have moved, it probably hasn't ripened sufficiently. In a stiff pre-ferment, it should be just beginning to recede in the center. In a looser pre-ferment, such as a poolish, look for lots of small fermentation bubbles and a noticeably pleasant aroma with a perceptible tang.

Converting to a Pre-ferment

A safe guideline for converting any recipe to use a pre-ferment is to take 25% of the total flour called for and use it in your pre-ferment. While this isn't a hard rule, 20% to 30% is fairly standard and will reliably yield good results. For the pizza recipe on page 44, 25% of the total flour would be 120 grams (1 cup) of our flour. We like to use a poolish with pizza doughs—an equal amount by weight of water and flour mixed with a pinch of yeast, then covered and rested overnight. The next day, add your poolish to the recipe, making sure to reduce the flour and water called for by the 120 grams you used the day before in your poolish. For the pizza recipe, that would mean adding only 360 grams of flour and 196 grams of water to the final dough.

Pizza Dough

Yield: two 12″ crusts

Pizza is endlessly variable and invariably delicious, and we could happily eat some form of it for every meal. We teach so many different pizzas in the school, with classes running from 3 hours to 2 days, so it's hard to choose just one to put in a cookbook. This version allows us to show you how to convert a straight dough to a pre-ferment (or the reverse, if you prefer); see sidebar. The added fermentation time builds flavor for the crust and has the bonus of making it easier to stretch. Specialty tools and ovens, while helpful, aren't necessary to make great pizza: Although a pizza peel does make transferring your dough easy, a baking sheet is just as effective! Here, you'll get comfortable working with a wetter dough than the previous breads; while more challenging to handle, the higher hydration contributes to an airier texture in the final dough.

480 grams (4 cups) unbleached all-purpose flour, plus more for dusting

6 grams (2 teaspoons) instant yeast

10 grams (a scant 2 teaspoons) salt

25 grams (2 tablespoons) olive oil

316 grams (1⅓ cups) warm water

Tip: We recommend using parchment paper as the neatest and most effective option for loading pizza.

1. Combine the flour, yeast, and salt in a large bowl.

2. Add the olive oil and water, stirring to make a cohesive dough. Add a bit more water if the dough seems dry or feels quite firm; you want it on the soft side.

3. Turn the dough out onto a lightly floured work surface and knead until smooth and springy.

4. Cover and let rise until doubled, about 60 to 90 minutes.

5. Preheat the oven to 450° to 500°F. Heat your baking surface (a pizza stone, steel, or baking sheet) in the preheated oven for at least 30 minutes before adding the pizza. If baking on a stone or steel, parchment will help prevent sticking.

6. Turn the dough out onto a floured surface, then divide it in half and preshape (see page 25).

7. Pat one piece of dough into a thin disk, then pick up by the edges with both hands, holding it vertically above your work surface. Rotate the disk of dough, stretching the edges until it's large enough to drape over the back of your knuckles.

8. Turn the dough on your knuckles, slowly moving your hands wider apart to gradually stretch the dough while preserving its round shape. This action provides the tension the dough needs to stretch fully. Try not to stretch to the point that the dough tears, though small holes can always be patched. Keep stretching until the dough is as thin as you like; exact thickness is a matter of personal preference. Place the stretched dough on a piece of parchment.

9. Top the pizza as desired. Use a peel or the back of a baking sheet to transfer your pizza to the stone, steel, or sheet and then bake. Watch carefully: A thin crust will bake more quickly than a thicker one. Consider, too, the topping that you've chosen for your pie: Heavily topped pizzas require a longer bake than those more lightly topped. Repeat with the second crust.

Pizza Toppings

When it comes to toppings, hold back! As a rule of thumb, every layer should be visible as you add the next: You should see some dough through the sauce, some sauce through the cheese, and some cheese through the toppings. Having an overly heavy hand with topping your pizza will weigh down the crust too much and inhibit proper baking. In the classroom, we teach the classic margherita, which allows students to really taste the dough without focusing too much on the toppings . . . but we also like to play! Here are a few of our instructors' favorite creative takes on pizza toppings:

- Mix ricotta with lemon zest and spread over the dough and top with thinly sliced summer squash.
- Brush the dough with olive oil, then top with sauce, pepperoni, and a drizzle of hot honey.
- Spread Thai peanut sauce over the dough and top with pickled daikon, pickled carrots, and any other thinly sliced vegetables you like.
- Brush the dough with olive oil, then add minced garlic and a shingling of roasted potatoes (slice them very thinly, rinse them in water, toss them in oil, and roast in the oven until starting to soften but not showing color). Sprinkle with crumbled goat cheese and chopped rosemary.
- Spread tomato sauce over the dough, then top with mozzarella, prosciutto, olives, and well-drained sauerkraut. Sprinkle a bit of brown sugar on top before baking for the trifecta of salty + sweet + sour.
- Spread béchamel sauce over the crust, then top with roasted mushrooms (roast them until golden with olive oil and a bit of thyme). Just before baking, crack an egg (or a few, depending on the size of your pizza) on top of the pizza.

Resting If Needed

If the dough resists stretching or handling at any time, place it on your floured surface and let rest for a minute or two to allow it to relax.

Spelt Pita

Yield: 8 pitas

Pita is about as instantly gratifying as a yeast bread gets. This recipe illustrates the use of a very short pre-ferment: Since we're using a whole grain (spelt) here, the sponge's role is to give the flour a little time to absorb the water. (Whole grains absorb more liquid, so we add more to the dough.) Once mixed, they come together quickly, and before you know it, they're magically puffing up in the oven and begging to be eaten!

---

174 grams (1¾ cups) whole spelt flour

227 grams (1 cup) water

½ **teaspoon** instant yeast

113 grams (1 cup) unbleached all-purpose flour

¾ **teaspoon** salt

13 grams (1 tablespoon) olive oil

1. Combine the spelt flour, water, and yeast in a large bowl and allow the mixture to rest for at least 10 minutes (or up to 2 hours).

2. Add the remaining ingredients and mix by hand to achieve a smooth, supple dough.

3. Allow the dough to ferment at room temperature for 1 hour.

4. Divide the dough into eight pieces and preshape into balls (see page 25). Let them rest for approximately 15 minutes while you preheat the oven to 500°F with a baking stone on the middle rack.

5. Roll the dough balls into 6˝ rounds.

6. Place the rounds directly on the hot stone; you'll bake in batches, so don't crowd them. Bake for a total of 3 to 5 minutes, turning over once they've puffed. A pair of tongs is useful here.

7. Cover the hot pitas with a towel so they remain soft and pliable as they cool.

French Bread

Yield: 2 loaves

How can just four ingredients create such a delicious mouthful? That's the endless mystery and challenge of French bread. This recipe builds upon the earlier ones by pulling together a variety of techniques to coax maximum flavor and texture from the simple ingredients in your bowl. We use a poolish to build flavor overnight, and a high ratio of water to flour to create a creamy mouthfeel. The kneading technique adds structure to the bread without adding flour, and we shape carefully and bake in a steamy oven to get that famously crisp crust.

POOLISH

236 grams (scant 2 cups) unbleached all-purpose flour

236 grams (1 cup) cool water

pinch of instant yeast

DOUGH

450 grams (3¾ cups) unbleached all-purpose flour, plus more for bannetons (optional)

227 grams (1 cup) water

5 grams (1½ teaspoons) instant yeast

13 grams (2¼ teaspoons) salt

Tip: This is a true pinch of yeast: less than 1/8 teaspoon. It's not an exact measurement, and we often talk about summer vs. winter pinches: If your kitchen is hot and steamy, use a smaller pinch.

POOLISH

1. The night before baking, combine the flour, water, and pinch of yeast and mix until well blended. Cover the bowl tightly and let ferment for approximately 15 hours at cool room temperature (60° to 68°F). When it's ripe and ready to use, the poolish will be very bubbly and fragrant (see photos on page 43).

DOUGH AND BAKING

1. Add the flour, water, yeast, and salt to the poolish, stirring to combine. The dough should be sticky (stickier than a basic bread dough), so add a bit more water if necessary to achieve that.

2. Turn the dough onto an unfloured surface to knead using the wet-dough kneading technique (see page 53). Resist the temptation to add flour even though the dough is sticky. After a short time, the dough will smooth out considerably and feel less sticky. (If desired, knead the dough for 3 to 4 minutes at medium-low speed in a stand mixer fitted with the dough hook.) When the dough is smooth and elastic, return it to the bowl, then cover. The dough temperature should be 75° to 78°F.

3. Let the dough rise for 1½ hours, folding once after 45 minutes (see page 24).

4. Preheat the oven to 500°F.

5. Divide the dough in half and preshape (see page 25). Let rest for 20 minutes, then shape into smooth rounds (boules; see page 59). Place the boules in floured bannetons or on parchment. Allow to proof, covered, until pillowy, 30 to 60 minutes.

6. Score the loaves (see page 32) and bake with steam (see page 60). After 5 minutes, lower the temperature to 425°F for the remainder of the baking time, about 30 to 35 minutes total.

Tip: Look for bubbling, slight doming, liquid separation, and crevasses on the surface—these are all signs that your poolish is ready.

TEMPERATURE

Why does temperature matter so much? Doughs rely on yeast—a living thing—so it's important to provide the right conditions to allow it to thrive. For that, you have two main inputs: water temperature and the temperature of the room.

It's difficult, and sometimes impossible, to control the ambient temperature of your kitchen, so instead we rely on controlling the water temperature.

Think of water temperature and kitchen temperature as two sides of a seesaw with your dough in the middle: To get consistent results, you want your dough to be the same temperature all year round. If your kitchen temperature rises, you'll need to lower your water temperature to offset it. In colder months, if your kitchen is chillier, you'll want to use slightly warmer water to compensate. You can do this by feel, adjusting the temperature of your water based on the conditions.

You can also measure it precisely, using a formula. Professional bakers use this formula to ensure their breads turn out as uniformly as possible, day in and day out, but home bakers don't need that level of control. Whether or not you do it often, measuring dough temperature is a helpful exercise to understand how environmental conditions affect your dough.

First, you need to know what your desired dough temperature is: For the best success with most yeast breads, it should be between 75° and 78°F.

Friction factor is the amount of heat that goes into your dough—either by hand or in a mixer—to bring it from just mixed to fully developed. In general, the friction factor is negligible if you're hand kneading and the mid-20s for most mixers.

WATER TEMPERATURE (if using a pre-ferment) = (4 × desired dough temperature) − (flour temperature + room temperature + pre-ferment temperature + friction factor)

WATER TEMPERATURE (if no pre-ferment) = (3 × desired dough temperature) − (flour temperature + room temperature + friction factor)

EXAMPLE: You're making a bread with a desired dough temperature of 78°F. You've measured the temperature of the room (72°F), the flour (72°F), and your recipe doesn't call for a pre-ferment. You'll be mixing in a mixer, and you know that the friction factor of your machine is 26°F.

Using the formula, determine the water temperature as follows:

WATER TEMPERATURE = (3 × 78°F) − (72°F + 72°F + 26°F) = 234°F − 170°F = 64°F

To achieve your ideal dough temperature in this example, you'd use 64°F water when mixing.

KNEADING WET DOUGHS

Wet doughs are harder to handle and mix, so we introduce a different technique than traditional kneading. Note: With some *very* wet doughs, like ciabatta, we recommend using a mixer to develop the dough—though you can still choose to knead by hand, if you prefer.

The "slap and fold" technique is commonly used to knead wet doughs. We teach a slightly different version, which introduces a "chopping" step before the slap and fold.

Both steps help build extra strength in loose and sticky doughs. We have a student to thank for the addition of the clever "chopping" step: He was attending one of our bread classes and had just returned from a trip to South America, where he'd watched local bakers make traditional bread. After they mixed the very loose, wet dough, they chopped it into small pieces using a sharp blade before continuing to knead and develop it.

We put the method to work and have used—and taught—it ever since. So, why does it work?

We often see students struggle with wet doughs, which feel stringy and sloppy. This interim chopping step helps to bring the dough together and make it more cohesive so you can better perform the slap and fold. It seems to run counter to what we know about gluten—that you don't want to cut the strands that have been developing—but here, chopping up the gluten encourages the smaller strands to "find" one another and align, which will actually end up giving you more strength in your dough.

STEP 1. THE CHOP

- After mixing but before beginning to knead, dump your soft, shaggy dough out onto an unfloured work surface.
- Chop it into small pieces with a bench knife, scrape it back together into a pile, and then repeat. Don't get hung up on getting the dough off of your bench knife as you work. Just chop all the way through the dough and carry on. It's helpful to angle the blade and push away from yourself a bit as you chop.
- Do this about six to eight times, until the dough begins to smooth out a bit and doesn't puddle out as much: You'll notice it begins to stand a bit taller. The changes are subtle, but will give you a head start on dough development before the next phase.

STEP 2. THE SLAP AND FOLD

- Pick up your dough from the top and bottom by scooping underneath it with your fingers together, supporting it on top with your thumbs, and moving as quickly and decisively as you can. If the dough were a cat, imagine that you would be picking it up just behind its front legs, not by the head, tail, or belly.
- Rotate the dough away from you.
- Now the "tail end" is hanging down toward the work surface (bench). Stick it to the bench and stretch the dough toward your stomach, using all your fingers together, supporting with your thumbs on top.
- Fold the dough in half away from yourself and rip your hands out to the sides, again moving quickly and decisively. Don't worry about the dough sticking to your hands—it will, but it'll get reincorporated as you work.
- Repeat these steps.
- As you get comfortable with the flow, you can speed up. As your dough gets stronger, rather than relying on gravity to get the dough to stick to the bench, you can slap that end of the dough on the bench, and then stretch and fold. This is where the "slap" in "slap and fold" comes in.
- Your dough will still be tacky when you are done, but will have developed some "muscle." When you grab a handful and tug, it should fight you a little and pull back rather than just ripping easily apart.

THE CHOP | **THE SLAP AND FOLD: STEP 1**

THE SLAP AND FOLD: STEP 2 | **THE SLAP AND FOLD: STEP 3**

SHAPING

Yeast doughs are flexible! They can be shaped in almost any way, regardless of what your recipe directs. For example, the dough in a sandwich bread recipe could easily be shaped into a bâtard (oval) and baked on a stone. You could take the dough for an artisan boule and make it into a pan loaf (the lack of direct heat will lead to a tighter crumb, which is great for grilled cheese). Or you could turn it into small rolls.

Varying the shape will vary the bake time: Baking in a pan will always slow it down a little since the metal forms a barrier to the heat. For non-pan breads, the more crust-to-interior ratio you have for your bread, the shorter your bake time will be (small rolls, for example, will bake much more quickly than a large hearth loaf).

Think of shaping as a destination—there are many paths to get there. While there are a lot of right ways to shape, choosing one is mostly a matter of comfort and preferences. All shaping has two goals: first, to create the final shape of the dough and second, to develop surface tension on the dough that will give the bread structure.

As you press the dough gently to shape it, you're getting rid of some of that gas that developed as it rose. This makes room for the yeast to continue to create new carbon dioxide as it bakes.

Most artisan breads will be shaped into round, oval, or oblong loaves. Pan loaves, like a sandwich bread, are shaped by rolling—in a similar way as an oblong loaf—but they need less surface tension, as the pan does much of the work of supporting the loaf.

Practice will guide you—the best shaping approach is the one that feels most comfortable to you. Observing the connection between what you've shaped and what comes out of the oven will help you improve your technique over time.

TO SHAPE A PAN LOAF

1. Give your preshaped, rested piece of dough a gentle stretch and place it in front of you on a very lightly floured surface. Have the seam side facing up with the dough in a rough vertical rectangle.

2. Fold the top edge of the dough about a third of the way down and give it a couple firm pats with your flat palm. You're trying to knock out the largest bubbles to begin building tension on the outside of the loaf.

3. Fold the "shoulders" of the dough (the two folded corners) down to the seam you created with the first fold. They'll overlap some, and the top of your dough will be roughly triangular at this point. Give the section you just folded another couple of firm pats with your flat palm.

4. Fold the point of the triangle down to the seam, but this time use the heel of your palm to seal it without flattening the dough.

5. You should now have a cylinder of rolled-up dough with a flap of dough on the edge toward you. Roll the cylinder toward you and seal. Depending on how much of a flap you have, this may take two to three steps. Roll a bit and seal with the heel of your hand, flouring your hand as needed. Repeat until the dough is fully rolled up and sealed. Place into a greased pan with the seam side down.

(Continued)

TO SHAPE A BÂTARD

1. Follow the first four steps as written for the pan loaf. Since you're not using a pan, firmer shaping is important to ensure enough tension to support the loaf as it rises.
2. With your palms facing down, make your hands form a triangle, with your thumbs pointing toward each other. Set your thumbs on the top of your loaf and roll the dough toward you as you gently press away to tighten up the roll. Keep your thumbs pointing toward each other, rather than into the loaf.
3. Repeat the second step three or four times until you've rolled the dough all the way up: You should have a cylinder of dough with a nicely taut surface.
4. You can stop here if you want a blunt bâtard, or you can taper the loaf by placing your hands over the ends of the dough and rolling out with a fair amount of downward pressure and a long rolling motion. Focus the pressure on the outsides of your hands.

TO SHAPE A BOULE

1. Start the same way you preshaped: Working around the dough, bring the edges to the center and pinch together.
2. Flip the dough over so the seam side is down and you have plenty of space between yourself and the dough. It's important that your surface is free of flour for this next step, but flour on your hands is a good thing.
3. With your palms facing you, plant your pinkies on your work surface behind your dough and drag the dough toward you in a long decisive motion. The front edge should catch, and as you drag the dough toward you, the top of the loaf will tighten up. If the dough slides instead of catching, make sure your surface is free of flour or give it a quick swipe with a damp towel to give yourself more traction.
4. Pick the dough up, rotating, and place it back farther away from you again with the seam side down.
5. Repeat Steps 3 and 4 until you have a nicely taut ball of dough.

OVEN HEAT AND STEAM

The ovens in our baking school are steam-injected with built-in stone hearths. The breads that come out of that oven are simply spectacular—high rising, crusty, and filled with holes. Of course, most of that is due to the skill of the bakers, but the oven certainly doesn't hurt! If you don't have access to that kind of oven, here are some methods to approximate similar results from your home oven.

The two most important characteristics of a bakery oven are its thermal mass and its ability to inject steam without losing heat by opening the door. You can increase your oven's thermal mass by using a baking stone or steel. A baking sheet will work, too, although it has less mass and won't conduct as much heat. These surfaces help the oven hold heat better, even when you open and close the door to load and steam the bread. They also drive the bread to rise up instead of pancake out when you place the dough directly on it. When you use a stone, steel, or baking sheet, it's important to preheat it along with your oven (check the instructions for your stone or steel for specifics.) This usually takes considerably longer than it takes to heat the air in your oven, so be sure to allow at least half an hour for pre-heating. When you move your shaped dough onto that preheated surface, it'll already have a high level of heat to transfer to the dough, creating a beautiful rise.

Introducing steam at the beginning of the bake is essential for successful hearth baking. Steam on the surface of your loaves keeps the exterior soft and pliable, which allows for maximum volume and an open interior structure. Steam also gelatinizes some of the starches on the outside of your loaf, giving it a nice crisp shine, rather than a matte, leathery exterior.

If your recipe calls for enclosed baking—meaning baking in a very small covered chamber, such as a Dutch oven—then you don't need to add steam; moisture released by the bread is being trapped close enough to the bread that it self-steams. With this method, you *do* need to vent the bread halfway through the bake by removing the cover; otherwise, you risk retaining too much moisture, preventing your crust from getting enough color and crispness. You can use the enclosed baking method even if the recipe doesn't call for it and you can do it without a Dutch oven by simply covering your loaf with a metal bowl or roasting pan. To use the enclosed baking method:

1. Place a baking stone, steel, or Dutch oven on the middle rack of the oven.
2. At least 30 minutes before baking, preheat the oven to 500°F.
3. When the bread is ready to bake, place it on a peel (or nonrimmed cookie sheet) lined with parchment or sprinkled with cornmeal if you're using a stone/steel, or onto a strip of parchment to use as a sling if using a Dutch oven.
4. Using the peel, deposit the loaf onto the hot stone/steel or lower it into your Dutch oven (parchment and all, if you're using it).
5. Place a metal cover over your loaf (either a bowl or roasting pan depending on size) or place it on your Dutch oven.
6. Set the timer for about 15 minutes. When the timer goes off, remove the cover or lid, opening it away from you. This will direct the steam toward the back of your oven, not toward your face and arms.
7. Continue baking until the bread shows all signs of doneness, such as recommended bake time, proper color, firmness, and relative lightness.

If you're not using an enclosed baking method, you'll need to add steam for hearth breads (and any recipes where you're after a very crisp crust). When adding steam, you'll need to be *very* careful, as the sudden and intense billowing of steam can crack the glass of your oven (we've seen this happen!)—you can prevent this by placing a baking sheet over the oven door while adding the water to protect the glass.

1. Place an empty cast-iron pan on the bottom rack of the oven. If you don't have cast iron, use the heaviest oven-safe pan you have (but do *not* use glass, as it can't handle the rapid temperature change).
2. At least 30 minutes before baking, preheat the oven to 500°F.
3. Boil approximately 1 cup of water.
4. Place the bread in the oven, then immediately pour the boiling water very carefully into the preheated empty pan, and close the oven door as quickly as possible.
5. Lower the oven to the baking temperature directed in your recipe and bake.

Ciabatta

Yield: 3 loaves

This is our wettest yeast dough, made with a biga, which is somewhat stiffer than the poolish in the French bread. The result is a slightly deeper flavor with an even lacier crumb. The dough is quite sticky, so you'll want to make it in a mixer, and the shaping is just a hint of length so you don't get stuck in the dough. The loaves are floured to keep them from sticking as they proof, and it's important to handle them with gentle confidence. The result? Crisp, caramelized, creamy bread you just can't stop eating. This is a very versatile dough—you can choose to make it into rolls or even a focaccia, or try the olive ciabatta variation below.

BIGA

255 grams (2⅛ cups) unbleached all-purpose flour

177 grams (¾ cup) water

pinch of instant yeast

FINAL DOUGH

all the biga

595 grams (5 cups) unbleached all-purpose flour, plus more for dusting

17 grams (1 tablespoon) salt

5 grams (1½ teaspoons) instant yeast

472 grams (2 cups) water

BIGA

1. In the bowl of a stand mixer, stir together the biga ingredients. It'll be a fairly stiff dough. Cover the bowl and let the biga rest at cool room temperature for 12 to 16 hours (see page 43); it'll be bubbly and aerated, crowning and just starting to recede.

FINAL DOUGH

1. Place all the dough ingredients in the bowl with the ripe biga.

2. Mix at low speed until the dough begins to hold together; it should be very wet and slack. You may need to add more water if conditions are dry.

3. Increase the mixer speed to medium-low and mix for about 4 minutes. Cover tightly and let rise for 2 hours, folding (see page 24) after 30 minutes, again at 60 minutes, and a third time at 90 minutes.

4. When the dough has risen, turn it out onto a well-floured work surface. Gently flatten and cut it into three pieces, shaping each into a rough 4″ × 10″ rectangle. These irregular rectangles, stretched to about ¾″ thick, are the finished shaped loaves. Cover the loaves and proof on well-floured boards or a parchment-lined baking sheet.

(Continued)

5. While the dough is rising, place a baking stone in the oven and set the temperature to 500°F. Allow the oven to heat for at least 30 minutes. If you're baking on a stone, slide the proofed loaves onto the stone. If you're not baking on a stone, simply place the baking sheet of ciabatta in the oven. Add steam (see page 60).

6. After 5 minutes, lower the oven temperature to 450°F. Bake the loaves until they're a deep golden brown, firm on the sides, and feel light and airy when you pick them up, approximately 25 minutes.

> ### VARIATION: FOCACCIA

Place one-third of the dough in a well-oiled 8″ or 9″ round cake pan or a 9″ × 13″ pan, depending on whether you like your focaccia thin or thick. Flip the dough to coat with oil. Proof until very puffy, then dimple and top as desired. Bake at 400° to 450°F for about 18 to 25 minutes, until golden brown and crispy on the bottom.

> ### VARIATION: CIABATTA ROLLS

Divide the dough into the size you like (we get about 6 rolls per loaf, or 18 for the full batch) and proof on a sheet of parchment. When they're very fluffy, lightly dust the tops with flour. Bake with steam at 450°F on a preheated surface for best results (see page 60). Baking time will vary depending on the size of the rolls, but take a peek after 15 minutes. Since these are smaller, they won't have the same deep color, but they'll be nicely golden all over.

> ### VARIATION: OLIVE ROSEMARY CIABATTA

Reduce the salt to 2½ teaspoons and fold in 177 grams (1¼ cups) chopped olives and 10 grams (¼ cup) chopped fresh rosemary at the end of the mixing stage.

Raisin Pecan Bread

Yield: 2 loaves

Hearty without being dense or dry, packed with flavor from a pre-ferment, whole grains, and added fruit and nuts, this highly customizable bread is hard to resist. We recommend making half of the dough into small rolls. Why? They cool faster, so you'll be able to rip one open and slather it with butter as soon as possible.

BIGA

132 grams (1 cup + 5 teaspoons) unbleached all-purpose flour

pinch of instant yeast

80 grams (⅓ cup) water

DOUGH

330 grams (2¾ cups) unbleached bread flour, plus more as needed

132 grams (1 cup + 3 tablespoons) whole wheat flour

66 grams (½ cup + 2 tablespoons) whole rye flour

15 grams (2½ teaspoons) salt

1 teaspoon instant yeast

414 grams (1¾ cups) water, plus more as needed

132 grams (1 cup + 3 tablespoons) pecans, chopped and toasted

100 grams (1 cup + 3 tablespoons) golden raisins

BIGA

1. Mix together the biga ingredients until thoroughly combined. Cover and let ferment for 12 to 16 hours at cool room temperature.

DOUGH

1. In a large bowl, mix together all the ingredients, except the raisins and pecans, with the biga. Add additional bread flour or water as needed to form a tacky, semifirm dough.

2. Allow to rest for 10 to 30 minutes before kneading until moderately developed (this should take about 1½ minutes by machine, 3 minutes by hand).

3. Once developed, knead in the raisins and pecans.

4. Bulk ferment the dough for 2 hours, with a fold after 60 minutes (see page 24).

5. Divide the dough in half.

6. Preshape into rounds (see page 25), cover, and let rest for 20 minutes.

7. Shape each round into a bâtard (see page 58) and place on a couche, in bannetons, or on parchment. Cover and proof for 60 to 90 minutes.

8. If proofed on a couche or in bannetons, carefully turn the risen loaves onto parchment. Score the loaves (see page 32) and bake with steam on a 500°F preheated stone for 10 minutes (see page 60).

9. Lower the oven heat to 400°F and bake for an additional 25 to 30 minutes, until a deep golden brown.

Master Class
Unkneaded Six-Fold French Bread (Baguette)

Yield: 1,051 grams dough, enough for 3 baguettes

THE BAKER

Jeffrey Hamelman was hired by King Arthur to open the Bakery and Baking School, both of which were the realization of a longtime vision of Frank and Brinna Sands, then owners of King Arthur. He was the director of the King Arthur Bakery from 2000 to 2017 and developed the professional curriculum for the Baking School, where he continues to teach. The author of *Bread: A Baker's Book of Techniques and Recipes* and a recipient of the Bread Baker's Guild Golden Baguette Award, he's one of a limited number of Certified Master Bakers in the United States and a past captain of Baking Team USA. Jeffrey's love of baking is at the heart of every class he teaches and has informed the Baking School since its inception.

THE BREAD

Here we see the culmination of all the lessons in this chapter: an understanding of how to achieve the proper dough, how to shape, the skill required for slashing, proper heat of the oven, and so on. You'll note in the recipe that Jeffrey has a column to list the baker's percentages of each ingredient and also includes the desired dough temperature. We use this format in our professional classes and he uses it in all his recipes. The percentages predict what the dough will be like before you make it, so you know what to expect and can check your dough if it seems off (see page 81 for more on baker's percentages and page 52 for dough temperature). Jeffrey teaches this recipe often because of its simplicity in ingredients and technique, requiring no equipment other than a plastic scraper and a bowl— no mixer involved. The real wow factor is the transformation of the initial shaggy mass of flour and water to a supple, developed dough. To get there, he teaches a deceptively simple technique of a series of folds. In his recipe here, Jeffrey shapes the dough as baguettes, but it can easily be made as round, oval, or pan loaves, as well as rolls and even pizza crust.

This recipe underscores how important time is as an ingredient in making very good bread. This particular bread isn't something impossible to achieve or esoteric—it's about the humblest loaf there is.

—JEFFREY HAMELMAN

INGREDIENTS	BAKER'S PERCENTAGE
600 grams (5 cups) unbleached all-purpose flour	100%
437 grams (1¾ cups + 1 tablespoon) water	73%
12 grams (2 teaspoons) salt	2%
2 grams (¾ teaspoon) yeast	0.4%

Desired dough temperature: 75°F

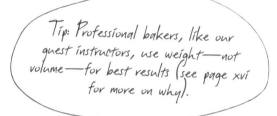

Tip: Professional bakers, like our guest instructors, use weight—not volume—for best results (see page xvi for more on why).

1. Place all the ingredients in a mixing bowl. Bring them together into a shaggy mass by running a plastic bowl scraper down the inside far wall of the bowl and bringing the ingredients up from the bottom of the bowl, then folding them on top of those that were on top of the bowl. Rotate the bowl about 20% with each stroke, so you are always working on a different portion of the dough.

2. Cover the bowl and let it bulk ferment at room temperature for 3 hours.

3. Every 30 minutes during the bulk fermentation period, give the dough 20 to 25 strokes with the bowl scraper. You should feel an increase in strength (a real tactile increase in dough development) as you go. By the time you perform the final fold, it should have considerably more elasticity than when you began.

4. Divide into three pieces, each weighing 350 grams. Lightly preshape each piece into a ball (see page 25), then let rest briefly.

5. When sufficiently relaxed (see page 71), shape into baguettes (see page 72).

6. Once shaped, cover lightly and let rest at room temperature (75°F) for about 1 hour. Ideally, the baguettes should rest on a couche or sheet pan between folds of baker's linen or a tea towel.

7. One hour before you're ready to bake, preheat the oven to 500°F with a baking stone set on a middle rack and an 8˝ to 10˝ cast-iron pan set on the lowest rack.

8. Load the bread onto the baking stone and immediately pour 1 cup of boiling water into the cast-iron pan. Bake for 22 to 25 minutes; if loaves are coloring too quickly, lower the oven temperature by 25°F.

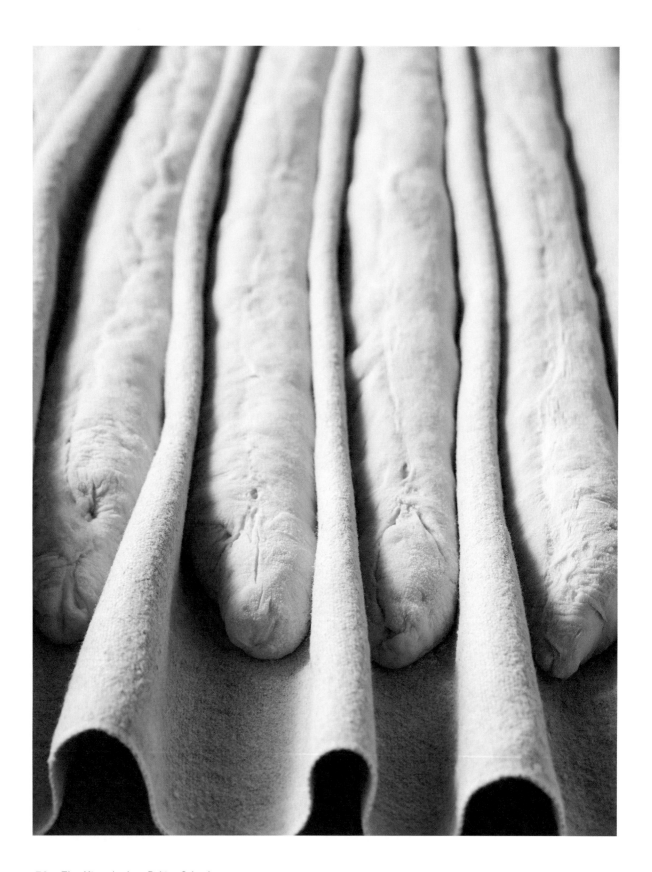

CHOOSE YOUR OWN BAKE

Jeffrey includes a time estimate for baking but uses this as a teaching moment for students. "I personally am a proponent of a bold bake and a crust you can trust," Jeffrey says. "But my philosophy is that you should bake to your own standard: People all have a preference. My preferred bake might be darker than someone else's, but do what works for you." His brilliance as a teacher is in how he imparts the importance of exploring the sensory aspects of baking. The more you bake—especially with simple recipes like this one—the more you begin to understand how dough behaves and how even a small change in method affects the final result. In that way, baking is a lifelong process that's a dance between truths of the craft and your own preferences and habits. Jeffrey notes that teaching is a matter of encouraging each student to go down the path of learning: "The best I can do is open up a little door with a key, and it's up to the student to walk through it and do the work."

Dough Relaxation

After you preshape your dough, you'll give it a brief rest (start with around 15 minutes). The recipe instructs you to wait until it's "sufficiently relaxed" before the final shaping step. To know when it *is* relaxed enough, try shaping it. If it fights you and shrinks back, it's not relaxed enough. On the other hand, if you've left it and waited too long, it'll lose too much of its structure. You want the dough to still provide some resistance, but it should also exhibit elasticity and adequate extensibility. It's a finely tuned sweet spot and one that practice will help you find. Remember that mistakes are incredibly valuable—they teach you the limits in either direction. Once you experience overly relaxed dough and not-relaxed-enough dough, you'll have a better sense of how to achieve the right balance.

Baguette Shaping

1. Place the relaxed, preshaped dough on a lightly floured work surface with the good side down.
2. Using gentle pressure with the flat part of one hand, flatten the piece into an oval shape of even thickness with the long sides in an east–west orientation.
3. Fold one-third of the dough toward you so that it rests on itself and gently pat out the air. Turn the dough around 180 degrees and again fold one-third of the dough toward you. Again, gently pat out the air. The dough should now be approximately rectangular and of even thickness.
4. Starting with the right end of the loaf (for right-handed bakers), begin to fold and press: The left thumb rests at the top of the dough with the fingers of the left hand holding the loaf from behind. The fingers fold a flap of dough over, covering the thumb, and the heel of the right hand presses the folded flap of dough to seal it. Repeat down the entire length of the dough. The seam should be tight and there should be a ½″ to ¾″ lip of dough along the bottom length.
5. Turn the dough around 180 degrees and repeat the folding and pressing process, this time bringing the seam right to the work surface. Again, the seam should be tight and more or less straight along the entire length.
6. Turn the dough over so that the seam is directly on the bottom. Place your right hand in the center of the dough, contouring your hand so that your fingertips and the heel of your hand are on the work surface and the palm of your hand is in contact with the dough. Roll the dough gently back and forth three or four times, in a manner more caressing than harsh, so that you slightly flatten the center of the dough.
7. Then take both hands and place them side by side on top of the dough with your index fingers touching, and the fingertips and the heel of each hand on the work surface. Begin to roll the dough back and forth, and at the same time, begin to elongate the dough. It's easy to see your hands rolling the dough back and forth; the outward pressure exerted by the hands is less visible, but very important.
8. When your hands have reached the ends of the dough, check the symmetry, proportion, and length of the baguette. If the dough is not yet long enough, bring both hands to the center of the loaf again and roll the dough back and forth and outward once more to continue to lengthen the baguette. Refine the shape by working directly on any areas that need attention: If there are areas that are too thick, work to thin them; if one end is bulbous, roll it back and forth until it has a similarity with the shape of the other end. Above all, the purpose of these refining strokes is to finish with a baguette that has a graceful appearance and harmonious taper with the high point in the center.

9. Throughout the process, take care to keep the dough from sticking to either your hands or the work surface. Lightly flour as necessary.
10. Once baguettes are shaped, allow them to rise on linen couches until fully proofed.

chapter 2.
SOURDOUGH

The Classroom

Our sourdough classes are essentially an extension of our yeast bread classes. All the fundamental lessons around mixing, kneading, shaping, and baking apply to both topics. Think of the yeast breads and sourdough chapters as parts one and two of "bread mastery": Working your way through the lessons in the yeast breads chapter will better prepare you to focus on the ins and outs of maintaining and using a sourdough culture, as you'll already be familiar with the skills of handling and baking bread dough.

Sourdough conjures up an almost mythical quest for many bakers, and it can be a lifelong journey. Because sourdough culture is a living thing, caring for it requires a unique blend of precision and intuition. Sourdough appeals to a broad spectrum of bakers: the very methodical, engineer-minded looking for precise formulas to capture every stage of the process; those who treat sourdough baking as a near-spiritual craft; and everyone in between.

Part of the challenge with teaching sourdough lies in the terminology. The word *sourdough* is used for different aspects of sourdough baking: It refers to the culture you maintain for baking, to the finished loaf of bread itself, and to the craft of baking with a sourdough culture. When someone in class raises their hand to ask a question about "sourdough," we know it's important to clarify which specific part of the process they're asking about.

For most of our sourdough classes, we start with a discussion of how to start and maintain a healthy sourdough starter, since that's at the heart of success with sourdough baking. Sourdough starter is a culture of wild yeast and bacteria that exist naturally in flour. By mixing flour with water, those naturally occurring yeast and bacteria are activated. This culture has two functions in baking: leavening and flavoring. The yeast provides leavening, and the bacteria, as they ferment, produce lactic and acetic acid, which impart flavor.

You need to feed your culture regularly with flour and water to keep it healthy and thriving. Caring for it, like caring for any living thing, requires you to watch and respond to it. You can follow a schedule and guidelines for feeding, but everyone's culture will behave somewhat differently (think of it as a family member!). The surest path to sourdough success is to practice and be attentive to the results.

Feeding your culture regularly at room temperature is the best way to become familiar with how it behaves and how to bring it to a robust ripeness. Once you understand what it takes to make a healthy, ripe culture, you can shift to a less frequent feeding schedule that utilizes the refrigerator for convenience. Remember, though, continuing to care for it is key. The more regularly you feed it, the better maintained it is, and the more resilient it will be. Think of it in the context of feeding yourself. If you're used to regular nutrition over a long span of time, your body can better handle a little neglect here and there. This doesn't mean you have to feed your culture daily to be successful, but it *does* illustrate the importance of regular care both for your culture and your ability to assess its health.

Once you have a thriving culture, there's no end to how you can use it. Its two functions (leavening and flavoring) can be put to use together or separately. Ripe culture can leaven breads without commercial yeast while also adding a wonderfully complex flavor. Discard culture doesn't necessarily have leavening power but can be used as an ingredient in any baking application: sweet or savory. You can add it to chocolate cakes, oatmeal raisin cookies, scones, quick breads, crackers (see page 90), flatbreads, waffles (see page 92), . . . and much more (see page 93).

The Lessons

In our sourdough classes, we emphasize the importance of caring for your culture. It's in the process of regular maintenance that you gain an intuition about how sourdough works—the more you witness the cycle of feeding and fermentation in your culture, the better equipped you'll be to put it to use in your baking. Our goals for you are to:

- Create a culture from scratch

- Practice basic maintenance of a culture, both refrigerated and at room temperature, adjusting care and feeding for different environments and circumstances

- Consider the effects of variations to your starter, including changes in hydration, feeding schedule, and flour selection

- Make breads using ripe sourdough culture as the primary leavener

- Utilize discard in a variety of baking applications

- Experiment with techniques to manipulate flavor in sourdough breads

- Build cultures to volumes needed for sourdough recipes

- Create schedules of feeding/builds to meet your baking needs

The Setup

The ingredients and equipment for our sourdough classes look the same as for our yeast bread classes (with the notable exception of storage containers for your culture; see page 86). In place of covering those basics again here (see The Setup, page 6), we'll start with a list of important vocabulary and an intensive mini-course on how to create a culture from scratch and maintain it. Then we'll dive into recipes so you can put your culture to work.

Here, as in all our classes, we *strongly* urge you to weigh your ingredients, particularly as you feed your culture. The proper ratio of flour to water is essential, and weights are the best way to ensure precision. This is especially true with sourdough; a measured cup of culture by volume can have drastically different weights depending on the hydration and stage of ripeness. Relying on weights is the only way to know exactly how much is going into your bread.

TERMINOLOGY

The topic of sourdough includes a swirl of vocabulary that's used interchangeably by different bakers. It can be confusing to switch between recipes and resources when the terms used aren't consistent. Even the word *sourdough* itself is bewildering to many bakers because it's used to refer to so many aspects of the process, from the culture to the bread itself. The important thing to remember is that all these words refer to the same basic fundamentals: They're all different ways to say the same thing.

SOURDOUGH CULTURE: In baking, *sourdough* refers to the culture of wild yeast and bacteria that leavens and flavors sourdough bread. "Culture," "sourdough culture," "starter," and just "sourdough" can all refer to the culture. *Synonyms: seed, levain, mother, inoculant.*

FEED: To maintain the health and effectiveness of the culture by regularly discarding (or using) a portion, and mixing flour and water into the remaining culture. *Synonym: refresh.*

BUILD: To increase the total weight and volume of a culture by adding enough flour and water to reach the amount required in a recipe. Build refers to both the act of increasing the amount and the stage itself. *Synonyms: levain, freshening, sour, full sour.*

UNDERRIPE: A fed culture that's not quite active enough yet for use in a recipe nor ready for its next feed. *Synonym: young.*

RIPE: A culture that's at its peak activity and ready for use in a recipe that requires leavening. *Synonyms: fed, active.*

OVERRIPE: A culture that's past its peak of activity and in need of feeding prior to use in a recipe that requires leavening. *Synonym: unfed.*

DISCARD: The portion of culture that's removed and replaced with fresh flour and water to feed the culture. Even without leavening power, discard can be used in a wide variety of baking applications (see page 93).

HYDRATION: Hydration indicates the ratio of flour to water in your culture or your dough, written in percentages—it's the total amount of water divided by the total amount of flour. In our classes, we use a 100% hydration culture, meaning equal parts water and flour by weight. You can maintain a stiffer culture (higher ratio of flour to water) or a wetter one; they'll still thrive. Using a 100% hydration culture is an especially accessible method to learn about keeping and baking with a culture. People may use stiffer or wetter cultures based on flavor and leavening characteristics, among other reasons. The Master Class for this chapter, **Miche Pointe-à-Callière**, uses a stiff (70% hydration) culture (see page 113).

Baker's Math

Baker's math is a common language for baking that makes it easy to scale recipes up and down. We call them percentages, but they're really a ratio system. The flour amount is always represented as 100%, and all other ingredients are a ratio of that. For example, if a bread recipe called for 1,000 grams of flour, 760 grams of water, 20 grams of salt, and 4 grams of yeast, the recipe in baker's percentage would be 100% flour, 76% water, 2% salt, and 0.4% yeast. Once you have the percentages, it's simple to increase or decrease the recipe.

Baker's math is also useful for quickly assessing the characteristics of a dough: If you have a dough that's supposed to have 70% hydration and your dough looks quite dry in the bowl in front of you, you'll know something is off. Percentages are a way to gauge, using your common sense and experience, the makeup of the dough. Although we don't include baker's percentages in all our bread recipes, we do teach them in our more advanced bread classes and always in our professional classes. We suggest you try applying them to your favorite bread recipes. You'll see them in the **Unkneaded Six-Fold French Bread** at the end of the Yeast Breads chapter, page 66. The more you bake using baker's math, the more familiar you'll be with the connection between percentages and how your dough should look and feel.

HOW TO CREATE A CULTURE FROM SCRATCH

Many of us have already purchased or been gifted a culture from another baker. If you haven't, making one from scratch is simple.

On **day one**, stir together 75 grams each of water and unbleached all-purpose flour. Cover and leave at room temperature for 24 hours.

On **day two**, discard all but 50 grams of the mixture and stir in 50 grams each of water and unbleached all-purpose flour. Cover and leave at room temperature for 24 hours. The discard isn't yet ready for use, so you'll need to compost or dispose of it.

By the **third day**, you'll likely see some activity—bubbling; a fresh, fruity aroma; and some evidence of expansion. It's now time to begin feeding twice a day, as close to every 12 hours as your schedule allows. Continue to discard all but 50 grams and stir in 50 grams each water and flour every 12 hours for a total of 14 days, leaving your culture at room temperature the entire time. You'll notice the culture becoming more active: It will start to look puffy, but it won't yet be ready to use.

After **7 to 10 days**, your culture will start to become predictable in both aroma and the time it takes to ripen, but continue the feeding schedule through the 14 days. At this point, you can begin to use the discard in recipes that don't require it to leaven.

After **14 days**, assuming you've been consistent in your feedings, your culture should be mature and ready to use for all your sourdough recipes. You'll know it's mature because you'll see a marked expansion in the culture—it should more than double in volume within 6 to 8 hours of feeding. This is the true indication that it has enough leavening power to make your bread rise. Now that your culture is ready to use for bread baking, be sure you build enough for each recipe to allow you to reserve 50 grams for perpetuating the starter.

Continue to store your culture at room temperature and feed it every 12 hours, or stash it in the refrigerator and feed it once a week as follows.

DAY ONE

FEEDING

NOT READY

MATURE

SOURDOUGH CULTURE CARE AND FEEDING

You have two options when it comes to basic maintenance of your culture: room temperature or refrigerated, and you can easily switch between the two. Say you're baking regularly and storing it at room temperature but decide to ease up on your baking. You can put the culture in the refrigerator and switch over to that schedule.

The goal in caring for your culture is to keep the yeast and bacteria in balance. Yeast leavens and acid-producing bacteria flavors; you don't want one to outpace the other.

Feeding is a cyclic process: Consistency and regularity are key. In ideal circumstances, you feed your culture when it's just ripe, then it slowly matures until it reaches peak ripeness, when you feed it again.

MAINTAINING YOUR CULTURE AT ROOM TEMPERATURE

To keep the balance of yeast and bacteria, room temperature is the ideal environment for your sourdough culture. If you store it at room temperature, you'll need to feed it twice a day, but this is a simple task and less demanding than you'd think. Remember that you can always stash your culture in the refrigerator when you need to, but we recommend you follow this room-temperature schedule when you're starting, as you'll learn a lot about your culture by observing it under these optimum conditions.

Feed the culture every 12 hours at roughly the same time each day: Stir the culture well and discard (or use) all but 50 grams. To that remaining 50 grams, add 50 grams each water and all-purpose flour, mix until smooth, and cover. How often you need to feed your culture at room temperature will depend greatly on the ambient temperature of your kitchen. If your kitchen is warm, the culture will ferment faster, and you'll need to feed it more often. If your kitchen is over 85°F, you'll want to keep your culture in the refrigerator. Keeping it refrigerated will slow its ripening and reduce the need for frequent feeding. The key is to reach it *before* it becomes overripe: In an ideal world, you'll discard and feed it at peak ripeness.

If you plan to use your culture to bake the next day, feed it as you normally would in the morning. For the second feeding, don't remove or discard any culture; instead, increase its quantity by stirring in equal weights flour and water to create the amount your recipe calls for, plus enough left over to feed and perpetuate the culture. The last feeding should take place 6 to 12 hours before you make your final dough, enough time for the culture to become ripe but not overripe.

MAINTAINING YOUR CULTURE IN THE REFRIGERATOR

If daily sourdough feeding is more of a commitment than you want to make, you can store your culture in the fridge and feed it once a week.

Once a week, preferably on the same day, take the culture out of the fridge, stir thoroughly, and remove all but 50 grams—remember you can save the discard to be used in other recipes. To that remaining 50 grams, add 50 grams each water and all-purpose flour, mix until smooth, and cover. Allow the culture to ferment at room temperature until it begins to show signs of activity, becoming a little bubbly before you put it back in the refrigerator. This could be just an hour or two or it might take all day, depending on your specific variables (ambient temperature, water temperature, total volume of culture, and especially the overall health of the culture).

Deciding when to remove your culture from the refrigerator to build its activity level before baking is one of the most challenging aspects of refrigerator maintenance. A day or two may be enough if you've been consistent with your weekly feedings and notice its activity level increasing quickly after feeding each week.

If your culture has been refrigerated without feeding for an extended period of weeks or months, you'll want to begin this process 3 to 5 days ahead of baking. Take the culture out of the refrigerator in the morning, feed it as usual to maintain the volume, and let it ferment for 12 hours at room temperature before the next feed. The next day, feed it twice, once in the morning and again about 12 hours later. If your starter is very active and increasing in volume rapidly, this may be all it needs before a final build to the weight your recipe requires. (Remember to allow for the amount you'll remove to perpetuate your starter!) If your starter isn't yet doubling in volume in 6 to 8 hours, continue the twice-daily feeding schedule until it does.

When it's active enough to bake, build to the volume you'll need for the recipe, plus enough for perpetuating your culture. Weigh out enough culture to use in your recipe and feed the remainder to continue the culture's maintenance. Mix until smooth, and once you see some activity, return it to the refrigerator to maintain as directed earlier.

BUILDING THE QUANTITY OF YOUR CULTURE

To increase the quantity of your culture for a large recipe or for use in more than one recipe at a time, simply feed the culture as usual without discarding any. You can also increase volume by increasing the amount of flour and water you add at each feeding, as long as you maintain the ratio of equal weights of flour and water. Remember that as your culture grows in volume, it will need proportionately more food: As you go, you'll have to increase the flour and water added to keep the feedings in balance with the size of your culture. As a rule of thumb, you'll want to add at least enough flour and water to equal the weight of your culture to keep it from overripening.

REVIVING A DORMANT OR NEGLECTED CULTURE

If your culture has gone far too long without feeding (which happens to the best of us!), you'll see signs of neglect. It might be covered in a clear but dark liquid, will lack bubbles or other signs of activity, and may have a very sharp aroma. Although the culture appears lifeless (or like something has gone very wrong), its microflora should spring into action again as soon as they get a few good meals.

To revive it, stir the liquid back into the culture, weigh out 50 grams (discard the rest) and feed the culture twice a day at room temperature until it's healthy, bubbly, and active. Sourdough cultures are very hearty and resistant to spoilage due to their acidic nature. The low pH of a sourdough culture discourages the proliferation of harmful microorganisms, and it's rare to irreversibly damage your culture. It *can* happen though. If your culture turns ominously pink or red, shows signs of mold growth, or smells decidedly putrid (rather than sharply acidic or strongly fermented), throw it away and begin again. A very strong, very unpleasant scent is a sign that non-food-fermenting bacteria have invaded the culture.

HOW TO STORE YOUR CULTURE

Ceramic sourdough crocks are a beautiful and traditional choice, but any nonreactive, 1-pint to 1-quart lidded container will do. We like to use clear containers because they allow you to easily see the activity beneath the surface. When feeding, mark the culture's level and the time on the outside of the container, then keep an eye on it as it grows. This makes it simple to determine whether your culture is doubling or tripling within 6 to 8 hours of feeding and helps guide you until you develop a good intuition and comfort level with your culture's needs.

Whatever container you choose, make sure its mouth is wide enough to easily add flour and water, stir, and pour out culture.

Commonly Asked Questions

When it comes to the world of sourdough, more than perhaps anywhere else in our classes, the answer to all the frequently asked questions is "Yes, and . . ." Regardless of what you do, you're almost always going to end up with bread coming out of your oven, though it might not be exactly the bread you were anticipating. The way you'll learn and progress is to track your results: Pay attention to what you did when maintaining the starter and making the bread, and what the resulting bread is like. Then adjust the next time you bake, and repeat!

HOW DO I KNOW IF MY STARTER IS RIPE?

Time is one way to get a sense of ripeness: A common method is to see when the culture has doubled in size. We teach students to rely on more than one cue, as cultures will vary depending on temperature and the overall health of the culture. Smell and sight are the best indicators of ripeness. The culture should have bubbles that will rise to the surface and pop. The culture will *just* have started to recede, and you'll notice rivulets on the top that may be a bit foamy. It'll have a fresh, tangy aroma.

CAN I USE A DIFFERENT FLOUR?

You can! But it's not necessary. We choose to use a 100% hydrated white flour culture because it's simple and less expensive than most whole-grain flours. If you're planning to make primarily rye breads, you may choose to keep a whole rye culture instead. If you're interested in keeping a whole-grain culture, keep in mind that whole grains accelerate both forms of fermentation (bacteria and yeast). That speedy fermentation can make your culture too acidic very quickly—for that reason, whole-grain cultures can be more high maintenance. If you choose this route, one way to manage it is to decrease the hydration of your starter: A stiffer starter will ferment more slowly.

DO I HAVE TO COVER MY CULTURE TIGHTLY?

Just like bread dough, it doesn't need an airtight cover. But you don't want too much airflow or the culture can dry out: A towel is too porous and will allow too much moisture to escape. With a sourdough culture, airtight isn't ideal because pressure can build up as fermentation occurs. A container with a top that allows some air to escape is ideal.

I'M GOING ON VACATION! WHAT ABOUT MY STARTER?

Enjoy your vacation and don't worry about your culture. Feed it before you go and then leave it in the refrigerator. When you return, pick up where you left off. It's very, very difficult to irreversibly harm your culture if you've been diligent in caring for it on a regular basis. Cultures, like bakers, are remarkably resilient.

CAN I FREEZE MY CULTURE OR DOUGH?

Freezing is a no-go. Freezing temperatures kill too many of the microorganisms in your culture. Remember, sourdough is a living thing.

DO I HAVE TO DISCARD IT?

You need to remove some of the culture when feeding for two reasons. First, you'll have too much culture if you don't remove some as you continue to feed. And because you need to keep feeding in proportion to the base amount of culture, the growth will be exponential. Second, discard is the metabolic waste—it's the flavor and carbon dioxide output of fermentation. While this can be a great baking component because it adds leavening and flavor to whatever you're baking, it's not good for the health of the culture. To encourage health in a culture, the levels of metabolic waste and fresh food need to be kept in balance. Yeast is more susceptible to acidity than bacteria: As the culture ripens, the bacteria keep producing acid. As the culture grows more acidic, the yeast's activity level will start to drop. We want to remove a portion of the culture and feed it to realign the activity levels of yeast and bacteria. That discard, though, can be used in many of the recipes that follow. You don't have to use it the day you feed—you can save it until you have enough for a recipe you have in mind or to use at a more convenient time.

Sourdough Crackers

Yield: 50 to 100 crackers depending on size

The concept of discard is a huge obstacle to getting into sourdough for many bakers. They simply can't bear the thought of throwing away all that starter, so having discard recipes on hand is critical. This recipe is a great one for that purpose: It's quick to make and can be easily scaled up and down to match the amount of discard you have. When you feed your starter, simply use any excess in the recipe below and have crisp, can't-stop-eating-them crackers within 40 minutes. Bonus—it uses whole wheat flour!

---

120 grams (1 cup) white whole wheat flour

5 grams (scant teaspoon) salt

60 grams (4 tablespoons) unsalted butter, cold or room temperature

230 grams (about 1 cup) discard culture

seeds or coarse salt for sprinkling (optional)

1. Briefly pulse together the flour and salt in a food processor just to combine.

2. Add the butter and pulse several times, just until the mixture is evenly crumbly, with perhaps a few larger crumbs showing.

3. Add the culture, pulsing to form a cohesive dough.

4. Alternatively, combine the flour and salt using an electric mixer or by hand. Work in the butter until the mixture is crumbly, then stir in the ripe culture to make a smooth dough.

5. Cover the dough and allow it to rest for at least 15 minutes at room temperature.

6. While the dough is resting, preheat the oven to 400°F.

7. Divide the dough in half. On a lightly floured surface, roll each piece about 1⁄16″ thick.

8. Transfer the dough to a parchment-lined baking sheet.

9. If desired, sprinkle the dough with seeds or coarse salt, pressing the topping in with a rolling pin.

10. Dock the dough all over by pricking it all over with a fork.

11. Using a pastry wheel or sharp knife, cut into equal-size rectangles.

12. Bake the crackers for about 9 to 12 minutes, until they're light brown all over (some will have some darker brown spots). Watch closely, as the crackers can go from underbaked to burned quickly.

13. Remove from the oven and let cool on the baking sheet.

Whole Wheat Waffles

Yield: Four 7˝ Belgian-style waffles

These waffles show how simple it can be to modify nonyeasted recipes to utilize your discard. We took a favorite waffle recipe from our website and did the math to incorporate the excess culture from a single feeding. This is a simple process to try for any recipe without yeast, sweet or savory (see sidebar). Since many of us maintain our culture in our refrigerator at home and feed once a week on Sunday mornings, this is a perfect way to use that discard for weekend breakfasts.

120 grams (1 cup) whole wheat flour

8 grams (2 teaspoons) baking powder

½ teaspoon salt

25 grams (2 tablespoons) granulated sugar

1 large egg

290 grams (1¼ cups) milk, lukewarm

100 grams (scant ½ cup) discard culture

71 grams (5 tablespoons) butter, melted, or 67 grams (⅓ cup) vegetable oil

1. Preheat your waffle iron while you make the waffle batter.

2. Whisk together the flour, baking powder, salt, and sugar in a large bowl.

3. In a separate bowl, whisk together the egg, milk, discard culture, and butter or oil.

4. Mix the wet ingredients into the flour mixture, stirring just until combined. The batter will be a bit lumpy.

5. Cook the waffles as directed in the instructions that came with your waffle iron.

How to Use Discard

You can use your discard culture in many recipes if you remember that it's equal weights flour and water. When you're adding discard, simply remove an equal weight of flour and liquid from the recipe as the weight of the culture you're adding. Here's how we did it for the waffle recipe: The original recipe called for 170 grams of whole wheat flour and 340 grams of milk. We used 100 grams of discard comprised of 50 grams of flour and 50 grams of water, and simply reduced the amount of flour and liquid in the recipe accordingly. Just remember that whatever you add, you must subtract the equivalent from the original to keep the recipe ratios equal. You'll want to combine the discard with the remaining liquid ingredients, and you'll find it works beautifully in many recipes—some of our favorites include crackers, cinnamon buns, pancakes, banana bread, and biscuits.

Sourdough English Muffins

Yield: 9 muffins

Homemade English muffins are surprisingly simple . . . and simply delicious. The addition of sourdough adds a depth of flavor and texture that's hard to beat. Here, we use a very small amount of commercial yeast in addition to the ripe culture. The yeast shortens the rise time, which also means a softer flavor since the tang of sourdough intensifies over time. You can leave the yeast out and lengthen the rise if you prefer a stronger flavor. This is a great first recipe for novice sourdough bakers and one you'll find yourself returning to again and again.

---

227 grams (about 1¼ cups) ripe culture

227 grams (2 scant cups) unbleached all-purpose flour, plus more for dusting

1 teaspoon instant yeast

7 grams (1¼ teaspoons) salt

14 grams (2 teaspoons) granulated sugar

21 grams (1½ tablespoons) unsalted butter, melted

170 grams (¾ cup) milk

cornmeal or semolina for dusting

1. Place all the ingredients in a large bowl and stir vigorously for about 1 minute. The dough will be too soft to knead.

2. Cover the bowl and let the dough rise at room temperature for about 1 hour, or until puffy but not fragile.

3. Turn the dough out onto a well-floured surface. Divide it into nine pieces, about 74 grams each.

4. Gently shape into lightly flattened rounds about 3½″ in diameter.

5. Lightly grease nine 3¾″ English muffin rings and dust them with cornmeal or semolina. Or lightly grease a baking sheet (or line it with parchment) and dust with cornmeal or semolina.

6. Place the rounds into the rings or onto the baking sheet. Dust the tops with cornmeal or semolina.

7. Cover the rounds and let them proof for 30 to 60 minutes, until puffy (the dough should still have some spring to it when pressed lightly). While they're rising, preheat a griddle to 300°F.

8. Cook the muffins in their rings, if using, on the griddle for 8 to 10 minutes per side, adjusting the griddle temperature as necessary to make sure the muffins are cooked all the way through but not burned.

9. Allow the muffins to cool completely on a rack before serving.

Tip: If your kitchen is warm, use slightly cooler milk. In cold months, you'll need slightly warmer milk.

Sample Build Schedule

Sourdough breads require advanced planning before you get to mixing and baking. It might be bewildering at first when you set out to bake a sourdough recipe only to realize that your recipe calls for ripe culture, which you would have had to start hours if not days ago. Making a build schedule helps you figure out when you need to start the process.

As we discussed in the care and feeding section (page 84), the health of your culture dictates how quickly you can build: If your culture hasn't been fed regularly or has been refrigerated for some time, it will need more time and regular feeding to gain strength and volume. If you've been feeding your culture regularly, it will respond more quickly, giving you more leeway in your build schedule.

When creating your build schedule, consider when you want to pull the bread from the oven, how much starter you'll need for the final dough, and about how long it will take to have your starter healthy enough to leaven the bread.

In the school we start with 100 grams 48 hours before class and know we can have 16 kilos of bubbly active starter in just four builds. This illustrates the exponential potential of a build schedule.

We start by calculating how much we need altogether and when we need it, then figure backward in 12-hour increments. We know we can triple the volume with each build, so we divide by 3 to work backward and figure the amounts needed for each build.

Let's see what this looks like for a possible real-life schedule. We'll use our English muffins recipe, which calls for 227 grams of ripe culture. Say you want to serve your muffins for a ten a.m. brunch. You'll want to mix your dough about 2 to 2½ hours ahead of that time, say at eight a.m.

Assuming your culture is healthy and chomping at the bit to leaven the bread, you'll want to build it to 277 grams (adding in the 50 grams needed to perpetuate your culture) at eight p.m. the night before, using 93 grams of ripe culture, 93 grams of water, and 93 grams of flour.

Moving back 12 hours earlier to eight a.m. that morning, you would feed 31 grams of culture to 31 grams of water and 31 grams of flour to get the 93 grams you need to use as the base that night.

If you're pulling your culture from the depths of your refrigerator, and it has a layer of dark liquid on top, you'll want to add a few days to the build schedule and start with smaller feedings to build strength. Instead of tripling the quantity for each 12-hour build, you feed a smaller amount each time, allowing more time for the culture to ripen.

You can adjust the timing of the process by shifting variables, including the amount of culture you use in each feeding—more culture ripens more quickly and less ripens more slowly. You can also speed or slow fermentation by using what you know about temperature. Or you can shift feedings as needed. It depends on your schedule needs, your kitchen, and above all, the health of your culture.

Note: These proportions for feeding and building work well in the relatively small quantities home bakers encounter. If you find yourself working with larger quantities or warmer environments with very active culture, you'll find you need to significantly reduce the quantity of culture in proportion to what you're feeding.

Sourdough Sandwich Bread

Yield: 2 loaves

When we say "sourdough bread," so many people think of crusty boules with a pronounced tangy flavor. This tall, tender, fine-grained loaf is a far cry from that! Because it relies on a sourdough culture to leaven the dough along with yeast, this loaf rises beautifully and has a far more complex flavor than a sandwich bread made entirely with commercial yeast. The use of bread flour and the added enrichments of butter, sugar, and milk make for a fantastic loaf for toast or sandwiches.

228 grams (about 1 cup) ripe culture

596 grams (5 cups) unbleached bread flour, plus more for dusting

15 grams (2½ teaspoons) salt

7 grams (2¼ teaspoons) instant yeast

45 grams (3 tablespoons) granulated sugar

45 grams (3 tablespoons) unsalted butter, at room temperature

350 grams (1½ cups) milk

1. Weigh the ingredients into a large bowl and stir together to make a cohesive mass. Adjust the hydration as needed, adding more flour or more milk to make a tacky (but not too soft) dough.

2. Transfer the dough to a very lightly floured work surface and knead it by hand for about 5 minutes, until it's smooth and elastic. Use as little flour on the work surface as possible.

3. Allow the dough to rise, covered, until it's doubled in bulk, about 2 hours.

4. Turn the risen dough out onto a lightly floured surface and divide it in half. Shape the pieces into pan loaves (see page 57) and place in two lightly greased 8½″ × 4½″ loaf pans.

5. Cover the loaves with plastic or a reusable cover and allow them to proof until they're puffy, with a soft marshmallow-like texture, about 2 hours.

6. Bake the bread in a preheated 375°F oven for 30 to 35 minutes, until the crust is golden brown and the sides of the loaf, when you remove one from its pan, are firm to the touch.

FLAVOR MANIPULATION

You can manipulate the flavor in your sourdough recipes, dialing up or dialing down the intensity as you like. To understand how to play around with flavor, it's important to remember where that flavor comes from. As your culture ferments, the bacteria within it are producing two types of acid: lactic and acetic. A common misconception is that lactic acid (the kind you find in yogurt) is milder in flavor than acetic acid, but this isn't true (we've taste-tested!). Both types of acid contribute strong, tangy flavor, and in combination they create a flavor that's fuller and more complex. An example we use in the classroom is applesauce: If you use two different kinds of apples to make it, you get a deeper, more pronounced apple flavor than if you were to just use one. Think of sourdough acids in the same way.

We teach three methods of flavor manipulation:

Adding whole grains: Whole grains speed up fermentation, but they also increase acetic acid production. More acetic acid can translate to a more pronounced sourdough flavor.

Temperature and time: A simple way to manipulate the flavor in any sourdough recipe is to do a slow, cold rise (typically an overnight rise in the refrigerator). Placing the dough in a cold environment like the refrigerator allows you to stretch the fermentation time longer, since it ferments more slowly. The longer the dough ferments, the more time there is for the bacteria to produce acids. Once shaped, you can leave your dough in the refrigerator for up to 16 hours (see opposite page for how long you can push it). After the cold rise, you can take it straight from the refrigerator to the preheated oven.

The introduction of commercial yeast: This will soften the flavor, making it less sharp and tangy. Why? Adding commercial yeast speeds up the fermentation time because it introduces more yeast cells (in addition to your culture's wild yeast). A shorter fermentation means less time for the bacteria to produce acids, which are responsible for flavor.

TIME

(SPEEDING UP OR SLOWING DOWN FERMENTATION)

Don't think of time as a fixed number in sourdough recipes. While there's a broad array of variables that will affect the fermentation in your dough, starting with a couple of easy-to-manage levers keeps things simple to control and track. To speed things up, use warmer water or ferment in a warmer location (80° to 85°F). To slow the process, use cooler water or consider letting your dough ferment slowly in the refrigerator. You can actively manipulate the time it takes for your culture to ripen *and* for your dough to ferment. Keep in mind that a quicker, warmer fermentation will yield a milder flavor, while a slower, cooler fermentation will be tangier.

How Long Do I Chill the Dough?

There's no exact time frame for how long to leave your dough in the refrigerator, just as there's no exact time frame for how long to proof your shaped dough at room temperature. Sixteen hours is a good guideline, but as with any dough, you should be checking to see when it looks fully proofed. Rely on visual cues here, just as you do with proofing at room temperature, knowing that cold refrigerated dough will feel stiffer than room temperature dough, so it won't seem as puffy and marshmallow-y when fully proofed (though it should feel more pillowy than when you started.) Instead, look for an increase in volume as a more reliable indicator. This might seem imprecise at first, but practice helps. The more you bake, the more you'll get a sense of how the dough changes as it proofs.

Since longer fermentation equals more flavor, it's understandable to wonder why you wouldn't want to keep your dough refrigerated for as long as possible. The reason is all about trade-offs. In the short term, the acid produced by bacteria will strengthen the gluten in your dough. In the long term, the acid will begin to break down the gluten, so in return for more flavor, you'll lose structure and strength in your dough.

Because the cold environment of a refrigerator slows the dough's rise (allowing us more time for the acids and flavor to develop), it's helpful to add a little "insurance" to kick-start the proofing process. After shaping, leave your dough out at room temperature for 15 to 30 minutes (but no longer), and *then* refrigerate.

Note that if you're working with a sourdough recipe that calls for commercial yeast and you want to use this cold fermentation method to intensify flavor, you can leave the yeast out—this ensures the dough won't overproof during that initial 15- to 30-minute rest at room temperature.

Crusty Sourdough Bread

Yield: 2 loaves

Here we transition into using a higher proportion of culture, and we see the impact on flavor and timing. Using a higher amount of starter, compared to the sourdough sandwich bread, means we need a shorter fermentation time since there's more culture at work. These loaves are baked on the hearth (meaning directly on a baking stone or surface)—the direct, intense heat allows you to pull crisp loaves from the oven in relatively short order. We love the added tang you get from chilling the shaped loaves overnight before baking.

---

454 grams (about 2 cups) ripe culture

595 grams (5 cups) unbleached all-purpose flour, plus more for dusting

85 grams (¾ cup) whole rye flour

397 grams (1¾ cups) water, plus more as needed

17 grams (2½ teaspoons) salt

1. Weigh the ripe culture into a large bowl.

2. Add the flours and water.

3. Mix the ingredients until all the flour is moistened and the dough has formed a cohesive mass. Add extra water as necessary: The dough should feel soft and tacky. It shouldn't be a batter, but it will be quite soft.

4. Cover the dough and let it rest for approximately 20 minutes.

5. Knead in the salt.

6. Transfer the dough to a very lightly floured work surface and knead it using the wet dough method (see page 53).

7. Place the dough back in the bowl, cover, and let rise until puffy, about 1½ to 2 hours. Halfway through the rise, fold the dough (see page 24).

8. Turn the risen dough out onto a lightly floured work surface and divide it in half.

9. Preshape each piece into a round (see page 25), cover, and let rest for 20 minutes.

(Continued) ⟶

10. Shape the loaves into boules (see page 59), or your desired shape. Allow them to proof, covered, until risen and airy but not too fragile, about 1 to 2 hours.

11. While the loaves are rising, preheat your oven to 450°F with a baking stone, steel, or Dutch oven in the middle. Score the risen loaves (see page 32) and bake with steam (see page 60).

12. Bake the bread until it's crusty and golden brown, about 35 to 40 minutes.

Tip: A proofing basket or couche is useful here (see page 9).

Holding Back the Salt/Autolyse

After bringing the ingredients together but before adding the salt and kneading, some recipes call for a short rest called an autolyse (usually around 20 minutes), which helps reduce the kneading time. Why hold back the salt? Because salt is hygroscopic, it pulls water away from the flour in the dough. A true autolyse also withholds leaveners, though that can be hard to do in doughs that have pre-ferments with large quantities of water (think poolish or a 100% hydrated culture).

Allowing the flour to hydrate in the absence of competition from other ingredients lets gluten formation begin and reduces the kneading time for the final dough. If you use a mixer for your dough, this means you're only mixing for a minute or two after the autolyse, which will greatly reduce the oxidation that can happen in a mechanically mixed dough. If you knead by hand, it's unlikely you'll overoxidize the dough, and the gluten development that accompanies hydration means you'll spend less time with your hands in the sticky dough so there's less risk you'll overflour the dough.

Whole Grains

Whole grains will ferment faster than white flour because they have more nutrients available for yeast to feed on. When properly hydrated and combined with the right proportion of culture and sweetener, this dough rises even *more* quickly, with an especially short final proof. As with any recipe, you want to rely on your senses to tell when your dough is ready at each stage of development and fermentation, but know that a whole-grain recipe is likely to proceed more quickly through those stages than a recipe without whole grains.

Whole Wheat Sourdough Bread

Yield: 2 loaves

In the classroom, we use a culture made with 100% all-purpose flour—for its predictability, ease of feeding, and resilience. But that doesn't mean you can't bake with whole grains. This recipe demonstrates how you can keep a white flour culture and still make spectacular breads with whole-grain flours. Here we use whole wheat flour and a bit of honey to create a complex, not-too-sour hearth bread. We make bâtards with this dough, but feel free to shape it into boules, or even rolls for a quick bake.

---

568 grams (about 2½ cups) ripe culture

340 grams (3 cups) whole wheat flour

284 grams (2⅓ cups) unbleached all-purpose flour

368 grams (1⅔ cups) water, plus more as needed

18 grams (1 tablespoon) salt

28 grams (1 generous tablespoon) honey

1. Weigh all the ingredients into a large bowl and mix to bring the dough together; it should be fairly soft and tacky. If it seems too dry, add a bit of water, 10 grams at a time. Once the dough comes together, cover it and allow it to rest for 15 minutes.

2. Knead the dough until it's smooth and elastic.

3. Cover the dough and let it rise for 2 hours, giving it a fold (see page 24) after 1 hour.

4. Start preheating the oven to 500°F. If you're using a baking stone, steel, or Dutch oven, position it on the center rack.

5. Divide the dough in half and preshape each half into a rough round or oval (see page 25). Let the loaves rest for 20 minutes.

6. Shape the loaves into bâtards (see page 58) or boules (see page 59), and place them on a parchment-covered baking sheet. If you'll be baking on a stone, place each loaf on its own piece of parchment, cut to size: The parchment should be large enough to hold the risen loaf but not so large that there's a lot of excess to potentially sear or smoke in the oven.

7. Proof the loaves until they're risen and puffy but not too fragile, about 20 minutes.

8. Score the risen loaves (see page 32) and bake with steam (see page 60). After 15 minutes, lower the temperature to 400°F and bake the bread until it's crusty and golden brown, about 20 minutes more.

Deli Rye Bread

Yield: 2 loaves

We love teaching this sourdough rye bread because it builds on the same important lesson we demonstrated in the whole wheat sourdough recipe: You can still get the flavor and benefits of whole grains while using a 100% white flour starter. Here, we use our standard white flour culture, then build with whole rye flour, which helps mimic the flavor and fermentation benefits of a stiffer rye culture. Even though we use whole rye in the recipe, the bread itself is a light rye (not too dark and intense in flavor) and flecked with caraway—you'll be impressed by how simple it is to turn out a professional-quality rye!

BUILD

5 grams (1 rounded tablespoon) ripe culture

142 grams (½ cup plus 2 tablespoons) water

170 grams (1½ cups) whole rye or pumpernickel flour, plus more for dusting

FINAL DOUGH

600 grams (5 cups) unbleached all-purpose flour

400 grams (1⅔ cups) water

14 grams (2 teaspoons) salt

1 teaspoon instant yeast

9 grams (1 tablespoon) caraway seeds

BUILD

1. About 12 to 16 hours before mixing the final dough, you'll want to make the build. To do this, mix together the ripe culture and water.

2. Add the rye flour and mix until smooth. This will be thicker than the culture you've been keeping, so be sure to scrape down the sides of the bowl and dust the top with flour before covering to ripen at room temperature overnight.

3. When ripe, this culture will look quite different than our white culture. The floured surface should have cracks all over from the expansion, and the aroma should be quite tangy. It won't be bubbly or foamy on top, but if you dig in a bit, you'll see a spongy interior.

FINAL DOUGH

1. Mix the ripened culture from the build with all the dough ingredients. Knead the dough using the wet-dough kneading technique (see page 53); the dough should be tacky and moderately developed.

2. Place the dough in a lightly greased bowl and let it rise at room temperature for about 1 hour, folding (see page 24) after 30 minutes.

3. Divide the dough in half and shape each piece into a boule (see page 59) or bâtard (see page 58).

4. Allow to proof, covered, until puffy and risen, about 45 to 90 minutes.

5. While the dough is proofing, preheat the oven to 450°F with a baking stone (if you're using one) on the second from bottom rack.

6. Just before baking, score the dough (see page 32).

7. Slide the dough onto the baking stone and bake with steam (see page 60).

8. Bake the bread for 35 to 40 minutes, until the sides are firm, the crust is golden brown, and it feels lighter than it did going into the oven.

9. Remove the bread from the oven and place it on a rack to cool. Cool completely before slicing.

Moderate Dough Development

After kneading, you're aiming for moderate dough development rather than *fully* developed (also called well-developed) dough. Your dough should be significantly stronger than when you started, and you should notice that it has more "muscle" to it. But if you pull on it, it should tear a bit. This is the difference between moderately developed and fully developed: A fully developed dough will resist you more robustly when you pull on it and will "fight back" without tearing or ripping as easily when stretched.

Building Flavor

When we talked about flavor manipulation within the dough itself (see page 98), we discussed how the addition of whole grains increases the production of acetic acid, which intensifies flavor. Here that same technique comes into play in the build rather than in the dough itself. We rely on whole grains to amplify flavor by using rye flour in the build, making a more pronounced rye taste. The culture and the dough use white flour; this demonstrates how introducing whole grains (rye) *only* in the build still has a strong impact on flavor.

Master Class
Miche Pointe-à-Callière

Yield: 1 large loaf

THE BAKER

James MacGuire works as a baking consultant and teacher and has held bread seminars for the American Institute of Baking, the Culinary Institute of America, and the Bread Bakers Guild of America. James taught the first-ever class at the Baking School in September 2000, featuring this *miche* recipe, and he remains a frequent guest instructor. With Dr. Ronald Wirtz, James translated Professor Raymond Calvel's last book, *The Taste of Bread*, from its original French into English. He opened an award-winning café, Le Passe-Partout, in Montreal in 1981, which featured exceptional house-made bread and *viennoiserie*. James now teaches, consults, and writes in-depth articles on all aspects of food for *The Art of Eating*.

THE LOAF

This bread has a fascinating historical context. James was invited to bake bread for an annual reenactment of an 18th-century market in Montreal at the archaeological museum in Pointe-à-Callière. His extensive research included Antoine-Augustin Parmentier's documentation of 18th-century French bread making, and this miche is the result: a robust loaf with a chewy interior and a dark golden-brown crust. Here, James uses a stiff culture and two additional stages of pre-fermentation to develop a depth of flavor in the final loaf that's unmatched by simpler breads. These loaves would traditionally have been made using what we now call high-extraction flour, where the coarsest bran particles are sifted out of the flour, but the germ is not. In this recipe, James mixes white and whole wheat as an approximation. If you have access to high-extraction flour, feel free to use it, but be aware that the dough might require slightly more water.

"

As yeast ferments, it produces acidity that has a firming effect on gluten strands, which will help give your dough its structure. For the stiff culture, you're essentially making a miniature dough, letting it ferment, and then mixing it into your dough. Why? It allows you to start off with all these organic acids, which means that you don't have to let your dough ferment for as long because fermentation has already been kick-started.

—JAMES MACGUIRE

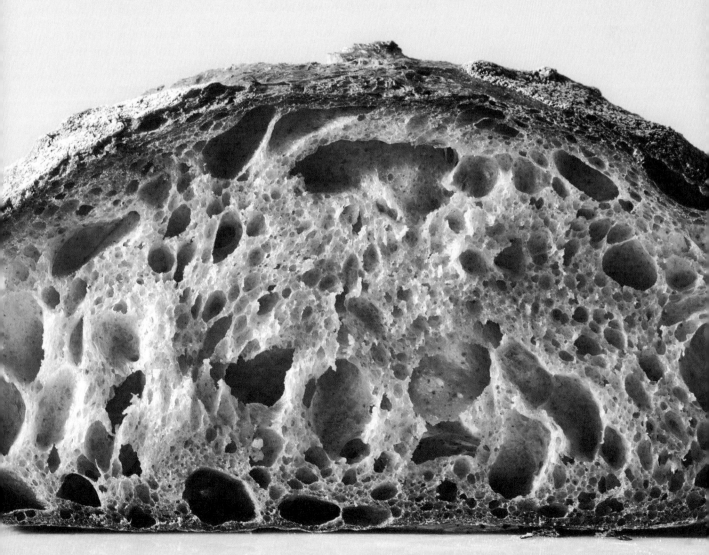

REFRESHER

25 grams (1 rounded tablespoon + 1 teaspoon) ripe stiff culture, fed 8 hours earlier

33 grams (¼ cup) unbleached all-purpose flour

23 grams (1 tablespoon + 1½ teaspoons) water

81 grams total refresher

LEVAIN

81 grams (¼ cup, rounded) refresher (above)

100 grams (¾ cup + 1 rounded tablespoon) unbleached all-purpose flour

70 grams (¼ cup + 2 teaspoons) water

251 grams total levain

FINAL DOUGH

717 grams (6 cups) unbleached all-purpose flour, plus more for dusting

150 grams (1⅓ cups) whole wheat flour

18 grams (1 tablespoon) salt

251 grams (¾ cup, rounded) total levain (above)

657 grams (2¾ cups) water

1,793 grams total dough weight

Tip: Professional bakers, like our guest instructors, use weight—not volume—for best results (see page xvi for more on why).

REFRESHER

1. Place all the refresher ingredients in a small bowl and mix well. The refresher is stiff and will require some kneading to bring together.

2. Cover and let ferment at room temperature for 8 hours.

LEVAIN

1. Mix the refresher with the rest of the levain ingredients. Like the refresher, the levain is stiff and will require kneading to bring together.

2. Cover and let ferment at room temperature for 8 hours.

FINAL DOUGH: MIXING

1. Combine the flours for the final dough in a large bowl and swirl in the salt. Make a well in the center of the dry ingredients, add the levain, and pour the water on top. Use a grabbing motion with one hand to break the levain up into the water and start bringing flour in from the sides using a stirring motion. Once there is no dry flour remaining, allow to rest for 5 to 10 minutes.

2. Instead of kneading, use one hand to pick up the dough from the sides and fold it into the center while the other hand turns the bowl. After 10 or 12 folds, the dough should form a loose ball and begin to come away, at least partially, from the sides. Now is the best time to make corrections if the dough is too firm or too liquid. The ideal consistency is looser and stickier than most people are used to but, when ready, should be relatively smooth, elastic, and not stick excessively to the hands or a work surface. The most important factor is the consistency because the fermentation will compensate for underkneading.

(Continued) ⟶

FINAL DOUGH: FERMENTATION

1. Cover the dough and let rest for 20 minutes.

2. Fold the dough over itself gently to de-gas and stimulate fermentation, then cover. Let rest for another 20 minutes.

3. Fold once again, cover, and let rest for another 20 minutes.

4. Yet another fold, cover, and let rest for 30 minutes this time.

5. A final fold, cover, and let rest 45 minutes.

6. By this point, the fermentation should appear very active (see sidebar). If it isn't, give the dough yet another gentle fold and wait for another 15 to 20 minutes. When the dough is ready, preshape it into a loose, round shape (see page 25; if you want to make smaller loaves, divide the dough into two or three pieces first).

7. Place the preshaped round on a lightly floured surface, cover, and allow to rest for about 30 minutes. This rest lets the dough "relax" so that it won't tear during shaping.

8. Shape as desired (see page 56). Place, with the seam up, into lightly floured banneton baskets or proofing linens. Cover and allow to rise in a draft-free place for 3 to 4 hours. Although the loaves will be denser than yeast-raised loaves, the criteria for oven readiness is the same: If you press your finger gently into the surface of the dough, the indentation should disappear slowly but completely after 2 to 3 seconds.

9. About half an hour to an hour before you're ready to bake, preheat the oven to 450°F with a baking stone or steel in it.

10. Just before baking, place the dough on a piece of parchment paper, seam side down, slide onto a peel, and slash the top.

11. Slide the dough from the peel onto the baking stone and bake with steam (see page 60) before quickly shutting the oven door.

12. After 10 minutes, lower the oven temperature to 400°F. The baking should take almost 90 minutes for a large loaf, 60 minutes or so if divided into two or three pieces. You can turn down the oven even further when the crust begins to color (about 20 minutes into the bake) to ensure a long bake and a crispier crust.

What Is a Stiff Culture?

James prefers a stiff culture for this bread, fed 8 to 12 hours ahead of its use in the recipe. He finds it gives a better rise and more rounded flavor to the bread. This stiffer culture best approximates the practices of bakeries since the 18th century, when they would use a bit of dough saved from the day's bread baking to begin building the next day's dough. The nickname for this bit of dough that powered the next day's bread came to be the "chef." This is wonderfully practical for bakeries making levain loaves daily but may not serve home bakers as well, since few of us bake bread that frequently.

Building and Maintaining Stiff Cultures

If you'd like to build and keep a stiff culture, you can refer to **How to Create a Culture from Scratch** on page 82, but instead use 70% hydration, meaning that for every 50 grams of flour you use, you'd add 35 grams of water instead of 50 grams. You'll have to knead the ingredients together, as it's more of a dough than the liquid culture. By the third or fourth day, you should see significant expansion in the culture. Continue to feed the culture every 12 hours until about day 7 or 8, when the culture should be ready to use in the refresher of the recipe (as well as other recipes calling for stiff culture). You'll know it's strong enough if it's rising to 3½ to 4 times the volume in 6 to 8 hours.

If you prefer to convert a liquid (100% hydration) culture to a stiff culture, it's best to give it a few days of feeding at room temperature at the lower hydration to give the lactobacilli a chance to establish themselves in the new environment and to provide the best flavor and rise for your bread.

Signs of Fermentation

In step 6, you're looking to assess whether there's enough active fermentation to move onto preshaping. The best way to know if the dough is ready is to watch for visual cues. When you've just mixed the dough, before bulk fermentation starts, it will just sit there without any strength. If you were to turn it out onto a work surface, it might even run right to the edge of the table. As it ferments, it will stand up more—toward the end it should look like a very tender sponge. At this point, if it sits on a work surface, you'll see it spread but only slightly. This is fermentation at work! The fermentation is adding structure, and you'll notice (and feel) this structure developing as you fold each time. The first time you fold after  20 minutes, you might need to fold closer to ten times—as you did when mixing the dough. As it sits, you might need only three or four folds by the end. Pay attention to the dough and you'll get a sense for what it needs—if it's very loose and wobbly, add more folds. If it seems to have developed some muscle, use fewer. And remember James's advice: "Good bakers mix little but ferment a lot. This is the key to good bread."

chapter 3.

LAMINATED
PASTRIES

The Classroom

If you can already feel the buttery flakes of a croissant on your fingertips or imagine the contrast of crisp pastry and velvety cream in the first mouthful of a napoleon, then you're in the right place. *Lamination* describes the process of layering dough and fat. When baked, the heat of the oven turns the water in the butter into steam, which makes pockets of air between the layers of dough and creates the flakiness we know and love in croissants and puff pastry.

In our laminated pastry classes, we go *a bit* beyond the classic laminated doughs—puff pastry, croissants, and Danish—to include phyllo dough and blitz puff pastry. These doughs all illustrate different forms of lamination: layering dough and butter to create varying degrees of flakiness.

We begin with phyllo dough because it's such a good introduction to the concepts underpinning lamination, and the dough is already made. The technique is simple—if you've ever brushed frozen sheets of dough with butter to make spanakopita or baklava, you've laminated! Here, we teach you to make your own dough as well.

Blitz puff pastry, sometimes called "rough puff," falls somewhere between pie crust and classic puff pastry. The dough is dotted with chunks of butter, then rolled and folded as in traditional lamination. The end result is flattened shards of butter that force the layers of dough to puff up in the oven.

Next up, classic puff pastry. Here, we rely on a slab of pliable butter and more folding to create many layers. Steam expands between each of those layers during baking, creating thin sheets of flaky pastry. When you bite into puff pastry, the dough shatters into delicate shards of crisp, buttery dough.

As we move into croissant and Danish, we add the flavor of an enriched, yeasted dough. These recipes show puff in a new light, relying on layers of pliable butter and dough *plus* the addition of yeast. Yeast helps drive rise and puff in the dough as it bakes.

Classic laminated doughs are made of a base dough (called the détrempe) and a butter block (literally, a large block of chilled butter, often called the beurrage). The détrempe varies in composition based on the type of pastry. Once the détrempe is mixed and allowed to rest, the fun begins.

The first step in lamination is a "lock-in," which simply refers to the process of placing the butter block onto the détrempe and folding the dough around the butter block to enclose it. (For an extra challenge, try the final recipe of the book, Gesine Bullock-Prado's **Gâteau St. Honoré** on page 370, where the butter is placed around the dough for an inverse puff pastry.)

Next, you laminate through a series of folds and turns (see page 137 for illustrations of each)—rolling out the dough, folding, rolling some more, folding again—until you've made multiple layers of dough-butter-dough-butter-dough. When baked, these layers puff up into thin sheets of buttery pastry.

The Lessons

The recipes in our laminated dough classes all hinge upon the same foundational skills, so we emphasize proper technique and lots of practice to get comfortable with the feel of each step. In this chapter, you will:

- Make and stretch phyllo dough by hand

- Practice single and double folds for blitz puff pastry

- Practice five stages of laminated dough production: creating the détrempe, producing a pliable block of butter, doing a lock-in, performing the "turns" to create flaky layers, and cutting/shaping

- Try different techniques for lock-in and folds for croissants, Danish, and puff pastry

- Gauge proper bake and assess degrees of doneness for laminated doughs

The Setup

KEY INGREDIENTS

Laminated doughs are, at their base, made primarily of butter and flour. The simplicity of the ingredient list helps offset the complexity of the technique, but it also means that we recommend you source the best quality ingredients you can—you'll taste the difference!

These are the functional ingredients we focus on as teaching points during our laminated pastry classes—and what students find waiting at the bench. For more on our ingredient philosophy, please see page xix.

BUTTER

Butter is widely available in two forms: standard supermarket butter and European-style butter. What we call standard butter is made up of about 80% fat and 20% water. European-style butters have more fat (closer to 83%) and less water (around 17%). For laminated doughs, you can use either type, but we prefer European-style butter if possible. Why? The higher fat content makes the butter more pliable, which helps it to "move" with us as we roll rather than fracturing into shards. As you laminate, you're aiming to create thin, even sheets of butter, so you don't want them to break apart.

FLOUR

Although pastries made with laminated doughs are ethereally light and shatteringly crisp, they don't require lower-protein pastry flours. In fact, we use all-purpose flour for our laminated doughs in the classroom, and it's what we recommend you use at home. Why? Because you need some gluten development to give the dough structure and support the butter as you layer it.

YEAST

Yeast isn't a component in all laminated doughs; puff pastry doesn't include it, but croissant and Danish doughs do. Yeast increases the rise of laminated pastry by leavening the dough itself, and it adds a depth of flavor as the dough ferments.

EQUIPMENT

BENCH KNIFE

When working with the butter blocks in classic laminated doughs, try to use tools in place of your hands as much as possible to keep the butter from softening or melting. Bench knives are your best friend here: They're excellent for squaring off butter blocks and rolled doughs, for quick measurements, and to keep surfaces clean as we work.

PASTRY BRUSH

Pastry brushes come with two different types of bristles: natural or nylon/silicone. A brush is an essential tool for brushing thin layers of melted butter onto phyllo dough, or applying an egg wash before baking or a glaze afterward. We also use a dry pastry brush to brush excess flour off dough during the lamination process.

PIZZA WHEEL/PASTRY WHEEL

Some pastry recipes, such as croissant or Danish, require precision in trimming your dough to a specific size for shaping. A pizza wheel or pastry wheel makes this task quick and easy.

ROLLING PIN

Rolling is an essential step in laminated dough recipes, and a good-quality rolling pin is a must-have. Choose one that feels the most comfortable in your hands, as you're the one putting it to use! See page 177 for more details on types of pins.

RULER

Laminated dough recipes are full of measurements! You'll need to keep track of your dough's dimensions as you roll, and a ruler allows you to check that you're on track rather than trying to eyeball the sizing.

The Bake

The final element of any recipe is the bake. We use this term in baking—and especially in professional bakeries—to refer to both the final stage of a recipe in the oven as well as the result. (We might say that a croissant has a lighter or a darker "bake," referring to its color and degree of doneness.)

Gauging the bake of laminated doughs is an important element in mastering the genre and requires your senses. In class, we show a spectrum: As students start to smell the tantalizing scent of butter wafting through the room, we pull one croissant from the oven around the time when the batch has started to take on a beautiful golden brown color, which is when many bakers think croissants are done. We wait a little longer, then take the rest out when they're baked to a deeper golden brown that extends all the way around the exterior of the pastries. We hold them up to show how one holds its shape while the other sags. We slice into each to show the difference in the cross section, how one sends flakes flying and one doesn't, and how one forms a dense layer toward the bottom of the croissant, where it didn't get the chance to fully puff and set before it was pulled from the oven. We let everyone taste both, so students can see and taste that the lighter one, while still buttery and delicious, doesn't have the degree of flakiness or the depth of flavor the darker ones do.

This is a pivotal teaching moment! Many of us are used to very pale pastries, like supermarket croissants that tend to be barely golden brown. This is because mass-produced commercial pastries often use shortening, which is cheaper than butter and yields a very tender texture (like a melt-in-your-mouth pie crust or soft, breadlike croissant), *but* doesn't brown well. Our laminated pastries call for butter exclusively, both because of its flavor and its water content, which helps drive all the puff we love in pastry. To create the steam for the layering to happen, the water needs to reach a high temperature, so we bake laminated doughs with butter at a high temperature. Butter also contains milk sugars that brown and caramelize during baking. Some doughs are also enriched with milk, sugar, and eggs, all of which contribute to browning. So, a "proper" bake will likely be darker than what you'd see in many commercial, mass-produced pastries.

Remember, though, that the bake is up to you! Maybe you like a lighter color to your croissants, and that's okay. Just be sure they've been in the oven long enough for the water in the butter to evaporate. Otherwise, you'll find your croissants fall once removed from the oven; have a more tender, underdone center without as many layers; and soften more quickly. If you prefer a more traditional croissant with a crisp exterior that shatters when you bite into it and well-defined layers that hold their loft even after cooling, challenge yourself to leave the croissants in the oven until they're a shade darker than you feel comfortable with, as we ask students to try in the classroom.

Commonly Asked Questions

ARE MORE LAYERS BETTER?

It's tempting to think that more layers are always better, but that's not necessarily the case. Each time you roll and fold the dough, you're creating layers of dough and butter. Those layers become thinner with each roll until eventually they become so thin they fuse together. Once you cross that line, you actually lose layers instead of making more. Our recipes are written to yield the number of folds that we've found just right for home bakers to master by hand. In a commercial setting, bakers use dough sheeters and blast chillers so they can get away with more layers. At home, with your own two hands, a rolling pin, and a regular refrigerator, it's best to aim for a more achievable number of layers to ensure success.

DO I NEED TO START OVER IF I FRACTURE MY BUTTER?

In a perfect world, we'd always have perfectly even, thin layers of dough and butter stacked together. In our world, however, there are many factors at play, including the type of butter you're using, the temperature and consistency of your butter block and détrempe, the room temperature, and the resting time between folds. All these variables mean that sometimes your butter may shatter. This is not a deal-breaker, and there's no need to start over. You might not win the Pastry World Cup with that batch of dough, but you'll still end up with a gorgeous, warm, flaky pastry.

I DON'T HAVE TIME! IS THERE A SHORTCUT?

It can take up to 3 days to make some laminated doughs, though much of that time is resting and chilling. Many bakers love the ritual and care that goes into longer, more involved recipes like this: There's comfort and mindfulness in tradition. But if you're looking for flaky layers fast, Blitz Puff Pastry (page 134) is the way to go. There are subtle differences between traditional and blitz puff, but blitz puff pastry comes together in about 20 minutes and needs only a quick 20 to 30 minutes of rest before it's ready to be rolled, shaped, and baked.

WHY DO I KEEP THE DOUGH COLD?

Pastry is notorious for needing to be *cold*, but it's helpful to remember why temperature matters and what effect it has. The butter is the biggest factor here: You want it to be cool but still pliable. If your kitchen is hot, the butter can soften, making the process messy and preventing distinct layers, which will affect the final texture of your pastry.

The dough, too, needs to be cool, and the butter block and détrempe should be matched in temperature and consistency when you perform the lock-in and the folding.

This means aligning the butter with the consistency of the dough, which varies by recipe.

Phyllo Dough

Yield: 1 batch, 327 grams, 30″ × 36″ square, enough for eight 9″ × 14″ pieces

Many people are familiar with lamination in the form of packaged phyllo: layers of frozen dough and melted butter that bake into a magically crisp result. Making the dough from scratch and using it fresh is a revelation. This recipe relies on kneading to develop the gluten, giving the dough sufficient strength to stretch without tearing. The dough will be a little thicker than store-bought sheets but makes a delicious, country-style pastry and, once stretched, brings an incredible sense of accomplishment. Before you begin, make sure you have a space large enough to let you stretch the dough to 30″ × 36″ and a smooth-weave cloth large enough to match.

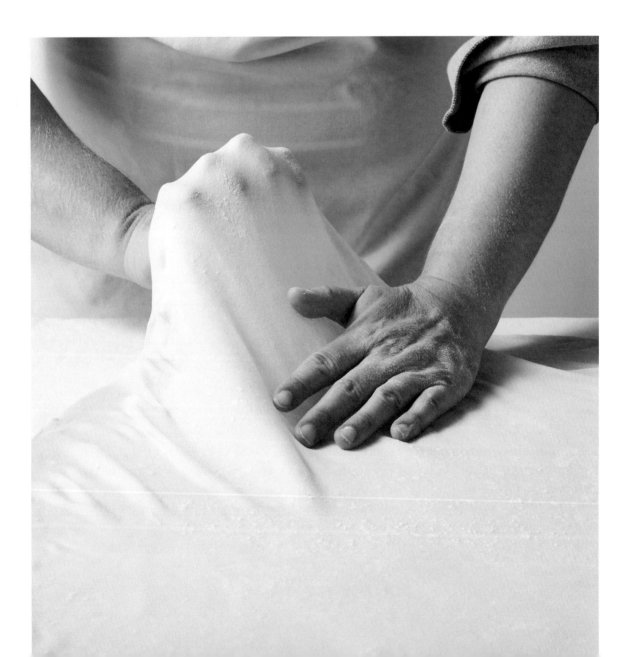

210 grams (1¾ cups) unbleached all-purpose flour, plus more for dusting

⅛ teaspoon salt

89 grams (6 tablespoons) water, plus more as needed

25 grams (2 tablespoons) vegetable oil

½ teaspoon white vinegar

Tip: The acid makes the dough more extensible and easier to stretch.

1. In a medium bowl, combine the flour and salt.

2. Add the water, oil, and vinegar, stirring to form a dry, shaggy mass.

3. Turn the dough out onto an unfloured work surface and knead until it's firm and smooth.

4. Cover the dough and allow it to rest at room temperature for at least 30 minutes, or up to a day.

5. Cover your work surface with a clean, smooth tablecloth or cotton sheet; it needs to be at least 3' square. Dust the cloth thoroughly with flour.

6. Place the dough in the middle of the cloth. Use a rolling pin to roll the dough into a circle about ¼″ thick and 8″ to 10″ in diameter.

7. Remove all jewelry and watches. Flour the backs of your hands. Lift the dough and drape it over the backs of your hands and wrists.

8. Turn the dough in a circular motion; the dough's weight will start the stretching process.

9. With the dough draped over the back of your hands, continue to stretch it by pushing one hand away from you while pulling your other hand toward you.

10. Use the same technique to stretch the dough left to right. Employ gentle pressure and resist the urge to use your fingers.

11. Your goal is to stretch the dough to at least 30″ × 36″. It will be tissue-paper thin; you should be able to read your recipe through it.

12. When you're done stretching, pull off any thicker dough around the edges.

13. Stretched dough should be cut or rolled immediately.

Tearing, Not Trimming

Tearing or pulling off the thicker dough around the edges is traditional and preferable to trimming the edges with a knife. Pulling at the phyllo allows the edges to taper, becoming thinner and thinner until they reach the ripping point, which ensures the dough is a uniform thickness; if you cut the edges of the phyllo, the edges tend to be blunt and thicker than the thinly stretched areas.

Proper Stretching Technique

When stretching phyllo dough, first place a clean cotton sheet or tablecloth on top of the work surface, then stretch the dough on top of it. The fabric helps keep the dough from sticking or tearing *and* makes it easier to cut and move (or roll and move if you're filling it). If you're adding filling, as with strudel, the sheet assists in getting the rolling started, since the dough is very thin and the filling is heavy. Using the sheet or cloth also gives you better leverage to transfer the filled strudel onto the baking sheet since you can roll it up to move it.

Don't worry too much if the dough does tear a bit as you stretch it. Tears *will* happen! Practice helps: The more you do it, the better you'll get. Most tears happen around the edges, and since we're tearing the edges off eventually, those aren't an issue. If you have multiple people stretching the dough (which isn't essential but can be helpful and fun), we recommend having one person heavily dust the palm of their hand with flour and place it over the hole. Then, another person continues to stretch the dough around the hole. If the hole continues to get bigger, it's best to move to another area of the dough. Phyllo is all about layering, so a few tears here and there won't make a big difference in the overall outcome. If you go into it knowing you're going to have tears, it takes a lot of the anxiety away. Removing any jewelry will help to reduce tears, as will focusing on using the flat top of your hand while keeping your knuckles slightly curled under instead of extending your fingertips.

Savory Strudel

Yield: 2 medium (15″) strudels

This strudel is traditionally made with ground lamb, but feel free to substitute other ground meats for the protein. The key to success here is keeping the dough buttered as you roll. Use the weight of the filling to help you roll—the heft of the filling gives you a little more leverage and momentum as you're starting out. A little trick to add even more flavor is to soak the raisins in a warm liquid other than water, such as chicken stock, apple juice, or even liqueur.

(Continued)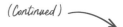

FILLING

43 grams (¼ cup) raisins

119 grams (½ cup) warm water

12 grams (1 tablespoon) olive oil

113 grams (1 medium) onion, peeled and cut into ¼" dice

454 grams (1 pound) ground beef or lamb

1 teaspoon cinnamon

1 teaspoon allspice

85 grams (6 tablespoons) full-fat Greek yogurt

28 grams (¼ cup) pine nuts, (toasted)

salt and pepper

DOUGH

1 batch Phyllo Dough (page 124)

ASSEMBLY

57 grams (4 tablespoons) unsalted butter, melted

FILLING

1. In a small bowl, combine the raisins and warm water. Set aside to let the raisins plump for about 10 minutes.

2. Heat the oil in a medium sauté pan over medium heat. Add the onion, cooking until transparent.

3. Increase the heat and add the meat, cinnamon, and allspice. Brown until cooked through, draining excess fat if necessary.

4. Remove from the heat and allow to cool to room temperature, then stir in the yogurt and pine nuts.

5. Drain the raisins, then add them to the mixture.

6. Season with salt and pepper to taste. Chill the filling until you're ready to assemble the strudel.

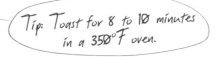

Tip: Toast for 8 to 10 minutes in a 350°F oven.

ASSEMBLY AND BAKING

1. Preheat the oven to 375°F. Butter a parchment-lined baking sheet and set aside.

2. Stretch the phyllo dough into a 30″ × 36″ rectangle, following the instructions on page 125. Pull off any thick edges, then add the filling mixture in a narrow column along one short side of the dough. Roll the dough around the filling, brushing the top of the dough with melted butter as you roll.

3. Once rolled, cut the strudel in half to make two 15″-long pastries.

4. Transfer the strudels to the prepared baking sheet and brush the tops with more melted butter.

5. With a sharp knife, score through the top layers of each strudel in 2″ segments until you reach the filling (but don't go through the filling).

6. Bake the strudels until their tops are golden brown and the filling is bubbling, about 25 to 30 minutes.

Rose Water Baklava

Yield: about 2 dozen 1½″ pieces

This recipe is our version of baklava. The lighter rose water simple syrup replaces the honey-based syrup. We teach it with frozen phyllo to introduce the concept of lamination: layers of dough interspersed with butter. You can, of course, use homemade phyllo dough—if you choose to use homemade, use fewer layers, since the homemade dough will be a bit thicker than store-bought. If you want a crisp yet saturated (and sweeter) pastry, pour the syrup over the baklava while hot as directed; for a crisp but not-so-sweet result, wait until the baklava cools to drizzle on the cold syrup.

SYRUP

149 grams (¾ cup) granulated sugar

89 grams (6 tablespoons) water

8 grams (1½ teaspoons) lemon juice

5 grams (1 teaspoon) rose water

FILLING

199 grams (1¾ cups) nuts (walnuts, pecans, or pistachios)

50 grams (¼ cup) granulated sugar

5 grams (1 teaspoon) rose water

DOUGH

227 grams (½ box) frozen phyllo dough

ASSEMBLY

170 grams (12 tablespoons) unsalted butter, melted

SYRUP

1. In a small saucepan, bring the sugar, water, and lemon juice to a boil over high heat.

2. Lower the heat to a simmer and cook for 5 to 10 minutes, until slightly thickened.

3. Remove the syrup from the heat and stir in the rose water.

4. Set the syrup aside to cool completely to room temperature.

FILLING

1. Place the nuts, sugar, and rose water in the bowl of a food processor or blender and process until the nuts are coarsely chopped. Set aside.

Tip: We cut the frozen sheets of phyllo in half on the long side because the full sheets won't lie flat in the pan, meaning you'd wind up with wadded dough along the edge. If you want to make a full 9″ × 13″ pan of baklava, trim the sheets so they'll lie flat and double the ingredient quantities, using a full box of frozen phyllo.

(Continued) ⟶

ASSEMBLY AND BAKING

1. Preheat the oven to 350°F. Lightly brush a 9″ × 13″ pan with melted butter.

2. Cut the phyllo sheets to make about forty 7″ × 9″ pieces (in half on the long side for store-bought sheets). Lay one sheet in the pan and brush with melted butter. Layer on three more sheets of phyllo, brushing each with butter. (The sheets won't fill every inch of the 9″ x 13″ pan—that's okay; see the tip on page 129.)

3. Sprinkle a thin layer of the nut mixture (about 28 grams) evenly over the buttered phyllo sheets.

4. Layer three more sheets of phyllo, brushing each with butter, on top of the nut mixture.

5. Sprinkle with a thin layer of the nut mixture.

6. Continue to layer four buttered phyllo sheets, then a thin layer of nut mixture until all of the phyllo and nuts have been used.

7. Using a sharp knife, cut the baklava into pieces. Start by making cuts at 1½″ intervals the length of the baklava along the short edge.

8. Next, make diagonal cuts at 1½″ intervals, starting from the top left corner. This will form diamond-shaped pieces. Use your hand to keep the cut pieces in place to prevent them from shifting as you continue to cut.

9. Bake the baklava for 20 to 25 minutes, until deep golden brown.

10. Pour the cooled syrup over the hot baklava as soon as it comes out of the oven. Using less syrup will result in a crispier baklava, while using more syrup will result in a softer baklava.

Working with Frozen Phyllo

When using frozen store-bought phyllo dough (which you might prefer in some applications, as it will be thinner than from-scratch dough), you should thaw it in the refrigerator overnight, then bring it to room temperature before beginning the recipe. This slow thaw cuts down on condensation, reducing the chances the dough will stick together when you try to separate the sheets.

Be sure to have all your ingredients prepped and ready to go before opening the package of dough since you'll want to work quickly to prevent it from drying out. You can also cover the phyllo once you've opened it with a piece of plastic wrap and a dry towel. Don't use a damp towel, as that will make the sheets of phyllo moist and gummy and *more* likely to stick together. Any unused phyllo sheets should be immediately folded or rolled and placed in a well-sealed bag, or well wrapped with plastic wrap. Store in the refrigerator and use within 1 or 2 days. If you keep it longer than that, it will start to dry out and become brittle.

Chocolate Phyllo Triangles

Yield: 6 triangles

These delectable bites come to us from Emily Luchetti, who taught at the school just before our move to our new classrooms. We use them to teach another shape for lamination—the triangular turnover. Here we fill them with chocolate, but you can easily vary both the filling and the size. The chocolate batons are a tidier way to add the filling, since you don't have to worry about bits of chocolate falling out as you fold, but chips or wafers will also work.

---

8 sheets (9″ × 14″ each) Phyllo Dough (page 124)

113 grams (8 tablespoons) unsalted butter, melted

12 chocolate batons or **60 grams, (about 6 tablespoons)** semisweet chocolate chips or dark chocolate wafers

confectioners' sugar for dusting (optional)

1. Preheat the oven to 350°F. Line a baking sheet with parchment paper.

2. Place one sheet of phyllo dough lengthwise in front of you. Brush the sheet with melted butter.

3. Place another sheet of phyllo on top, brushing it with butter. Repeat this stacking and buttering with two more sheets of phyllo, for a total of four layers.

4. Using a pastry wheel or sharp knife, cut the phyllo lengthwise into three equal (3″) strips.

5. Place two chocolate batons, broken in half (or 1 tablespoon of chocolate chips or wafers) at the bottom of one strip.

6. Fold the end of the phyllo, with the chocolate inside, diagonally up to the edge of the strip. Next fold the triangle straight up, along its base. Then fold again on the diagonal; if you've ever folded a flag, this is the same series of folds.

7. Repeat folding, alternating the direction with each fold, until you reach the end of the strip. You'll end up with a triangular packet of phyllo-enclosed chocolate.

8. Repeat with the remaining two strips of phyllo to make two more triangles. Place the triangles on the prepared baking sheet.

9. Repeat with the remaining ingredients, stacking four buttered phyllo sheets, cutting lengthwise, filling with chocolate, and folding as directed above.

10. Place the triangles on the prepared baking sheet and brush the tops with melted butter.

11. Bake the triangles until golden brown, about 15 minutes. Serve warm.

Blitz Puff Pastry

Yield: 1 batch pastry, about 590 grams

While traditional puff pastry can be quite time consuming to make, this version (literally translated from German as "lightning") comes together in under an hour, with half that time spent resting in the refrigerator. Here, the lamination comes from the larger pieces of fat in the dough. When you roll the dough, the butter elongates and stays relatively intact through the series of folds, producing layers of fat and dough that puff when baked. Many of our instructors refer to Blitz Puff Pastry as their "ace in the hole" because it uses just three pantry ingredients (flour, salt, and butter) and can be used in sweet or savory applications for everything from desserts to appetizers.

---

240 grams (2 cups) unbleached all-purpose flour

½ teaspoon salt

227 grams (16 tablespoons) unsalted butter, cold, cut into ½˝ dice

119 grams (½ cup) water, cold

1. In a medium bowl, combine the flour and salt.

2. Toss the butter into the flour mixture to coat.

3. Gently flatten the butter pieces with your fingers, being mindful to keep them intact. You're aiming for a combination of flour and flattened chips of cold butter. As you work the dough later, the butter pieces will flatten out even more and create "planes" of butter.

4. Mix the water into the flour mixture with a few quick strokes. The dough won't be cohesive at this point (see sidebar).

5. Turn the crumbly dough out onto a lightly floured work surface and pat it into a rough rectangle.

6. Use a floured rolling pin to gently roll the dough into a 6˝ × 20˝ rectangle. Position it with a short side closest to you.

7. Perform a letter fold (see page 136).

8. Turn the dough 90 degrees so the folded edge is on your left.

9. Again, roll the dough into a 6˝ × 20˝ rectangle.

10. Perform a book fold (see page 136).

11. With the folded edge on your left, roll one more time and perform a second book fold.

12. Wrap the dough and chill it for at least 30 minutes before using.

13. Store Blitz Puff Pastry in the refrigerator, covered, for up to 2 days or freeze for up to 3 months. Thaw the pastry overnight in the refrigerator before using.

A Very Rough Puff

Blitz Puff Pastry is a dough that looks worse before it looks better. If it's falling apart and doesn't look cohesive as you begin to roll it out, don't panic: You're on the right track. Resist the urge to add more water. Because the butter pieces are left intact, the flour isn't coated with fat as you mix the dough. So, it absorbs water quite quickly and won't get incorporated smoothly into the dough until you've performed a few turns. Use a bench knife or spatula to fold your dough in the beginning when it's messy looking. As you continue to roll and fold, it will come together into a smoother, layered dough.

Direction Matters

As you read through the recipe, it may seem overly fussy to pay such close attention to which way the folds are oriented before you roll each time, but it does matter. We stress dough orientation because it's the best way of ensuring that the dough is getting rolled and "turned" in opposite directions each time. Let's use the letter fold here as an example: If you picture the dough in front of you with the short side facing you, you'd be taking the "top" and "bottom" short sides and folding them over each other like a letter. In class, we instruct students to roll directly in front of them, which is the easiest way, then move the dough as needed before folding and rolling again. That's why we specifically call out checking if the folded edge is on the left before proceeding—it ensures that you're not continuously rolling the same direction each time.

FOLDING TERMINOLOGY

The words *turn* and *fold* are tossed around a lot in pastry production, and it can get confusing to keep track of what they mean. Different recipes use different terminology to mean the same thing, so we like to break down the method for students so they know what to look for regardless of the recipe source.

The letter fold, sometimes called a single fold, is performed by folding the top third of the dough down and the bottom third up, as you'd fold a business letter. The book fold, sometimes called a double fold, has you fold both ends in to meet in the center, then fold in half from the top or bottom to make a book.

Once the dough is folded, turn it 90 degrees to keep the folded edge on the left (see sidebar, page 135), then roll out again and perform another fold. It's important to use enough flour to keep the dough from sticking, which can result in the loss of layers. Be sure to brush that flour away with each step so that raw flour is never folded into the turns.

Some bakers refer to the entire step for each (rolling + folding + turning) as a "turn," and some as a "fold," though the full step involves both folding *and* turning! For our purposes, we refer to it as a fold. Just keep in mind that the entire step for either a letter or a book fold requires several small folds, rolling, and turning the entire dough to reorient it.

LETTER FOLD: STEP 1

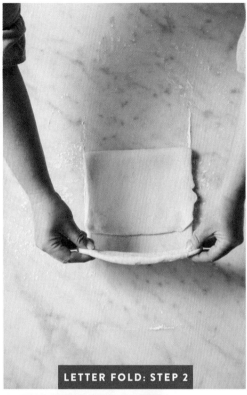

LETTER FOLD: STEP 2

BOOK FOLD: STEP 1

BOOK FOLD: STEP 2

BOOK FOLD: STEP 3

Laminated Pastries 137

Apple Galette

Yield: one 7″ × 10″ galette

If you have puff pastry on hand in the freezer, this is a wonderful go-to template for a very quick and very elegant dessert. It has all the same qualities as a pie—juicy fruit filling, buttery pastry—but without all the rolling and crimping and care that pie crust requires. We love the simplicity of an apple galette, but you can vary the fruit according to the season—just remember to use less juicy fruits to avoid a soggy pastry.

½ batch Blitz Puff Pastry (page 134), chilled

1 large apple, peeled (or not), cored, and sliced ⅛″ thick

1 large egg white

12 to 25 grams (1 to 2 tablespoons) granulated sugar or cinnamon sugar

1. Preheat the oven to 400°F. Line a baking sheet with parchment paper.

2. On a lightly floured surface, roll the pastry into an 8″ × 12″ rectangle about ⅛″ thick.

3. Cut a ½″ strip off each of the four sides and set them aside. Brush the edges of the rectangle with egg white and lay the strips on top to create a low "wall" all around the border of the pastry.

4. Arrange the apple slices on the pastry, overlapping slightly.

5. Sprinkle the apple slices with the sugar, to taste.

6. Bake the galette for 20 to 25 minutes, until it's nicely browned and puffed. The bottom will be golden brown, and the apples should be tender and starting to caramelize.

Savory Parmesan Palmiers

Yield: about 24 palmiers

This shaping technique can be used with both sweet and savory flavors. Here, we pair the blitz puff with mustard and Parmesan for a quick appetizer. Feel free to substitute pesto or tapenade for an equally delectable bite. Keep in mind, you'll want to use fillings that pack maximum flavor so the pastry isn't overwhelmed by the quantity of filling—a thin layer works best. We teach sweet palmiers with Traditional Puff Pastry (see page 142), but you can swap sweet fillings into this recipe as well.

---

28 grams (2 tablespoons) Dijon mustard

¼ to ½ teaspoon cayenne pepper or smoked paprika

½ batch Blitz Puff Pastry (page 134), chilled

50 grams (½ cup) grated Parmesan

1. Preheat the oven to 400°F. Line a baking sheet with parchment paper.

2. In a small bowl, stir together the mustard and cayenne. Set aside.

3. On a lightly floured surface, roll the pastry dough into an 8″ × 12″ rectangle about ⅛″ thick.

4. Spread the mustard mixture in a thin, even layer to the edges of the pastry.

5. Sprinkle the Parmesan evenly over the mustard.

6. Using both hands, gently lift one long edge of the pastry and fold it (firmly) and evenly over itself in 1″ sections until you reach the center of the pastry.

7. Repeat, folding the other long edge in the same manner to meet in the center. Then fold the two edges together to form a U shape.

8. Slice the pastry into ½″-thick slices. Place them about 2″ apart on the prepared pan.

9. Bake the palmiers for about 15 minutes, or until they're puffy and a deep golden brown.

10. Remove the palmiers from the oven and transfer them to a rack to cool completely.

Tip: Fold the dough sharply, like creasing a piece of paper, to ensure it holds its shape.

Traditional Puff Pastry (Pâte Feuilletée)

Yield: 1 batch pastry (about 520 grams)

Traditional puff pastry is a multiday process, but as with so much of baking, the majority of the time isn't hands-on, as the dough rests in the refrigerator. Here, the fat is sealed into the dough, then rolled and folded repeatedly to make the many layers (289 here!) that puff when baked in a hot oven. During the initial kneading of the détrempe, you only knead enough to bring the ingredients together, not to fully develop the gluten, since gluten formation continues during the lamination process. Once the recipe is complete, you can freeze the pastry to have on hand up to 3 months ahead of time.

DÉTREMPE

225 grams (1¾ cups + 2 tablespoons) unbleached all-purpose flour, plus more for dusting

6 grams (1 teaspoon) salt

28 grams (2 tablespoons) unsalted butter, room temperature

119 grams (½ cup) water, cold

BUTTER BLOCK

142 grams (10 tablespoons) European-style unsalted butter, cold

DÉTREMPE

1. In a medium bowl, combine the flour and salt.
2. Cut the butter into the flour until it's fully worked in, and the mixture looks like a coarse meal.
3. Add the water and mix to make a shaggy dough.
4. Turn the dough out onto a lightly floured surface and knead gently for about 1 minute. The dough should be cohesive and slightly elastic with no visible dry patches of flour. It might look like the outside of an orange: slightly bumpy and not smooth—that's okay.
5. Shape the dough into a disk (it doesn't need to be too precise).
6. Place the détrempe in a plastic bag or airtight container and refrigerate for at least 5 hours, or overnight.

BUTTER BLOCK

1. Place the butter on an unfloured surface and pound it with a rolling pin until it's pliable.
2. Working quickly to avoid warming the butter too much, mold the butter into a flat 4″ square, about ¾″ thick. If it's starting to soften or melt, place it in the refrigerator to stay cool while you roll out the détrempe. Remember, you're aiming for the butter and the dough to be equally pliable, so don't chill to the point that it's hard.

LOCK-IN

1. Remove the détrempe from the refrigerator and, on a lightly floured surface, use a sharp knife to score a deep X through the top, being careful not to cut all the way through.

2. Gently press the edges of the dough outward to resemble a four-leaf clover; you're trying to open and flatten the dough a bit here without activating its gluten.

3. Using a rolling pin, gently roll the dough into a 5″ square about ¼″ thick, big enough to enclose the butter block.

4. Brush away all excess flour and place the chilled butter in the center of the dough at a 45-degree angle so it looks like a diamond in a square.

5. Working clockwise, fold the dough over the butter one section at a time so that the dough just comes together and the butter is completely enclosed. Seal in the butter by pressing the dough together at the seams.

(Continued)

TURNS

1. Place the square of dough in front of you with the seams up (see sidebar below). With your rolling pin, tap the dough a few times across the top, working from the center outward.

2. Roll the dough about ¼″ thick into a rectangle roughly 6″ × 16″. Position the dough so one of the short sides is closest to you.

3. Perform a letter fold.

4. Turn the dough so that the folded edge is on your left, then tap it with your rolling pin before rolling it into a 6″ × 16″ rectangle about ¼″ thick.

5. Perform a second letter fold.

6. Wrap the dough in plastic wrap and refrigerate for at least 45 minutes to relax the gluten.

7. When ready to continue, place the dough on a lightly floured surface and repeat the process of tapping and rolling. This time, roll the dough into a rectangle about 6″ × 20″, making sure that the folded edge is always on the left when you start rolling and when you fold.

8. Perform a book fold.

9. Refrigerate the dough for at least 45 minutes, again to relax the gluten.

10. For the final fold, with the folded edge on the left, roll the dough into a 6″ × 20″ rectangle about ¼″ thick and repeat the book fold.

11. Rest the wrapped dough in the refrigerator for 5 hours (or overnight) before using it in a recipe.

Time

Traditional laminated dough can take up to 3 days to make, as the process of folding over and over to create multiple layers of dough/butter/dough/butter is labor-intensive and requires plenty of resting time. Many recipes involve two types of folds (letter folds and book folds) to give the baker flexibility in timing. The resting time is inactive, but don't be tempted to skip it—it's crucial for allowing the dough to relax, making it possible to continue the series of folding and rolling that yields layers in the dozens or even hundreds.

Palmiers

Yield: about 24 palmiers

These are the traditional sweet palmiers, also known as elephant ears. We bake them a little differently here than we do in the savory palmiers (page 140) by placing another sheet pan on top to keep them flat and even. This serves two purposes: It gives them a more professional-looking finish (whereas the savory palmiers will look slightly more rustic), and it helps to crisp and caramelize the sugar, resulting in a gorgeously burnished, crunchy sugar exterior.

Demerara sugar for sprinkling

½ **batch** Pâte Feuilletée (page 142), chilled

1. Preheat the oven to 400°F. Line a baking sheet with parchment paper.

2. Sprinkle your work surface heavily with Demerara sugar. Place the dough on the sugar, then sprinkle it heavily with additional sugar to keep it from sticking as you roll it into an 8″ × 12″ rectangle approximately ⅛″ thick.

3. Sprinkle the dough heavily with more sugar, then use your rolling pin to gently press the sugar into the dough.

4. Score a superficial line midway through the dough, lengthwise, and fold each of the long sides toward the middle in 1″-wide folds, eventually sandwiching the two sides together in the center of the dough to make a U shape.

5. Using a sharp knife, cut the log into ½″-thick slices.

6. Place the palmiers about 2″ apart on the prepared baking sheet.

7. Top the palmiers with another piece of parchment paper and an additional baking sheet to weigh them down.

8. Bake the palmiers for 10 to 12 minutes, then remove the top baking sheet and parchment, flip the pastries over, and continue to bake until they're a deep golden brown, an additional 5 to 7 minutes. The sugar will be nicely caramelized.

9. Remove the palmiers from the oven and let them cool right on the pan.

Napoleons

Yield: five 2″ × 4″ pastries

Napoleons are the pinnacle of the puff pastry dessert world. This traditional version layers baked pastry with pastry cream. The finishing touch is a distinctive design of white icing swirled with chocolate. As you get comfortable with assembling the pastry, you'll find yourself thinking of delicious ways to vary the recipe and create your own signature dessert. You can flavor the cream or add layers of fruit or jam to create your own showstopping versions.

½ **batch** Pâte Feuilletée (page 142), chilled

1 recipe Pastry Cream (page 213)

1 recipe White Icing (recipe follows)

28 grams (2 to 3 tablespoons) semisweet or bittersweet chocolate chips or wafers, melted

1. On a lightly floured surface, roll the dough into an 11″ × 14″ rectangle about ⅛″ thick.

2. Dock (prick) the dough all over (this ensures an even bake), then chill for about 30 minutes; there's no need to cover it.

3. Preheat the oven to 425°F.

4. Place a piece of parchment on top of the pastry, then put a second baking sheet on top.

5. Bake the pastry for 20 to 25 minutes; it should be starting to brown around the edges. Remove the second pan and parchment and continue to bake until the pastry is golden brown and crisp throughout, an additional 5 to 10 minutes.

6. When cool, use a serrated knife to trim the pastry edges. Cut it into three equal strips on the long edge, each strip measuring approximately 4″ × 10″.

7. Place one pastry strip on a flat surface.

8. Pipe or spread it with Pastry Cream, then cover with another strip. (Piping will give you a more professional look.)

9. Pipe or spread pastry cream on the second strip.

10. Place the last strip of pastry on top, then cover with White Icing. The icing should be room temperature, not cold; you don't want the melted chocolate garnish to immediately harden when piped on top.

(Continued)

11. Pipe several thin stripes of melted chocolate atop the icing lengthwise. Use a toothpick or the back edge of a paring knife to drag the stripes in a perpendicular direction, starting at the top. After cleaning off your toothpick/knife, move to the right about ½″ and pull up, starting at the bottom of the chocolate lines to the top. Repeat this pattern of pulling up, then down through the lines of chocolate to create a herringbone pattern (see page 148 for illustration).

12. Allow the pastry to chill, uncovered, for at least 1 hour before cutting and serving.

13. Using a serrated knife and a sawing motion, carefully cut the pastry into individual 2″ × 4″ napoleons.

14. Napoleons are best eaten the day they're assembled. They may be stored, covered, in the refrigerator for up to 1 day; the pastry will soften as it sits.

White Icing

Yield: about 350 grams (2½ cups)

227 grams (2 cups) confectioners' sugar, sifted

1 teaspoon vanilla extract

119 grams (½ cup) heavy cream, room temperature, or more as needed

Tip: Room temperature is key here; otherwise, the chocolate will seize up.

1. Place the confectioners' sugar in a medium bowl.

2. In a separate bowl, whisk together the vanilla and cream.

3. Whisk the cream mixture into the confectioners' sugar to create a thick but spreadable icing that dissolves back into itself. Add additional cream, if necessary, to reach the correct consistency. The higher the butterfat of your cream, the more cream it will take to reach the desired consistency.

4. White icing may be stored in an airtight container in the refrigerator for up to 4 days; freezing isn't recommended. Bring the icing to room temperature before assembling and cutting the napoleons.

Trimming

The dough will shrink some as it bakes (ending up smaller than the original 11″ × 14″), and the edges will not be perfectly straight. In order to make it look precise and uniform, we trim one long edge and one short edge to create a straight starting point. After trimming, the short ends should measure about 10″. The long side is cut into three equal pieces, about 4″ across for each.

Assembling a Napoleon

To give yourself some breathing room, you can make the pastry cream for napoleons up to 3 days ahead of time. Just before using it, whisk it or mix it briefly in a stand mixer with the paddle attachment on low to get it smooth. When you're ready to assemble everything, have all of your components set up and ready to go before you begin. The melted chocolate should be hot (around 120°F), which will make it easier to create a precise design. Save the prettiest, most uniform piece of pastry for the top layer and the second-best piece for the bottom. Use the more uneven layers in the middle, as you can offset them with pastry cream.

Cutting Flaky Pastries

Slicing your masterpiece is one of the most challenging parts of working with laminated pastry, and we have some suggestions to help minimize the crumb factor. First, though, you'll need to accept that some crumbs are inevitable and they can even help build anticipation for that crisp crunch that comes with each delectable bite.

We recommend using a sharp serrated knife with a blade long enough to cut through your pastry. Start your cut with a steep angle, and once you've got the cut started, you can flatten out the angle to gently saw through the pastry.

For napoleons, we suggest holding each pastry layer as you cut through it, before moving to the next layer. The bottom layer is the easiest to cut through, so you can cut straight through that one. Because there's pastry cream in a napoleon, too, you'll want to clean your knife between pieces—use a moistened tea towel or paper towel.

Croissants

Yield: 8 croissants

Croissants build on the lamination techniques of basic puff pastry. The addition of yeast lightens the final product and adds a depth of flavor that comes from the fermentation of the yeast as the dough rests. As with puff pastry, the entire process can be time-consuming, but you can fit it into your schedule—and the spectacular finished pastries are worth the effort and care.

DÉTREMPE

255 grams (2 cups + 2 table-spoons) unbleached all-purpose flour, plus more for dusting

25 grams (2 tablespoons) granulated sugar

8 grams (1¼ teaspoons) salt

1¼ teaspoons instant yeast

28 grams (2 tablespoons) unsalted butter, room temperature

59 grams (¼ cup) milk

89 grams (⅜ cup) water

BUTTER BLOCK

113 grams (8 tablespoons) European-style unsalted butter, cold

EGG WASH

1 large egg

15 grams (1 tablespoon) water

⅛ teaspoon salt

DÉTREMPE

1. In a medium bowl, combine the flour, sugar, salt, and yeast.

2. Cut in the softened butter.

3. Add the milk and water, mixing to form a shaggy dough.

4. Turn the dough out onto a lightly floured surface and knead gently until it's cohesive and no patches of dry flour remain. The dough should spring back when gently pressed but won't be completely smooth.

5. Place the détrempe in a plastic bag or lidded container large enough for it to rise, and refrigerate for at least 5 hours, or overnight.

BUTTER BLOCK

1. Shape a pliable block of butter by placing the butter on an unfloured surface and pounding it with a rolling pin until it's the consistency of modeling clay.

2. Working quickly, mold the butter into a smooth, flat 5½″ square. You can leave the butter out while you prepare the détrempe in the next step, but if you notice it starting to soften, place it in the refrigerator briefly.

(Continued) ⟶

LOCK-IN

1. On a lightly floured surface, gently de-gas the détrempe and roll it into a 6″ × 12″ rectangle about ½″ thick.

2. Turn the dough so the long side is parallel to you, then place the butter block on the right half of the dough. Fold the left half of the dough over the right, enclosing the butter. Pinch the edges to seal in the butter.

TURNS

1. Keeping the folded edge on the left, re-roll the dough into a 6″ × 16″ rectangle.

2. Perform a letter fold (see page 136), then cover and refrigerate the dough for 20 minutes.

3. Remove the dough from the refrigerator and place it on a lightly floured surface. Position the dough so that the folded edge, running the length of the dough, is on your left.

4. Tap down on the dough to make the butter more pliable, then roll it lengthwise into a 6″ × 16″ rectangle.

5. Perform a second letter fold, then cover and refrigerate the dough for 45 minutes.

6. Repeat this process (rolling to 6″ × 16″, then performing a letter fold) one more time. Cover the dough and allow it to rest for at least 5 hours (or overnight) in the refrigerator before rolling out and forming the croissants.

CUTTING AND SHAPING

1. Roll the dough into a rectangle approximately 8½″ × 16½″ and ¼″ thick. Trim the dough to an even 8″ × 16″.

2. Mark the dough at 4″ intervals along the long edge. Cut the dough into four 8″ × 4″ strips, then cut each strip in half diagonally to form triangles.

Tip: You roll larger than the needed dimensions, then trim to give straight edges and precise measurements for shaping.

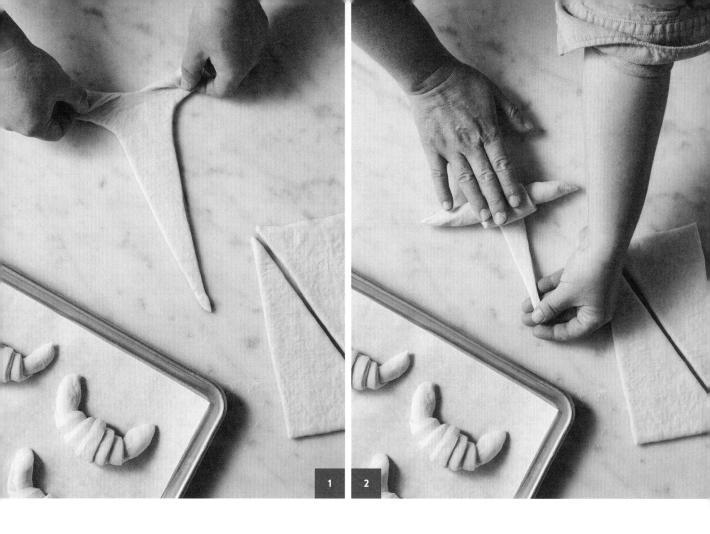

3. Cut a 1″ notch midway along the base of each triangle. Pick up the dough piece and gently stretch it by pulling from the bottom of the triangle to the tip. Stretching the dough before rolling the croissant will result in more rolls and a more layered croissant.

4. Working with one piece of dough at a time and starting at the base of the triangle, fold ¼″ of the dough over onto itself by angling your hands to roll outward from the center notch to stretch the triangle's base, before rolling the triangle up to its point (see photos above).

5. Repeat this process with the remaining triangles.

6. Arrange the croissants on a baking sheet, leaving plenty of room for them to expand. Be sure to lay the croissants with their tips down so they don't unfurl as they bake. Lightly cover the croissants.

PROOFING

1. Allow the croissants to rise until they've almost doubled in bulk, about 1 to 2 hours.

Tip: Rising times vary depending on temperature and humidity, so observe the croissants for signs of puffiness. When risen, they should feel airy and marshmallow-like to the touch.

EGG WASH AND BAKING

1. Preheat the oven to 400°F.

2. Whisk together the egg, water, and salt. Brush the croissants all over with the egg wash.

3. Bake the croissants for about 20 minutes, or until they're a deep golden brown. Remove them from the oven and transfer to a rack to cool.

❯ VARIATION: CHOCOLATE CROISSANTS

A pastry shop favorite, the chocolate croissant pairs gooey melted chocolate with flaky pastry in an irresistible combination. We teach two basic ways to shape a chocolate croissant, both using a 4″-square of dough. For the "fold over" method, you simply lay the first baton on the side of the square closest to you, then pick up that closest edge and roll it over the chocolate. When the baton is enclosed, lay the second baton down on the piece of dough that's not yet rolled and continue the motion of rolling away from you to enclose the second piece. Place the croissant on the sheet pan with the smooth side up. For the second, or "tuck in," method, lay both pieces of chocolate on the square in parallel, one on each side. Roll each side from the edge over the baton to meet in the center. Press to seal the seams before placing on the sheet pan with the smooth side up. With either method, you can use chocolate batons *or* chocolate chips, although batons are easier to work with. We use two pieces of chocolate so that you get chocolate in every bite regardless of the side of the pastry.

Tarte Flambée

Yield: one 12″ × 16″ tart

The Alsace region of northeastern France, bordering southern Germany, is known for its rich dishes. Butter, eggs, milk, cream, cheese, lardons (matchstick pieces of slab bacon), and onions are the stars of its daily cuisine. Using laminated dough adds yet another layer of richness. Our version of this classic "pie baked in the flames" uses thinly rolled croissant dough: The result is an indulgent dish that is ideal for special occasions.

---

25 grams (2 tablespoons) olive oil

113 grams (1 medium) onion, peeled and sliced ⅛″ thick

2 teaspoons herbes de Provence

227 grams (1 cup) cream cheese, room temperature

1 batch Croissant Dough (page 153), chilled

45 to 90 grams (2 to 4 slices) bacon, cooked just until the fat is rendered, drained, and roughly chopped

Tip: Dimensions aren't exact—aim to roll the dough as thin as you can.

1. In a sauté pan over medium heat, heat the olive oil, then sauté the onion until softened. Remove from the heat and set aside to cool.

2. In a small bowl, stir together the herbs and cream cheese until thoroughly combined.

3. Preheat the oven to 400°F. Line a baking sheet with parchment.

4. On a lightly floured surface, roll the dough into a ⅛″-thick rectangle, about 12″ × 16″. Place it on the prepared baking sheet.

5. Spread the dough evenly with a thin layer of the herbed cream cheese, leaving a thin border around the edge of the tarte.

6. Sprinkle the onion and bacon on top.

7. Bake the tarte for 20 to 25 minutes, until it's a deep golden brown and puffy.

Tarte Technique

Baking the tarte directly on a preheated pizza stone will ensure that the bottom crust is fully cooked through without charring the toppings. If you don't have a stone, place your tarte on a baking sheet on the lowest rack of your oven. You can easily vary the flavors of the tarte by adding different herbs or spices to the cream cheese and changing the toppings. Or mix another soft cheese with the cream cheese (goat cheese, Boursin, or ricotta, for example). Just be sure the toppings are parcooked to keep the tarte crisp.

Danish Pastry

Yield: 8 Danish

Danish pastry is an enriched version of croissants, with an egg added to the détrempe. This makes for a somewhat softer dough, and it's best to work with the butter at a softer texture as well to avoid the shattering you can encounter when the butter is firmer than the dough. If you find your butter is too cool and firm, let it sit out for 10 minutes to warm up slightly before starting the lamination process. There are so many fillings and shaping methods for Danish; the following are just a few of our favorites.

DÉTREMPE

255 grams (2 cups + 2 table-spoons) unbleached all-purpose flour, plus more for dusting

25 grams (2 tablespoons) granulated sugar

1¼ teaspoons salt

6 grams (2 teaspoons) instant yeast

1 large egg

59 grams (¼ cup) milk

59 grams (¼ cup) water

BUTTER BLOCK

113 grams (8 tablespoons) European-style unsalted butter, cold

FILLING

jam or other filling of your choice

EGG WASH

1 large egg

15 grams (1 tablespoon) water

⅛ teaspoon salt

GLAZE

85 grams (¼ cup) apricot jam

15 grams (1 tablespoon) water

DÉTREMPE

1. Combine the flour, sugar, salt, and yeast in a medium bowl.

2. Add the egg, milk, and water, mixing to form a shaggy dough.

3. Turn the dough out onto a lightly floured surface and knead gently for about 1 minute, until it's cohesive and no patches of dry flour remain. The dough should spring back when pressed but won't be completely smooth.

4. Cover the dough and refrigerate it for at least 5 hours, or overnight.

BUTTER BLOCK

1. Form a pliable block of butter by placing the butter on an unfloured surface and pounding it with a rolling pin until it's the consistency of modeling clay.

2. Working quickly, mold the butter into a smooth, flat 5″ square.

LOCK-IN

1. On a lightly floured surface, gently de-gas the détrempe and roll it into a 6″ square.

2. Brush away any excess flour and place the butter in the center of the dough at a 45-degree angle so it looks like a diamond in a square.

3. Working clockwise, fold the corners of the dough over the butter one section at a time so that it's completely enclosed. Seal in the butter by pressing the dough together at all the seams.

TURNS

1. With the seam up, roll the dough lengthwise into an 8″ × 16″ rectangle.

2. Perform a letter fold, brushing away any excess flour.

3. Cover and refrigerate the dough for 20 minutes.

4. Place the dough on a lightly floured surface with the seam up and the folded edge on your left.

5. Tap the dough a few times with the rolling pin to make the butter more pliable, then roll the dough into an 8″ × 16″ rectangle.

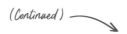

(Continued)

6. Perform another letter fold, then cover the dough and refrigerate for 45 minutes.

7. Repeat the process of rolling and folding the dough one more time.

8. Cover and let the fully laminated dough rest for at least 5 hours (or overnight) in the refrigerator before shaping the pastries.

CUTTING AND SHAPING

1. Place the chilled dough on a lightly floured work surface, tap it down, and roll it into an 8½″ × 16½″ rectangle.

2. Use a ruler and a pastry wheel to mark and trim the dough, then cut it into eight 4″ squares.

3. Shape each square as desired; some classic Danish shapes are rounds, pinwheels, bear claws, and diamonds.

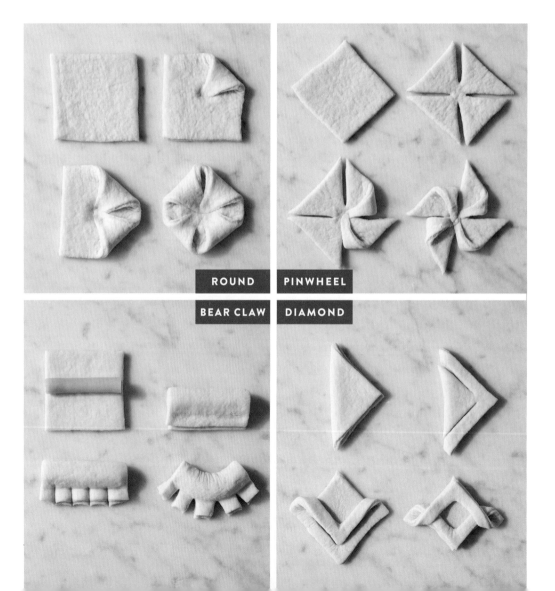

ROUND PINWHEEL

BEAR CLAW DIAMOND

PROOFING

1. Cover the pastries and let them rise in a warm spot until they're visibly puffy and feel marshmallow-like. Depending on room temperature, this will take 1 to 2 hours.

2. Partway through the rise time, preheat the oven to 400°F.

FILLING

1. Using a well-floured finger, gently depress the center of each pastry to make a cavity for the filling.

2. Fill each cavity with about 1 tablespoon of filling.

EGG WASH AND BAKING

1. Whisk together the egg wash ingredients. Gently brush the Danish with the egg wash.

2. Bake the Danish for 18 to 22 minutes, until they're a deep golden brown. Remove from the oven and transfer them to a rack to cool slightly while you make the glaze.

GLAZING

1. In a small saucepan, heat the jam and water over medium heat until the mixture liquefies and comes to a boil. Strain out chunks or purée the mixture.

2. Brush the warm Danish with the glaze.

3. Allow the Danish to cool completely before serving.

Filling Methods

There are two main schools of thought on how to fill Danish: Some bakers prefer to shape and fill the Danish before proofing and baking them. Others prefer to proof first, then fill and bake. We find that some fillings (particularly jam fillings) tend to run out and overflow onto the baking sheet if added before proofing. This happens when the force of the dough as it rises *plus* the heat of the oven combine to push the filling up and over the sides. We recommend you first shape the Danish, then proof them. Once proofed, you gently deflate the centers to make a well for the filling. In this method, the already-proofed dough holds the shape of the well better so you can make a larger well. This makes for more filling and less overflow, yielding more flavor per bite!

Prune Filling

Yield: about 500 grams (2½ cups)

This recipe for the traditional prune filling makes more than you'll need for your Danish, and the extra is a wonderful bonus! Stir it into yogurt or oatmeal; use it as a filling for cookies; or freeze it, then blend to make a quick sorbet. For variations, try mixing prunes and dried sour cherries (or any dried fruit, such as apricots, cranberries, apples, and so on).

---

65 grams (⅓ cup) granulated sugar

340 grams (2 cups) pitted prunes

237 grams (1 cup) water

1 teaspoon orange zest

60 grams (¼ cup) orange juice

1. Combine all the ingredients in a small saucepan and bring to a boil over medium-high heat.

2. Lower the heat to a simmer and continue to cook until the liquid is syrupy, about 3 to 5 minutes.

3. Purée the mixture using a food processor or immersion blender.

4. Let cool completely before using.

5. Store the filling, covered, in the refrigerator for up to 1 week, or wrap and freeze for up to 3 months. Thaw overnight in the refrigerator; stir before using.

Cream Cheese Filling

Yield: about 340 grams (1½ cups)

Creamy and smooth, this filling is an excellent match for the rich dough. For the best, smoothest texture, be sure to have your cream cheese and egg at room temperature because cold cream cheese and cold eggs can cause lumps in the filling. Feel free to play with different flavors, such as almond extract, rum, or even citrus oil.

---

227 grams (1 cup) cream cheese, room temperature

99 grams (½ cup) granulated sugar

1 teaspoon vanilla extract

1 large egg yolk, room temperature

1. In the bowl of a stand mixer, mix the cream cheese and sugar on medium speed until smooth.

2. Mix in the vanilla and egg yolk.

3. Cover the filling and chill until ready to fill pastries.

4. Store the filling, covered, in the refrigerator for up to 1 week. Freezing is not recommended.

STORAGE AND HANDLING OF LAMINATED DOUGHS

Having laminated dough on hand and ready to use is a boon for any baker. You can make all manner of sweet or savory recipes in no time and you can freeze and store your dough at almost any point in the process. Follow these guidelines for storing at different stages:

DÉTREMPE: Within 48 hours of making the détrempe, you may choose to begin the lamination process, or you can wrap it well and freeze it for up to 1 month.

FULLY LAMINATED DOUGH: Within 48 hours of finishing the lamination process, you may choose to use it immediately in your recipe or wrap it well and freeze it for up to 1 month.

SHAPED PASTRIES: To make croissants or Danish 1 day ahead, roll, cut, and shape the croissants or Danish in the evening, spacing them out on a parchment-lined baking sheet. Cover the pastries lightly with plastic wrap, then refrigerate overnight. In the morning, bring the pastries to room temperature to finish the proofing process. Egg wash the croissants, or egg wash and fill the Danish, and bake as directed.

To freeze shaped croissants or Danish, roll, cut, and shape the pastries, then place them on a parchment-lined baking sheet and freeze. Once frozen solid, place the pastries in an airtight container and freeze for up to 1 month. The night before you'd like to bake, remove them from the freezer and place them on a parchment-lined baking sheet. Cover lightly with plastic wrap, then place in the refrigerator to thaw and begin the overnight proofing process. In the morning, bring the pastries to room temperature to finish proofing (for more on proofing, see page 11). Egg wash the croissants, or egg wash and fill the Danish, and bake as directed.

Tips for Success

Because they include yeast, it's best to freeze croissant or Danish dough only once during the entire process. If you've frozen the dough at the détrempe stage, you'll need to continue through the recipe without freezing again.

To minimize condensation, always allow frozen dough to thaw overnight in the refrigerator before using rather than going directly from the freezer to room temperature.

Master Class
Kouign Amann

Yield: 12 kouign amann

THE BAKER
Jackie King is an author and owner—along with her husband, Andy—of A&J King Artisan Bakers in Salem, Massachusetts. A&J King has won multiple Best of Boston awards (*Boston* magazine) and supplies bread and pastries to some of the region's top restaurants and shops. Authors of *Baking by Hand*, the Kings first came to King Arthur to teach at the school's annual Bakers' Harvest Conference and now regularly teach classes for both professional and home bakers at the Baking School.

THE PASTRY
Since opening in 2006, the Kings' bakery has specialized in laminated doughs, particularly croissants. This sparked the idea to introduce *kouign amann* ("butter cake" in Breton) to their menu: Why not take all that lamination work in another direction? This recipe leans into the same techniques you've learned throughout this chapter, with a few detours that make it a distinctive pastry. The dough has a higher hydration than many laminated doughs, which helps the pastry to rise quite high. A simple method of folding a square piece of dough and pressing it into a jumbo muffin tin creates a beautiful floral shape. The exterior—and all the layers—are coated in sugar that caramelizes in the oven, but the pastry itself is incredibly light. Bread flour might seem like an unusual choice in a tender pastry, but the Kings find it gives the dough more structure without sacrificing its delicate quality.

> I've always loved the physicality of the work of making laminated doughs: the simplicity of two elements (butter and dough) coming together and the soothing, rhythmic process of folding after that.

Jackie King

—JACKIE KING

DOUGH

680 grams (5⅔ cups) unbleached bread flour

7 grams (2¼ teaspoons) instant yeast

15 grams (2½ teaspoons) salt

440 grams (1¾ cup + 1 tablespoon) water, 78°F

LAMINATION

454 grams (1 pound) European-style butter, cold

300 grams (1½ cups) granulated sugar

SHAPING

50 grams (¼ cup) granulated sugar

Tip: Professional bakers, including our guest instructors, use weight—not volume—for best results (see page xvi for more on why).

DOUGH

1. Combine the bread flour, yeast, and salt in a medium bowl and toss them together with your hands.

2. Pour the water into the bowl of a stand mixer fitted with the dough hook, then add the dry ingredients on top.

3. Mix on low speed for 3 to 4 minutes. The final dough should be fairly smooth and not shaggy, but not completely developed.

4. Transfer the dough to a lightly greased, covered container and let rest at warm room temperature for approximately 90 minutes, or until doubled in size.

5. Turn the dough out onto a baking sheet and gently punch/press it to de-gas. Shape it into a rough rectangle (it doesn't have to be perfect, but shaping at this stage makes it easier to shape precisely later) and refrigerate—the dough needs to be fully chilled before starting lamination. The longer you rest it, the more flavor you'll develop.

Tip: Add dry ingredients on top of the wet when mixing dough to prevent dry ingredients from getting stuck at the bottom of the bowl.

LAMINATION

1. Lightly grease a 12-well jumbo (Texas-style) muffin tin. Soften the butter by pounding it out with a rolling pin. Flatten it out and fold it back onto itself a number of times until it feels lump-free and pliable.

2. Flatten the butter onto a piece of parchment paper so that it measures roughly 7½″ × 9½″.

3. Check the butter temperature. It needs to be at approximately 58°F before you fold it into the dough.

4. Place the dough on a lightly floured surface and use your hands to flatten the dough out to a rectangle measuring 10″ × 14″—aim to have this be as even a shape as possible.

5. Place the flattened butter onto the bottom half of the dough. Fold the top half of the dough over the butter and seal the three edges.

6. Roll the dough out to 11″ × 18″ and perform a letter fold, brushing off the excess flour.

7. Turn the dough 90 degrees so that the seam of the dough is facing away from you. Repeat step 6 for a second letter fold.

8. Cover the dough, place in the refrigerator, and chill for 30 minutes.

9. Remove the dough from the refrigerator and place it on your work surface so that the seam of the dough is facing away from you.

10. Repeat step 6 for a third letter fold.

11. Cover the dough and chill it for 30 minutes.

12. Have the 300 grams of sugar ready at your work surface. Place the chilled dough on the work surface so that the seam is facing away from you.

13. Perform a sugared letter fold by rolling the dough out to 11″ × 18″, brushing off excess flour, and sprinkling half (150 grams) of the sugar over the entire surface of the dough.

14. Use the rolling pin to lightly press the sugar onto the surface of the dough.

15. Fold the dough into thirds, like a letter. Try to keep the sugar as even as possible when folding.

16. Turn the dough 90 degrees so that the seam faces away from you and repeat steps 14–16 for a second sugared letter fold.

17. Cover the dough, refrigerate, and let rest for 2 hours.

Sugared Letter Folds

Sugar is integral to a kouign amann; otherwise, it would basically be a twistier version of a croissant. You'll notice that this is a very lean dough—no sugar is added to the dough itself, and it's not enriched with eggs or dairy. An essential characteristic of a great kouign amann is the sugary coating on the outside, which gives it a bit of a salted caramel vibe. When you sugar during the folding process, it allows the sugar to stay in between the layers instead of just covering the top—sometimes this even creates pockets of sugar, and some of it oozes out and encrusts the bottom of the pastry, all of which really sets the kouign amann apart.

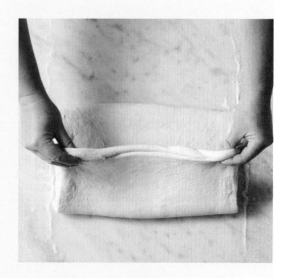

SHAPING AND BAKING

1. Remove your dough from the fridge and roll out to 13″ × 17″.

2. Sprinkle the dough with the 50 grams of sugar. Use the rolling pin to press the sugar onto the surface.

3. Let the dough relax for a few minutes.

4. Trim the outside edges of the dough so that you end up with a squared-off rectangle that measures 12″ × 16″.

5. Cut the dough into 12 squares measuring 4″ × 4″ each.

6. Fold the four corners of each piece into the center and place one in each prepared well of the muffin tin, pressing the very center down firmly to adhere the corners together as you put each square into the pan.

7. Wrap a bag loosely around the pan (you can also loosely wrap with plastic wrap—you don't want the covering to be tight but it should be well sealed) and refrigerate overnight.

8. The next day, remove the pan from the refrigerator and let it sit at room temperature for 30 to 45 minutes while you preheat the oven to 375°F.

9. Bake for about 40 minutes, until golden brown all over.

Shaping Tips

When you're cutting out the squares for the final shaping, it's important that they maintain their shape and don't bounce into rectangles. Sometimes the dough will want to fight you and shrink out of a square. To prevent this, the dough should be rolled out, relaxed briefly, and then trimmed. If you don't let the dough relax before cutting it, the squares will always shrink a bit. Jackie's tip is to roll the dough out a little bigger than you need (she recommends 13″ × 17″ in the recipe) so that as it relaxes, you have some room for error in case it shrinks a bit. You're aiming to trim the dough to a 12″ × 16″ rectangle, so if your dough shrinks a lot, you can start with an even larger rectangle.

chapter 4.
PIES AND TARTS

The Classroom

The first question we ask students in our pie classes is what they consider to be the best pie, and the answers run the gamut, with people sharing stories of their family favorites, cloaked in the memories of past holidays and gatherings. We hear about their grandmother's incredible mincemeat pie made from memory every year at Christmas, and never recorded. Or about the challenges people encounter when it's their turn to bring pie to their in-laws' for Thanksgiving. It's immediately obvious why pie is such an emotional and sometimes intimidating topic for so many of us. One of the greatest joys of our work is watching these nerves turn to ease and confidence as students discover they really can make pie.

So, what *is* the best pie? Maybe you grew up with a tender, melt-in-your-mouth crust with a filling that slices cleanly and holds its shape. Or maybe a buttery, golden brown, flaky crust and a juicy filling is more to your liking. There's no right or wrong here.

The challenge in teaching pie is that every expert who thinks they've found the perfect pie has found *their* perfect pie, and it may not match *your* vision of perfect pie at all. We guide you through the fundamentals in this chapter. As instructors, our goal is to help you understand how the ingredients you choose and the techniques you use affect the outcome of any recipe you try. So, whether you like tender or flaky, thick or juicy, or any combination thereof, after a little practice, you'll find making it really is as easy as pie.

The Lessons

We start with mastering crust, then delve into fillings and toppings, touching throughout on the effect of varying ingredients and techniques. Woven into it all is the advice of our instructors to empower you to make each pie your own as you do the following:

- Explore the function of ingredients in pie crust, with an emphasis on the interplay of flour and fat

- Practice a variety of techniques for making crust and note the variation in results

- Practice rolling crusts, including pressing in by hand and finishing by sealing, crimping, and venting

- Experiment with fillings and thickeners to see what best matches your palate

- Mix and match with crusts, fillings, and toppings, then vary ingredients according to the seasons and your own personal tastes

The Setup

KEY INGREDIENTS

Pie doughs contain only a few ingredients, so understanding the role each one plays is key. A simple swap can give you the texture and flavor you want—you just have to know the characteristics each ingredient brings to the table.

These are the functional ingredients we focus on as teaching points during our pie classes—and what students find waiting at the bench. For more on our ingredient philosophy, please see page xix.

FATS

Fats play a critical role in your dough, providing flavor and texture as well as the degree to which your crust browns. When you cut fat into flour, it coats the flour and reduces gluten development, making for a tender mouthfeel. At the same time, the water content in some fats can provide flakiness in the finished crust. When the cold fat heats up in the oven, the water it contains evaporates to create small puffs of steam that push against the dough as it bakes. These small air pockets in the dough give us that flaky texture and look in our crust. In the school, we choose butter for most of our crusts because we love the flavor, color, and the layers of flakiness you can get from an all-butter crust, but we encourage you to think about the pie you're trying to create. If you grew up with your grandmother's Crisco-based crust, you may crave that tender, melt-in-your-mouth texture. In that case, you could try using 50% butter and 50% shortening to get the best of both worlds: Butter will give you flavor, flakiness, and superior browning, whereas shortening will add tenderness. Or perhaps you like the incredible tenderness of a lard-based crust, but you'd prefer not to use lard. In that case, you could use 100% butter and cut it *very* finely into the flour, adding just enough water for the dough to hold together; here, you'll be relying on physical manipulation rather than water to bring the dough together and mimic the tender texture you get with lard. The key is to understand how each fat behaves so you can handle it to achieve the results you want.

BUTTER

What characterizes butter is flavor, browning, and its capacity to create flakiness. As the fat with the highest water content (15%–25%), butter gives the most flakiness as water/steam evaporates. It yields excellent flavor and browns beautifully through the caramelization of its milk sugars and solids, so all-butter crusts need only an egg-white wash for finishing, or nothing at all. We use unsalted butter in our crusts and add the salt separately to give more control over the flavor.

LARD AND SHORTENING

Lard imparts a slightly savory flavor and makes a very tender crust, but it doesn't brown well, so for color, finish lard crusts with an egg wash or milk wash. Lard has a higher water content (12%–18%) than shortening, so it can be used to achieve flake, but not as much as butter. It has a larger crystal structure than other fats and a higher melting point, meaning it won't break down as easily even as you knead and handle the dough, making it a good candidate for sturdier savory pie crusts. The higher melting points of these fats mean the crusts are less likely to slump. Adding a bit of shortening to your butter crust can add tenderness while helping to hold its shape. It's particularly good for decorative or crimped crusts, but as with lard, it won't brown well, so try an egg wash or milk wash to add color.

MARGARINE AND OIL

Margarine can be difficult to work with, as it stays soft even when chilled. It has more water and some added milk solids in its attempt to mimic butter, but its fat isn't solid, so it doesn't produce the same degree of flakiness as butter. Oil doesn't brown well and can be, well—oily! It will look better with an egg wash or milk wash for finishing. It makes a crisp, somewhat cracker-like crust.

FLOUR

In the classroom, we use unbleached all-purpose flour for most of our pie crusts because it's easily accessible to all bakers and it adds the right amount of structure. Some crusts, as for meat pies or hand pies, call for bread flour to add more structure from the increased gluten content. For a more tender crust, you can buy a little insurance by using pastry flour (aim for 25% to 50% of the flour weight called for). We don't recommend using all pastry flour, as its lower gluten content can make the dough harder to handle, especially for novice pie bakers. Alternative flours can bring new flavors to your crusts but can also change the texture. If you want to experiment, start by swapping 25% of the flour called for with an alternative (e.g., a nut flour or rye) and see how you like the results before adjusting any further.

Flour also shows up as a thickener in pie fillings. Added in the proper proportion, it makes for a softer set than other starches.

LIQUID

You need liquid to bring the dough together and to promote some gluten formation for structure and ease of rolling. Most crust recipes call for water, which is an easily accessible and inexpensive option. You can also use milk, either dairy or nondairy. Egg yolk is also an option that will tenderize your crust and promote browning.

THICKENERS

Our go-to thickener for many of our fillings is flour. We like the gentle thickening it offers, and it doesn't dramatically change the flavor of the filling. If you're looking for a firmer set, you'll want to give cornstarch a try, and we offer it as the thickener in several of the recipes here. Interested in trying other thickeners? See the thickener chart on page 204 for more.

EQUIPMENT

BOWLS

When mixing your dough, it's best to use a medium to large bowl, the shallower and wider the better. You'll want plenty of room as you cut in the butter and a larger bowl will best contain the flour as you work.

PANS

We prefer to use metal or glass pie pans rather than ceramic, which tend to vary greatly in size and dimension. Metal is the best conductor of heat and helps crusts brown well. Glass pans don't conduct heat quite as well as metal, but they have the added benefit of allowing you to see how the crust is baking on the bottom. Ceramic pie pans, while beautiful for presentation, take a long time to heat up in the oven. If you're using ceramic, try baking directly on a preheated baking stone to ensure the bottom of the pie bakes.

As for tart pans, look for ones made of tinned steel with a removable base. In the classroom, and for our recipes in this book, we use 9˝-diameter, 1½˝-high round pie pans and 9˝ round standard tart pans. (For more about swapping pan sizes, see page 179.)

ROLLING PINS

There are many different kinds of rolling pins, from French-style to marble pins. While this choice is largely a matter of preference, it's helpful to know what's out there. In the classroom, we use tapered French or traditional ball-bearing wooden rolling pins and recommend students try both. When choosing a pin, select what feels most comfortable for you. (And use what you have. Anything cylindrical and longer than 16˝ works well; we've had instructors share stories of using wine bottles or broom handles in a pinch on vacation!) **Ball-bearing pins** are the most traditional, and most common, option. The sturdy, heavy barrel takes care of the hard work, requiring only gentle pressure on the handles to roll along easily. **French-style pins**, either tapered or straight, offer more control: Your hands are positioned closer together right over the dough, allowing you to apply pressure directly where you need it. **Marble pins**, often used for pastry, are beautiful but very heavy. If chilled, they can help keep doughs cold. You'll sometimes see **silicone-coated pins**, which can help prevent your dough from sticking, though generously flouring any rolling pin will do the trick.

UTENSILS

We recommend keeping a bowl scraper close at hand: It's useful for everything from dividing dough to mixing and folding to transferring rolled-out crusts. You can use a number of different tools to cut in fat. A pastry blender is our classroom choice as opposed to our hands, since it's the most efficient at cutting in fat without heating up or softening the butter. Be sure to choose one with blades rather than a wire blender, as those wires aren't strong enough to cut through cold butter. If you don't have a pastry blender, you can use a fork or just your fingers. If you use your fingers, be sure to use your fingertips (the coolest part) and to work quickly.

PRE-BAKING CRUSTS

Many recipes require you to bake your crust *before* adding the filling. Sometimes, you'll fully bake the crust if your filling is already cooked, as with a custard or cream pie. Other times, you'll want to bake the crust only partially before adding your filling and continuing to bake to ensure a crisp, fully baked crust for more delicate fillings that don't require as long of a bake (such as a quiche custard or some tarts).

Start by preheating the oven to 375°F. Once you've placed your crust in your pan, dock the bottom of it by pricking it all over with a fork; this helps steam escape from the crust as it bakes, which will prevent it from puffing up. No need to obsess here; the goal is to do this evenly, leaving about ½" to 1" between pricks.

Line the crust snugly with parchment paper or foil. In the classroom, we use large basket-style coffee filters. They're already the perfect size and shape, and they function just as parchment will, with the bonus that often you'll already have them on hand and they can be reused. Fill the lined crust with dried beans (you can use the same beans over and over again) or pie weights to weigh it down.

Once the crust is prepped, chill it for 30 minutes before baking—this allows the fat to solidify, which helps prevent shrinkage.

Bake the crust for about 15 minutes, or until it's set. The dough will be matte and starting to take on a bit of color; it should be a very light golden brown.

Remove from the oven and remove the weights and liner. If you're only partially pre-baking, let the crust cool, then proceed with your recipe. If you're baking fully, return the pan to the oven and continue to bake until the crust is a medium golden brown and looks (and feels) dry; this should take an additional 10 to 15 minutes. Remove from the oven and let cool fully before adding your filling.

Commonly Asked Questions

WHAT ABOUT VODKA?

Bakers often ask about using vodka in their crust, having heard someone swear that it yields the most tender crust. It does, but use a small amount. Vodka, compared to water, promotes very little gluten development, which makes a tender crust, but it doesn't give the dough much structure, making it harder to handle and roll out.

WHAT ABOUT VINEGAR?

Adding acid in the form of vinegar or lemon juice is another technique bandied about in the pie world. In small amounts, it doesn't improve the crust's tenderness but instead strengthens proteins and makes the dough tougher. To promote tenderness, you'd have to use a high enough quantity that it would also introduce an acidic flavor.

CAN I USE A FOOD PROCESSOR?

Yes, absolutely! The trick is not overprocessing your dough, which can happen very quickly. See more about using a food processor on page 196.

SHOULD I FREEZE THE BUTTER?

If temperature is key to success, why not take things a step further and use frozen butter? It's a logical jump to make but not one we find practical. It's almost impossible to cut in frozen butter unless you grate it, which will produce small shards of butter. But it won't coat the flour with fat as when you cut in the butter by hand, so the resulting crust will be flaky but not tender.

CAN I SWAP PAN SIZES?

Let's say your recipe is written for a pie pan, but you want to make a tart, or vice versa. A 9″-diameter, 1″-deep tart pan holds about half the filling of a 9″ pie pan that is 1½″ deep, so you'll need to at least double the filling amount when moving from a tart to a pie or halve it when moving from a pie to a tart. You'll also want to adjust the bake temperature and time: a lower temperature and a longer time for a larger amount, and vice versa for the smaller quantity.

WILL MY CRUST SHRINK?

Avoiding shrinkage is *all* about time and temperature. The longer you rest and chill your dough in the pan, the less likely it is to shrink. Half an hour is the minimum time you'll need to chill your crust—more time is better.

Crusts

Most students in our pie classes are there because they're anxious about making pie crust. Part of the anxiety comes from not being sure how to achieve the texture and taste they hold in their memory. Making a tender yet flaky crust with a beautifully burnished bake is the foundation of a great pie, and we believe the key to success here is knowledge: the why and how. The most empowering way to baking success is to understand the role of each ingredient and how to coax different results from them—more flakiness, more tenderness, a darker bake, and so on. Although the ingredient list is short (or perhaps because of it), technique is paramount when it comes to making a great crust.

Pie crust is essentially the sum of <u>flour + fat + liquid</u>; varying the ratios (and types) of each will move you along the spectrum from tender to flaky. For the most tender crust, you want very small particles of fat so that the flour gets as coated as possible, reducing the gluten development. You'll need very little water to bring this dough together. On the opposite end of the spectrum you have the flakiest crust, which you achieve by leaving the fat in much larger flattened shards. The larger pieces create more flakiness but don't coat the flour in fat as much; you'll need to use more liquid to bring it together and you'll lose a degree of tenderness.

Basic All-Butter Crust (One-Stage)

Yield: One 9˝ double crust

This rich, buttery crust manages to be exceptionally tender with some flake; it works beautifully with both sweet and savory pies. We love the depth of color and flavor using all butter brings to pie crust, and as we show in the classroom, you're able to dial in the degree of tenderness you prefer—in this crust, we dial up the tenderness by cutting the butter into smaller bits (the water content in butter allows for some flake as well). Bonus: This is the perfect recipe for learning the techniques you'll need to succeed at most any crust you choose to tackle. Consider doubling the recipe every time you make crust. Any extra dough can be frozen, and it's great to have on hand. More pie for later!

---

300 grams (2½ cups) unbleached all-purpose flour

½ teaspoon salt

227 grams (16 tablespoons) unsalted butter, cold, cut in ½˝ cubes

119 grams (½ cup) water, cold; more as needed

1. Combine the flour and salt in a large, shallow bowl.

2. Add the butter, tossing to coat it thoroughly with the flour.

3. Cut in the butter with a pastry blender by pressing straight down on the cubes, cutting and flattening them against the sides of the bowl. As the cold butter breaks into smaller pieces, more and more of the flour becomes coated in fat, which is key to this crust's tender, melt-in-your-mouth texture.

4. Keep cutting in the butter until the mixture is the consistency of coarse meal (aim for the texture of coarsely grated Parmesan).

5. Add the cold water all at once. Working quickly to keep the ingredients cool, toss the mixture together, then press the dough against the sides of the bowl and fold it over on itself a few times to bring it together. Once the dough comes together, grab a handful and squeeze. If it falls apart, add additional water a little at a time until it holds together when squeezed but is still noticeably dry.

6. Take the dough out of the bowl and place it on an unfloured work surface. Squeeze together any dry bits that remain in the bowl and add them to the main piece of dough.

7. Use a bowl scraper or bench knife to fold one side of the dough up and over onto itself, pressing down firmly. This brings the dough together further and creates layers, which will eventually contribute to the crust's flakiness.

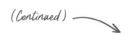

(Continued)

8. Fold the dough over and gently press it down on the work surface a few more times; your goal is a cohesive dough with no bits falling off. <u>Avoid stirring</u>; focus on folding instead. Once the dough starts to feel at all sticky or tacky, stop: it's ready.

9. Cut the dough in half. Flatten each piece into a 6″-diameter disk about 1″ thick.

10. Wrap each disk tightly in plastic wrap and flatten just a bit more to force it to the edges of the wrap; this will help prevent cracks around the edges later. You can also roll the disk on its side across a countertop to further smooth the edges. Refrigerate the dough for at least 30 minutes before rolling. This resting period chills the fat, allows the flour to absorb the water fully, and relaxes the gluten, all of which will contribute to the crust's tender, flaky texture.

Tip: When we say "tacky," imagine the feel of the back of a sticky note.

TEMPERATURE

A common refrain in the classroom is _keep it cool_. Temperature is key when working with pastry dough. Keep your ingredients cold throughout the entire process; this will both make the dough easier to work with and give you the best results. Keeping your fat and your liquid cold is most important. If you're working in a very warm environment, you can go a step further and chill your flour and your tools as well: the mixing bowl, the pastry blender or fork, the rolling pin, and so on. If you're really struggling to keep your dough cold, try placing a bag of ice or frozen vegetables on your work surface for a few minutes before rolling. (Just be sure to wipe up any wet spots before rolling!)

TIME

One important yet intangible component to crust-making success is time: Chilling and resting your dough is essential. This cannot be expedited or skipped! Make your crust ahead of time or use the chilling/resting time to prep the filling.

   You should always rest your crust, refrigerated, for at least 30 minutes after you make it before rolling it out. This resting time allows the fat to firm up, the gluten to relax, and the flour to hydrate sufficiently. You do this before rolling the dough, and then we recommend doing it again and chilling for another 15 to 30 minutes after assembly but before baking. This further prevents the crust from shrinking or slumping and helps any crimping or decorative crust design to hold its shape and definition better.

Extra-Flaky All-Butter Crust (Two-Stage)

Yield: One 9″ double crust

Can't get enough flake? Increasing the size of the butter particles adds flakiness to your crust. While still tender, this crust is a little sturdier, making it a good choice for juicier fruit fillings. One consequence of leaving the butter in larger pieces is that with the flour less coated in butter, you'll find you need more liquid than with the previous recipe (about 30 grams [2 tablespoons]) to bring the dough together.

300 grams (2½ cups) unbleached all-purpose flour

½ teaspoon salt

227 grams (16 tablespoons) unsalted butter, cold, cut into ½″ cubes

119 grams (½ cup) water, cold; more as needed

1. Combine the flour and salt in a large bowl.

2. Cut in half of the chilled butter. Work quickly, incorporating it into bits about the size of dried currants.

3. Cut in the remaining butter, this time leaving it in larger pieces, roughly the size of cranberries.

4. Using your floured fingers, flatten the larger pieces into flakes, working quickly to keep everything cool.

5. Add the water and toss just until a rough, shaggy dough begins to form. Grab a handful of the dough and squeeze. If it falls apart, add additional water a little at a time until it holds together when squeezed but is still noticeably dry.

6. Transfer the dough to a clean, unfloured work surface. Fold it over on itself a few times, then bring it together with a few quick, gentle kneads.

7. Cut the dough in half. Flatten each piece into a 6″-diameter disk about 1″ thick. Wrap and chill for at least 30 minutes before rolling.

Rolling Tips

When you're ready to roll, remove the dough from the refrigerator and place on a lightly floured surface. Use your rolling pin to firmly tap down on the dough, making it pliable, easier to roll, and less likely to crack. Flour your pin and begin rolling from the center out, taking care not to roll over the edges. Rotate the dough one-eighth of a turn between strokes to ensure it's not sticking to the work surface and retains its round shape. Return the pin to the center of the dough each time rather than rolling back and forth, which can agitate the gluten in the dough, causing it to tighten up and shrink back.

How wide? For a pie pan, roll the dough out about 2″ to 3″ wider than the top of your pan to allow for crimping—even more if it's a deep-dish pan. If making a tart crust, roll the dough about 1″ to 2″ wider than the pan. The dough should be about ⅛″ thick: Visualize a thickness somewhere between a Wheat Thin and a Ritz cracker.

To transfer the dough to the pan, first brush off excess flour, then fold the circle into quarters. Place the point of the dough in the center of the pan and gently unfold.

Trim the crust to make a 1″ border of dough all around the edge of the pan. Lift the edge of the dough, fold it underneath itself, and pinch it to leave a rim about ½″ in height.

From here, you can flute or crimp the crust before filling and baking (see page 188).

We hate wasting crust. You can use scraps as decorative toppings for your pie, or fill with jam for turnovers, or sprinkle with cinnamon sugar and bake separately for a quick treat.

OUR FAVORITE CLASSIC CRIMP

While there are myriad ways to dress up the edges of your pie, in the classroom we focus on the classic fluted edge crimp. There's really no right or wrong way to crimp: What feels and looks best to you is most important. It's crucial to keep in mind the type of fat you're using: Lard- and shortening-based crusts hold the definition of intricate shapes and designs best and are least likely to slump over the edges of the pan, while butter-based crusts are best suited to simple designs and need to be thoroughly chilled before baking to reduce slumping. In addition, the thickness of your crust will affect the crimp: Thicker crusts show less definition and may end up slightly underbaked, while thinly rolled crusts may burn with the pie's extended baking time.

To make a classic fluted edge crimp: Trim your crust to about 1˝ longer than the edge of the pie plate. Fold the crust under itself, then pinch the fold to seal the edge. Starting from the inside ring of the crust, use the pointer finger of your dominant hand to gently press the edge of the crust outward. Keeping your pointer finger steady, use the thumb and pointer finger of your nondominant hand to gently pinch the dough around the tip of your dominant hand's pointer finger, making a V shape. Continue doing this along the entire edge of the pie. Chill, then bake your pie as directed.

Changing the Crust's Flavor

Feel free to add spices, extracts, or other flavorings to these basic crusts to customize your dough to match your filling. Add dry ingredients with the flour; try 1 teaspoon ground spice (e.g., cinnamon or cardamom), 1 teaspoon citrus zest, or other ingredients, like poppy seeds or chopped herbs. Start small with any additions and see how much the crust tolerates; flour gives the crust its structure and holds it together, so too many additions can compromise the flour's function. For liquid ingredients, try replacing some of the water called for with any of the following: 2 tablespoons orange blossom water, 1 tablespoon flavored liqueur, or ½ teaspoon almond extract. Tweak the quantities to your taste.

Cheddar Crust

Yield: one 9″ double crust

The rich, nutty flavor of cheddar makes this crust the perfect foil for any savory filling—or even a delicious cloak for apple pie! Of course, adding cheese for flavor means we need to reduce the butter, so we cut the fat into small pieces to keep this mouthwatering crust tender.

---

300 grams (2½ cups) unbleached all-purpose flour

½ teaspoon salt

170 grams (12 tablespoons) unsalted butter, cold, cut into ½″ cubes

170 grams (1½ cups) grated sharp cheddar

119 grams (½ cup) water, cold

1. Combine the flour and salt in a large bowl.
2. Cut in the butter until the mixture resembles coarse meal.
3. Add the cheese, tossing to combine.
4. Add the water and toss just until a shaggy dough forms. Grab a handful of the dough and squeeze; if it falls apart, add more water a little at a time until it holds together.
5. Transfer the dough to an unfloured work surface. Fold it over on itself a few times, then bring it together with a few quick, gentle kneads.
6. Divide the dough in half, flatten each half into a 6″-diameter disk about 1″ thick, and wrap in plastic wrap. Chill the dough for at least 30 minutes before rolling.

Storing Dough

If you want to make your dough ahead of time and refrigerate the wrapped disks, use them within 1 to 2 days. If you're not planning on using it within 2 days, wrap it tightly in a second layer and freeze it for up to 3 months. Why not refrigerate it longer? Your dough will begin to oxidize after a few days in the refrigerator and can take on a grayish tinge. The gray color is just visual and will disappear during baking as the crust browns.

If you do freeze your dough, remove it from the freezer the night before you plan to bake and thaw it overnight in the refrigerator. Set it on the countertop at room temperature for 10 minutes before starting to roll it out. If you're in a rush, you can thaw the dough for a few hours on the countertop at room temperature, but keep it wrapped to avoid condensation getting on the dough, which can make it wet/gummy and difficult to work with.

If you have the freezer space, you can also roll out your dough, place it in the pan, and freeze it that way so your pie shell is ready to go.

Tender Tart Crust

Yield: one 9″ tart crust

This buttery, sweet tart crust yields enough dough so you can easily fill your tart pan and have scraps left for cookies or decorations. The increased tenderness here comes from both ingredients and process. Using room temperature butter instead of cold allows the flour to become fully coated with fat, minimizing gluten development. The dough is enriched with both egg and sugar to add richness and tenderness. With such a tender dough, you'll need to handle it with care, but you'll agree the result is well worth the effort! We like to press this dough into the pan using well-floured fingers, which is easier than rolling since it can be a challenge to roll without cracking, though a rolled crust does give a more professional look (aim for a thickness of ⅛″ to ¼″).

---

113 grams (8 tablespoons) unsalted butter, room temperature

57 grams (¼ cup) granulated sugar

⅛ teaspoon salt

½ teaspoon vanilla extract

1 large egg yolk

150 grams (1¼ cups) unbleached all-purpose flour

1. Combine the butter, sugar, salt, and vanilla in the bowl of an electric mixer and mix until smooth. If you don't have an electric mixer, you can make this dough by hand if the butter is truly room temperature.

2. Add the egg yolk and mix until completely incorporated, scraping down the sides of the bowl once or twice as necessary.

3. Add the flour, mixing to make a cohesive dough.

4. Wrap the dough tightly in plastic wrap, then refrigerate or freeze until ready to use.

Tip: If it's still cool, give it a few whacks with a rolling pin.

Cornmeal Tart Crust

Yield: one 9˝ tart crust

This crust features the toasty flavor of cornmeal and illustrates how to swap out some of the flour. When you're using non-wheat flours, you'll need to keep the structure of the crust in mind. The more cornmeal, the more tender and difficult to handle the crust will be. We also use this crust to teach students how to use a food processor for making crusts since there's less risk of overworking it (see sidebar).

---

180 grams (1½ cups) unbleached all-purpose flour

69 grams (½ cup) whole-grain cornmeal

½ teaspoon salt

12 grams (1 tablespoon) granulated sugar

113 grams (8 tablespoons) unsalted butter, cold

1 large egg yolk

59 grams (¼ cup) milk, cold; more as needed

1. Combine the flour, cornmeal, salt, and sugar in a large bowl.

2. Cut the butter into the flour mixture until the butter pieces are the size of currants.

3. Add the egg yolk and milk. Mix quickly and lightly to make a dough that just holds together, adding additional milk as necessary.

4. Cut the dough in half, form into disks, wrap, and refrigerate until cool but still pliable, about 30 minutes, before rolling.

WHAT ABOUT A FOOD PROCESSOR?

We teach two other methods of combining fat and flour in the cornmeal tart crust (and for other tart and pie doughs): the food processor method and fraisage.

To use a food processor, pulse your dry ingredients together in the food processor bowl. Add the cold butter (or other fat) and pulse to cut the butter into pieces the size of currants. Once you've cut in the fat, you can either add your liquid and pulse lightly a few times just until the dough comes together or dump it all into a bowl and add the liquid by hand. After you add the liquid it's easier to take the dough too far in the food processor, as that's when the gluten begins to develop; switching to your hands at this point can help prevent that.

If you don't have a food processor you can try fraisage to bring your dough together instead. Fraisage is a French technique whereby you use the heels of your hands to smear the fat and flour together rather than adding more liquid, which might toughen your crust.

To do it, make your crust in the bowl, cutting in the fat as instructed, then add your liquid. Turn the shaggy dough out onto an unfloured surface. Use the heel of your hand (where the wrist meets the hand) to *smear* the dough a tablespoon or two at a time across the work surface, moving away from you. The heel is a cooler part of your hand, so using it will help reduce the effect of handling the dough. Move quickly and work just until the dough comes together, or you risk toughening the crust.

Nut Crust

Yield: one 13¾″ × 4½″ rectangular tart crust or one 9″ round tart crust

Ground nuts lend this iconic crust tons of flavor, but also increased tenderness. Almond or hazelnut are the traditional choices for a classic Linzer torte, but you can swap in other nut flours as long as their fat content is similar. You can use toasted or untoasted flour—toasted yields a slightly nuttier flavor. During the winter, try toasting the nut flour for a heartier holiday flavor. In the summer, leave the nuts untoasted and lighten up on—or even eliminate—the spice to make a tart that pairs well with fresh fruit. Since we use this dough most often for a Linzer torte with a lattice top, the recipe yields enough dough for the bottom crust plus about 25% extra for a lattice crust.

---

170 grams (12 tablespoons) unsalted butter, room temperature

66 grams (⅓ cup) granulated sugar

168 grams (1¾ cups) nut flour, untoasted or toasted

¼ teaspoon salt

1 teaspoon cinnamon

zest of **1 large** lemon

1 large egg

180 grams (1½ cups) unbleached all-purpose flour

1. Combine the butter, sugar, nut flour, salt, cinnamon, and lemon zest in the bowl of a stand mixer. Mix on medium speed until smooth.

2. Add the egg, mixing on medium-low speed until incorporated.

3. Add the flour, stirring to make a soft dough.

4. If you're planning to press the dough into your tart pan, do that now and then chill before using. If you'll be rolling it out, first press the dough into a disk, wrap tightly in plastic wrap, and chill until cool but still pliable before using, about 20 to 30 minutes.

Nut Crust Classic: The Linzer Torte

Preheat the oven to 325°F. With lightly floured fingers, press about three-quarters of the dough into the pan; it'll be ⅛″ to ¼″ thick. Spread 340 grams (1 cup) jam (red currant or raspberry are traditional, but use your favorite) evenly into the tart. Shape the remaining dough into strips or ropes and place them on the tart in a crisscross pattern for a mock lattice. Trim excess dough from the edges and bake the tart until the crust is golden brown and fragrant and the jam is actively bubbling in the center, about 45 minutes. Remove the tart from the oven and allow it to cool completely. Remove from the pan and dust the top with confectioners' sugar.

Fillings and Toppings

These are the fillings and toppings we teach most frequently in our pie classes, as they best illustrate important lessons, such as the effect of different thickeners or how to make a foundational pastry cream. While the world of flavors and recipes is nearly endless, this offers a good opportunity for mixing and matching. The recipes we teach in our basic Easy as Pie class are based on seasonality: The crust remains the same, but the fillings change. We have students who sign up each season for the exact same class, eager to learn the changing fillings. We laugh (and we love them!) because it reminds us that some people are *all* about the filling, not the crust, and bakers need a little guidance in that department, too!

Why We Vent the Crust

Venting the crust allows steam to escape. Cutting a few small slits (five or so) is all you need, but the top of your pie can also be a canvas if you're artistically inclined—try cutting decorative designs or patterns instead of straight slits. For more elaborate designs, it's helpful to cut them into the top crust after rolling it out but before transferring the dough onto the top of the pie.

Proper Baking Tips

A soggy bottom is a common stumbling block with pie. To ensure your bottom crust is baked thoroughly, follow a few guidelines.

If possible, bake your pie on a preheated baking stone or steel. If you don't have either one, bake the pie on the lowest rack of your oven. We recommend you bake on a baking sheet or parchment paper to catch any drips.

For fruit pies, mix your filling just before you assemble the pie. This cuts down on the amount of juice the fruit releases, which can lead to a wet, underbaked bottom crust.

Bake your pie until the filling is actively bubbling in the center. Don't be afraid of a little color! Butter browns as it bakes; that browning is a sign of caramelization and delicious flavor that awaits. See page 217 for more tips on browning.

Crust getting too dark too quickly? Lower the oven temperature by 25°F or tent the top with foil.

A NOTE ON YIELDS

Our filling recipes are all written to just fit a 9″-diameter pie pan (with about 4 cups of filling). We do this so that we can bake the pies within the time constraints of the class schedule—we want every student to go home with a pie they've made from start to finish. If you prefer a taller or fuller pie, you can increase the fillings accordingly. Increasing the amounts by 150% will yield a heaping pie, but remember you'll need to drop the temperature by 25°F and bake as much as a third longer than the time called for in the recipe.

THE ASSEMBLY

In the classroom, we assemble pies in a certain order due to the constraints of time and logistics, and our recipes reflect this. We make the dough; while it chills, we make the filling. Then we roll out the bottom and top crusts, pre-bake if needed, fill the pie, and bake. At home, you'll have the luxury of a bit more time, so rely on your common sense and judgment. In Vermont, we tend to take for granted a cool, dry kitchen environment. But this can vary greatly depending on where you are—be attentive and your dough will tell you what it needs. If you notice that it's slumping and softening, then consider adjusting the assembly timeline: You may want to chill the bottom crust after it's rolled out to keep it cool while rolling out the top crust and making the filling.

Apple Filling

Yield: one 9″ pie

Students always ask what apple varieties to use for pie. There are different types of apples found in different locations, so there's no single best answer. We're lucky to teach in both Washington State and Vermont, where orchards full of wonderful fruit abound, and we enjoy experimenting with different varieties, so we encourage students to bravely explore what's available locally. A mix of soft, firm, sweet, and tart apples delivers a pie with complex textures and flavors. It's especially nice to include some tart apples in the mix to heighten the flavor. But remember that you're in control: Say you want a saucier filling—use softer apples that will release more juice, and mix your filling before rolling out the dough to allow the fruit to macerate. Want a firmer filling? Use traditional baking apples, such as Cortland or Granny Smith, and mix the fruit just before adding it to your rolled-out crust.

FILLING

66 grams (⅓ cup) granulated sugar

71 grams (⅓ cup) brown sugar

30 grams (¼ cup) unbleached all-purpose flour

1 teaspoon cinnamon

¼ teaspoon nutmeg

⅛ teaspoon salt

4 large (800 to 900 grams) apples, peeled, cored, and sliced ⅛″ thick

ASSEMBLY

1 batch Extra-Flaky All-Butter Crust (Two-Stage), chilled (page 186)

egg wash (optional)

18 to 36 grams (1 to 2 tablespoons) sparkling sugar (optional)

1. Preheat the oven to 400°F.

2. In a medium bowl, combine the sugar, brown sugar, flour, cinnamon, nutmeg, and salt.

3. Add the apples, tossing to combine. Set aside until you're ready to assemble your pie.

4. Roll out half of the chilled dough to a 13″ circle and place it in a 9″ pie pan.

5. Spoon the filling into the crust.

6. Roll out the remaining dough to a 13″ circle and place it over the filling. Lift the edge of both top and bottom crusts together, fold them under, and press to seal; this helps prevent the juices from escaping as the pie bakes. Crimp the edges of the crust, then vent the top crust by cutting a few small slits.

7. Brush the top of the pie with egg wash and sprinkle with sparkling sugar. Refrigerate for 20 to 30 minutes before baking.

8. Bake the pie for about 1 hour, or until the pastry is golden brown and the filling is actively bubbling in the center.

> ### ⟩ VARIATION: BROWN SUGAR APPLE PIE

> For a classic apple pie with a deeper caramel flavor, use all brown sugar instead of a blend of granulated and brown sugars. This simple change yields a surprising shift in the final result.

Fruit Pie Thickener Guide

FRUIT	THICKENER	FOR 1 CUP OF FRUIT
Apples Need the least amount of thickener since they're less juicy. They're also high in natural pectin; pectin helps filling thicken.	All-purpose flour	1¾ teaspoons
	Instant ClearJel	½ teaspoon
	Cornstarch	½ teaspoon
	Quick-cooking tapioca	¾ teaspoon
	Pie Filling Enhancer	1½ teaspoons *Reduce sugar by ¾ teaspoon*
Blackberries and Raspberries These are very juicy and release even more liquid if they've been frozen; they need more thickener than apples.	All-purpose flour	1 tablespoon + 1 teaspoon
	Instant ClearJel	2¾ teaspoons
	Cornstarch	1 tablespoon
	Quick-cooking tapioca	1 tablespoon
	Pie Filling Enhancer	1 tablespoon + 2 teaspoons *Reduce sugar by 2½ teaspoons*
Blueberries These have a lot of pectin; they'll need a little less thickener than other berries.	All-purpose flour	1 tablespoon
	Instant ClearJel	2 teaspoons
	Cornstarch	2½ teaspoons
	Quick-cooking tapioca	1½ teaspoons
	Pie Filling Enhancer	1 tablespoon + 1 teaspoon *Reduce sugar by 2 teaspoons*

FRUIT	THICKENER	FOR 1 CUP OF FRUIT
Cherries Fresh cherries will need slightly less thickener than canned or frozen.	All-purpose flour	1 tablespoon
	Instant ClearJel	2½ teaspoons
	Cornstarch	2½ teaspoons
	Quick-cooking tapioca	1¼ teaspoons
	Pie Filling Enhancer	1 tablespoon + ½ teaspoon *Reduce sugar by 2 teaspoons*
Peaches and Stone Fruits Don't have quite as much pectin as apples; they're also juicier, so will require more thickener.	All-purpose flour	2½ teaspoons
	Instant ClearJel	2½ teaspoons
	Cornstarch	2½ teaspoons
	Quick-cooking tapioca	1½ teaspoons
	Pie Filling Enhancer	1 tablespoon + 2 teaspoons *Reduce sugar by 2½ teaspoons*
Strawberry/Rhubarb These have a lot of pectin; they'll need a little less thickener than other berries.	All-purpose flour	1 tablespoon + 1½ teaspoons
	Instant ClearJel	2½ teaspoons
	Cornstarch	1 tablespoon + ¼ teaspoon
	Quick-cooking tapioca	2½ teaspoons
	Pie Filling Enhancer	2 tablespoons *Reduce sugar by 1 tablespoon*

Cherry Filling

Yield: one 9˝ pie

We cannot tell a lie—it took us a long time to get a cherry pie in our classes since it was so hard to find fresh sour cherries in season in Vermont. This version uses frozen cherries, and you'll notice a shift in the thickener we use here—we love the jewel-like clarity Instant ClearJel brings to this pie. It's a specially modified cornstarch that's available online (kingarthurbaking.com) and from baking retailers. It allows the fruit's natural beauty to shine through and makes it especially beautiful when topped with a lattice. When you use frozen fruit, our preference is to partially thaw the fruit, allowing it to release some juice, which helps encourage the sugar to start to dissolve as the pie bakes.

FILLING

124 grams (½ cup + 2 tablespoons) granulated sugar

24 grams (3 tablespoons) Instant ClearJel

¾ teaspoon cinnamon

½ teaspoon salt

650 grams (5¾ cups) frozen pitted sour cherries, partially thawed but not drained

1 large lemon, zested and juiced

1½ teaspoons almond extract (optional)

ASSEMBLY

1 batch Extra-Flaky All-Butter Crust (Two-Stage), chilled (page 186)

egg wash (optional)

18 to 36 grams (1 to 2 tablespoons) sparkling sugar (optional)

Tip: To prevent clumping, first combine ClearJel with sugar, then mix well as soon as you add to liquid ingredients.

FILLING

1. Combine the sugar, ClearJel, cinnamon, and salt in a small bowl. Set aside.

2. In a medium bowl, combine the thawed cherries with their liquid, lemon zest, lemon juice, and almond extract.

3. Add the sugar mixture to the cherry mixture, stirring to combine.

ASSEMBLY

1. Roll out half of the dough to a 13˝ circle and transfer to a 9˝ pie pan.

2. Add the filling, then roll out the second piece of dough and cut the dough into 1˝-wide strips.

3. Weave a lattice top (see sidebar).

4. Brush the lattice with egg wash and sprinkle it with sparkling sugar.

5. Preheat the oven to 400°F. Refrigerate the pie (while the oven preheats) for at least 15 minutes.

6. Bake the pie on a parchment-lined baking sheet for about 50 to 60 minutes, until the crust is golden brown and the filling is actively bubbling in the center.

7. Remove the pie from the oven and allow it to cool on a rack for at least 2 hours before slicing.

WEAVING A LATTICE TOP

To weave a lattice, roll out your top crust about ⅛″ thick. Using a ruler and a pastry wheel or sharp knife, cut the dough into 1″-wide strips (see photo 1, opposite page). Place the strips vertically over the filling, about 1″ apart.

Fold back the odd-numbered strips, then place a strip of dough horizontally on top of the filling (see photo 2, opposite page). Return the odd-numbered strips to their original place.

Fold back the even-numbered strips, then place a strip of dough parallel to the first horizontal strip (see photo 3, opposite page). Return the even-numbered strips to their original place.

Repeat this process of folding back the odd- then even-numbered strips and placing horizontal strips about ½″ apart until the top of the pie is covered with the lattice (see photos 4 and 5, opposite page).

Trim the lattice so there's a 1″ overlap all around the edge of the pan. Fold the ends of the lattice strips under the bottom crust and press to seal, then crimp as desired (see photo 6, opposite page).

Brush the lattice with egg wash and sprinkle it with sparkling sugar.

While the oven preheats, refrigerate your pie for at least 15 minutes. This will help ensure that the crust holds its shape during baking.

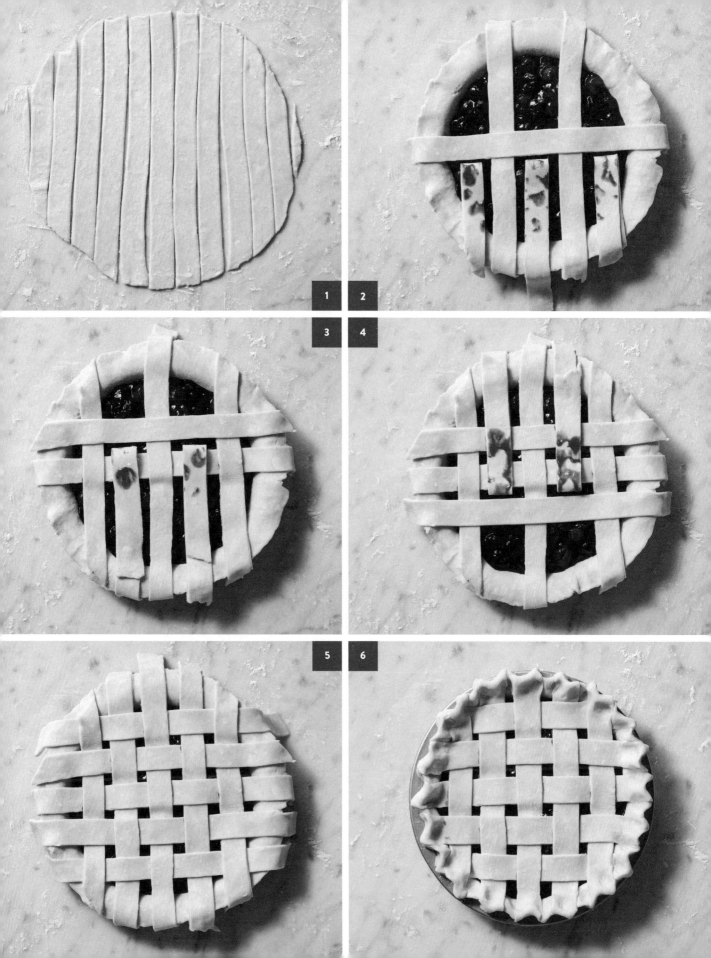

JUICY FRUIT

You can control the juiciness of any fruit pie filling by adjusting when you mix the filling. The longer the filling sits before you add it to the crust and bake, the juicier the filling will be. If you mix and add the filling just before baking, you'll cut down on some of the juiciness. Once baked, it's tempting to dive in, but have patience! Resting allows the filling to set. Looking for perfectly set slices? Consider chilling the pie overnight before cutting.

Peach Blueberry Filling

Yield: one 9″ pie

Nothing says summer quite like peaches, and with blueberries in season at the same time, the pairing is inevitable. The increased liquid from the summery fruits means you'll want a stronger thickener—cornstarch fits the bill here, giving the pie a thick, sliceable consistency.

FILLING

99 grams (½ cup) granulated sugar

28 grams (¼ cup) cornstarch

⅛ teaspoon salt

zest and juice of **½ large** lemon

340 grams (2 cups) blueberries, fresh or frozen

340 grams (2 cups) peaches, fresh or frozen, peeled, pitted, and sliced ⅛″ thick

ASSEMBLY

1 batch Extra-Flaky All-Butter Crust (Two-Stage), chilled (page 186)

egg wash (optional)

18 to 36 grams (1 to 2 tablespoons) sparkling sugar (optional)

FILLING

1. Combine the sugar, cornstarch, and salt in a large bowl.

2. Add the lemon zest and juice, berries, and peaches, tossing to coat the fruit.

ASSEMBLY

1. Roll out half of the dough to a 13″ circle and place it in a 9″ pie pan.

2. Spoon the filling into the shell, then roll out the remaining dough and place it over the filling.

3. Seal, crimp, and vent the top of the pie.

4. Brush the pie with egg wash and sprinkle it with sparkling sugar.

5. Preheat the oven to 400°F. Refrigerate the pie (while the oven preheats) for at least 15 minutes.

6. Bake the pie for 45 minutes, or until the crust is golden brown and the filling is actively bubbling in the center.

7. Allow the pie to cool for at least 2 hours before slicing.

Tip: Thick-skinned peaches? Score an X on the bottom of each with a paring knife. Drop them in a pot of boiling water for about 30 seconds, then into a bowl of ice water. Once cooled, drain and peel.

Pastry Cream Filling

Yield: 1½ cups (enough for one 9″ tart)

There are so many versions of this fundamental recipe, each with its own avowed adherents. We like this particular one because of its versatility: Using all cornstarch as the thickener yields a firmer filling that holds its shape when sliced. While this filling yields enough to fill a 9″ tart, if you choose to use it for a 9″ pie, use one and a half times the recipe.

474 grams (2 cups) milk

99 grams (½ cup) granulated sugar, divided

35 grams (5 tablespoons) cornstarch

⅛ teaspoon salt

2 large eggs

1 large egg yolk

10 grams (2 teaspoons) unsalted butter, room temperature

1 teaspoon vanilla extract

½ batch Tender Tart Crust, fully baked (page 193)

1. Place the milk and ¼ cup (50 grams) of the sugar in a saucepan and bring to a boil over medium-high heat.

2. Whisk together the remaining sugar, cornstarch, and salt in a heatproof bowl.

3. Add the eggs and yolk to the cornstarch mixture, whisking until very smooth.

4. Temper the egg mixture by pouring about half of the hot milk over it, stirring to combine. Return this hot mixture to the saucepan and bring it back to a boil, whisking constantly. Boil for 1 minute, then remove from the heat. Stir in the butter and vanilla.

5. Fill the baked tart shell with the pastry cream, cover, then refrigerate until set and cold, about 1 hour. To prevent a skin from forming, place plastic wrap directly on the surface of the pastry cream.

Tip: If you notice any small lumps, press the mixture through a sieve.

Thickening Pastry Cream

In class, we demonstrate how cornstarch gives a firmer, more sliceable texture to pastry cream and its many variations. It's excellent to use for tarts, pies, and pastries that'll be sliced. Think of pastry cream as essentially homemade pudding. If you want a softer set, use half cornstarch and half flour. Some instructors prefer the more satiny mouthfeel of pastry cream made with flour, though it won't hold its shape as well. Remember that fillings made with cornstarch or flour mixtures all need to come to a full boil to activate their maximum thickening power, and flour needs to be cooked slightly longer to lose its "raw" taste. On the other hand, if you cook cornstarch more than a minute or two after it boils, it will break down, become soupy, and won't thicken the mixture.

> **VARIATION: FRUIT TART**

Top the tart with 340 grams (2 cups) fresh berries or cut fruit arranged in a decorative pattern; glaze the fruit by puréeing together 85 grams (¼ cup) apricot preserves with 30 grams (2 tablespoons) water. Once puréed, transfer the mixture to a small saucepan and bring it to a boil over medium-high heat. Remove the hot glaze from the heat and let cool slightly before brushing over the berries.

> **VARIATION: CHOCOLATE CREAM TART**

Decrease the cornstarch to 21 grams (3 tablespoons) and stir in 113 grams (⅔ cup) semi-sweet chocolate chips with the butter and vanilla, stirring until smooth. Omit the fruit and glaze, and top with whipped cream and chocolate shavings or a dusting of cocoa powder just before serving.

> **VARIATION: EGGNOG CREAM TART**

Add ½ teaspoon nutmeg along with the cornstarch and salt. Use only ½ teaspoon vanilla extract and add ½ teaspoon almond or rum extract along with it. We like to serve the tart with a billowing pile of rum whipped cream (237 grams [1 cup] cold heavy cream whipped to stiff peaks with 14 grams [1 to 2 tablespoons] confectioners' sugar, 15 to 30 grams rum, and ½ teaspoon vanilla) and a dusting of freshly grated nutmeg.

Storing Custard Tarts

It's best not to freeze cream or custard tarts like this one, as the luscious and silky texture suffers during the thawing process.

Maple Cream Filling

Yield: one 9″ tart

A favorite of our Vermont instructors, this variation on pastry cream uses brown sugar instead of white to add a depth of flavor that underscores the caramel notes of maple syrup. Maple is the star, so use the best you can find and be sure it's real maple syrup, not maple-flavored or pancake syrup. To really up the New England vibe, add an optional splash of maple extract or maple flavor. Be sure to use whole milk here, or even a mixture of whole milk and cream; the fat prevents the acidity of the brown sugar from curdling the cream. *(See photo on page 223.)*

FILLING

473 grams (2 cups) whole milk

78 grams (¼ cup) pure maple syrup

50 grams (¼ cup) brown sugar

35 grams (5 tablespoons) cornstarch

⅛ teaspoon salt

2 large eggs

1 large egg yolk

10 grams (2 teaspoons) unsalted butter, room temperature

1 teaspoon vanilla extract

¼ teaspoon maple extract or flavor (optional)

ASSEMBLY

½ batch Tender Tart Crust, fully baked (page 193)

whipped cream for garnish (optional)

1. Place the milk and maple syrup in a saucepan and bring to a boil over medium-high heat. Remove from the heat and set aside.

2. Meanwhile, whisk together the brown sugar, cornstarch, and salt in a medium bowl.

3. Add the eggs and yolk to the cornstarch mixture, whisking until very smooth.

4. Temper the egg mixture by pouring about half of the hot milk mixture over it, stirring to combine. Add it back to the saucepan and bring to a boil over medium-low heat, whisking constantly. Boil for 1 minute. Remove from the heat.

5. Stir in the butter, vanilla, and maple extract.

6. Pour the filling into the baked tart shell and cover with plastic wrap, placing it directly on the surface of the filling. Refrigerate the tart until thoroughly chilled, about 2 hours. The tart may be refrigerated for up to 4 days.

7. Garnish the tart with whipped cream up to 1 day prior to serving. If not serving immediately, refrigerate the tart, covered, until ready to serve.

> **VARIATION: GINGERBREAD**
>
> Omit the maple syrup and increase the brown sugar to 100 grams (½ cup). Instead of all milk, use 237 grams (1 cup) each heavy cream and whole milk, adding half of the sugar to it and bringing to a boil. Add the remaining brown sugar to the cornstarch and salt, along with ½ teaspoon cinnamon, ¼ teaspoon ginger, and ⅛ teaspoon each cloves and nutmeg. Continue with the recipe as written, adding 2 tablespoons molasses along with the butter and vanilla, omitting the maple extract.

Brown Butter Cranberry Filling

Yield: one 9˝ tart

We love this brown butter filling, which is the star of this tart and is beautifully complemented by little bursts of jewel-like cranberries. We enjoy teaching the filling because of its versatility, making it a great go-to recipe. It pairs well with most tart crusts and mastering it empowers you to make uniquely seasonal tarts, as it's an excellent base for any type of sour or tart fruit, like apples or sour cherries. If using frozen fruit, partially thaw it first and drain any excess liquid. *(See photo on page 195).*

FILLING

57 grams (4 tablespoons) unsalted butter

85 grams (⅓ cup + 2 tablespoons) granulated sugar

¼ teaspoon salt

1 teaspoon vanilla extract

1 large egg

21 grams (3 tablespoons) unbleached all-purpose flour

75 grams (¾ cup) cranberries, fresh or frozen

ASSEMBLY

½ batch Tender Tart Crust, partially baked (page 193)

confectioners' sugar (optional)

1. Preheat the oven to 375°F.

2. In a small pan, simmer the butter until it's deep brown and fragrant (see sidebar below). Remove from the heat and set aside.

3. In a medium bowl, whisk together the granulated sugar, salt, vanilla extract, and egg.

4. Whisk in the flour.

5. Slowly stream in the browned butter, whisking until fully incorporated.

6. Scatter the cranberries into the partially baked shell.

7. Pour the browned butter mixture evenly over the berries.

8. Bake the tart until the crust is deep golden brown and the filling is puffed and set, about 45 minutes.

9. Remove the tart from the oven and let it cool to room temperature. Remove from the pan and dust with confectioners' sugar just before serving.

Tip: There should be more filling than fruit, allowing the beautiful berries to dot and accent the filling.

Browning Butter

Brown butter is like liquid gold to a baker! As you slowly cook the butter, the milk solids caramelize, yielding a beautiful dark golden color and a nutty flavor. Before you begin, be sure you're using a large enough pot to help reduce spatter, and have a heatproof container or bowl ready on hand nearby—the butter will go from just right to too dark quite quickly, so you'll need to be prepared to transfer it from the pan. Start and remain on medium to medium-low heat the entire time, using a silicone spatula to stir as you go. The butter will foam at first, then subside and turn clear. Continue to cook and stir, stopping when it reaches the color of an amber beer with browned flecks—there may still be some foam on top. Transfer it immediately to your waiting container to help cool the butter and stop the cooking so it doesn't burn.

Meringue Topping

Yield: enough for one 9″ pie or tart

This ethereal topping transforms an already baked pie into a mile-high glory. You'll get the best volume from your whites if they're at room temperature. You can brown the top with a quick bake under the broiler or, if you have a hand torch, use it to get a nicely caramelized tone just where you want it.

---

70 grams (2 large) egg whites

99 grams (½ cup) granulated sugar

⅛ teaspoon salt

½ teaspoon vanilla extract

1. Place the egg whites, granulated sugar, and salt in a heatproof bowl or in the bowl of a stand mixer. Set the bowl over a pan of simmering water.

2. Whisk gently and constantly until the egg whites are hot (about 161°F) and the sugar is dissolved, about 2 to 3 minutes.

3. Remove the bowl from the heat. Using the whisk attachment, beat the mixture at medium-high speed until it's thick and glossy, about 2 to 3 minutes. The mixture should feel just warm to the touch.

4. Stir in the vanilla.

5. Spread the meringue atop your pie or tarts, making sure it goes all the way to the edges and meets the crust.

6. If desired, toast the meringue with a small kitchen torch, or place the pie or tarts under the broiler for a few seconds to caramelize the meringue.

7. Store the pie or tarts in the refrigerator for up to 2 days. Freezing is not recommended.

Oat Crumble

Yield: enough for one 9″ pie

The humble crumb topping can elevate any fruit pie with its contribution of spice and crunchy texture. Feel free to make the streusel your own by shifting spices, adding nuts, or even mixing up the sugar you use. Granulated sugar will change the texture: The topping will be crisper and won't clump as much, whereas brown sugar adds a caramelized flavor (the darker, the more robust the flavor). Think about the fruit you're using and what would complement it nicely. Be creative! Try a bit of candied ginger for a peach pie, perhaps, or crunchy additions other than nuts.

---

30 grams (¼ cup) unbleached all-purpose flour

107 grams (½ cup) brown sugar

½ teaspoon salt

1 teaspoon cinnamon

½ teaspoon nutmeg

¼ teaspoon cardamom

57 grams (4 tablespoons) unsalted butter, room temperature

99 grams (1 cup) rolled oats

CRUMBLE

1. Combine the flour, brown sugar, salt, cinnamon, nutmeg, and cardamom in a medium bowl.

2. Rub in the butter. The mixture should hold together when pressed but still maintain a crumbly texture.

3. Add the oats, tossing to combine.

ASSEMBLY

1. Sprinkle the oat crumble evenly over the pie filling and bake the pie as directed, or until the crumble is lightly browned.

2. The crumble needs about 30 minutes to brown; if your pie needs to bake longer than that, tent the top lightly with aluminum foil or consider adding the crumble for just the last half hour of baking.

Tip: Use whichever oats you have on hand: instant, quick, or old-fashioned. It's a matter of personal preference—old-fashioned oats yield a chewier texture, whereas quick-cooking or instant oats offer less bite.

HOW TO MIX AND MATCH

Once you get comfortable with the various components of crust, filling, and topping, you can go anywhere. Think about the characteristics of each element and how to combine them to achieve the result you want. You can tailor your pie or tart to match your taste. In class, we teach specific combinations that work well as a way to demonstrate the different techniques, and we encourage students to think of all the different ways to use them. A cheddar crust, for example, would be excellent paired with savory fillings or with some fruit fillings, such as apple. Flakier crusts do well with more delicate fillings; a more tender and crisp crust can be a good pairing for a sturdier filling.

Take it one step further and personalize each component to open up even more potential for combinations. To guide you with some inspiration, here are a few favorite combinations from our instructors:

APPLE CHEDDAR: Combine the Apple Filling (page 203) with the Cheddar Crust (page 190).

HERB: Try snipping a teaspoon of fresh herbs into your flour when making your crust dough. Pair flavors to complement your filling.

BRANDIED CHERRY: Add 57 grams (¼ cup) cherry brandy or rum to the Cherry Filling (page 207) and increase the Instant ClearJel to 48 grams (¼ cup plus 1 tablespoon).

VANILLA-ROASTED PEACH: Toss 1,420 grams (6 cups) peeled, sliced peaches with 198 grams (1 cup) brown sugar, 57 grams (¼ cup) butter, 1 tablespoon vanilla bean paste, 2 tablespoons lemon juice, and a pinch of salt. Spread on a baking sheet and roast at 400°F for 15 to 25 minutes, until the fruit just begins to caramelize. Refrigerate the fruit mixture until chilled, then pair the filling with a Basic All-Butter Crust (One-Stage; page 182) and top it with Oat Crumble (page 221).

MAPLE CREAM CORNMEAL: Combine the Maple Cream Filling (page 215) with the Cornmeal Tart Crust (page 194), fully baked.

EGGNOG MERINGUE: Make the Eggnog Cream Tart (page 214) as written. Once cooled, top with Meringue Topping (page 218), swapping in rum for the vanilla and adding a pinch of freshly grated nutmeg, torching to brown.

Classic Quiche Custard

Yield: one 9˝ quiche

All you need for the most tender quiche is a partially baked crust and this creamy custard. With those in hand, you can come up with your own favorite combinations of meat, vegetables, and cheeses. The most important lesson here is ratio: Use the right amount of liquid to eggs, which creates a delicate and wonderfully wobbly custard rather than one that's too stiff. To know when it's ready, shake the pan slightly and remove it from the oven while it's still a bit jiggly, as the custard will continue to cook from the residual heat.

FILLING

2 large eggs

119 grams (½ cup) whole milk

59 grams (¼ cup) heavy cream

⅛ teaspoon salt

⅛ teaspoon nutmeg

freshly ground black pepper

3 grams (1 tablespoon) fresh parsley, chopped

ASSEMBLY

85 grams (3 slices) bacon, chopped

71 grams (½ large) onion, peeled and sliced

57 grams (½ cup) cheddar

½ batch Basic All-Butter Crust (One-Stage), partially baked in a 9″ tart pan (page 182)

FILLING

1. Whisk together the eggs, milk, cream, salt, nutmeg, pepper, and parsley. Set aside.

2. Preheat the oven to 375°F.

ASSEMBLY

1. Cook the bacon in a large sauté pan over medium-high heat until the fat begins to render. Add the onion and continue to cook until the bacon is crispy and the onion has softened. Remove from the heat and set aside to cool.

2. Scatter the bacon mixture and cheese evenly over the bottom of the partially baked crust, then pour the custard on top.

3. Bake the quiche for 25 to 30 minutes, until the crust is golden brown and the custard is just slightly jiggly in the center.

4. Remove the quiche from the oven and allow it to cool slightly before slicing.

Quiche Filling Variations

Quiche can be made with a variety of fillings with a few general guidelines. Always use cooked vegetables, as raw vegetables will release too much liquid and keep the custard from setting properly. We suggest ingredients with stronger flavors; they'll give you more flavor impact with less quantity. Lightly sprinkle your filling ingredients (including any added cheese) into the partially baked shell, taking care not to pack them down. Bring the level of added ingredients up almost to the height of the pan and then pour your custard over the top. You can always scatter more cheese on top. For inspiration, here are a few instructor favorites:

CRAB AND CARAMELIZED ONION: Gently mix together crabmeat, caramelized onion, shredded mozzarella, chopped asparagus tips, and smoked paprika (or hot sauce); scatter this lightly into your crust, then add the custard.

HAM AND CHEESE: Sprinkle roughly chopped cooked ham and shredded Gruyère into your crust. Whisk a teaspoon or two of whole-grain Dijon mustard into the custard before pouring it over the filling.

CAPRESE: Spread 2 to 4 tablespoons pesto over the bottom of the crust. Lightly pile chopped roasted tomatoes and chunks of fresh mozzarella on top of the pesto before pouring the custard over the top.

Cornish-Style Pasties

Yield: 3 large pasties

These traditional hand pies use the humblest ingredients to create pure pleasure—a fitting tribute to the miners who made them famous. We lightly adapted this traditional version of the classic pasty from the Cornish Pasty Association (the true experts!). You'll notice that suddenly we break a cardinal crust-making rule—handling lightly and working quickly—and instead we treat the crust like bread dough. Kneading, while it may go against all your pastry-making instincts, will give the crust the strength necessary to hold the filling and retain its shape. To further encourage structure, we use bread flour for its higher protein content. Although high-quality lard can be hard to find, it's worth seeking out here. This filling isn't highly seasoned, staying true to its plain roots, so feel free to season to your taste. Depending on the size of your vegetables, you may find you have some extra filling that won't fit in the crusts. Put it in a covered baking dish and braise in the oven until everything is tender and browned, then top with a fried egg—heaven!

CRUST

250 grams (2 cups + 1 table-spoon) unbleached bread flour, plus more for dusting

½ teaspoon salt

65 grams (5 tablespoons) unsalted butter, cold

60 grams (¼ cup) lard, cold

79 grams (⅓ cup) water, cold

FILLING

225 grams (8 ounces) skirt steak or beef tips, cut in ¼″ dice

225 grams (1 large) potato, peeled and cut in ¼″ dice

125 grams (½ medium) rutabaga or turnip, peeled and cut in ¼″ dice

100 grams (1 medium) onion, peeled and cut in ¼″ dice

½ teaspoon salt

¼ teaspoon freshly ground black pepper

egg wash

CRUST

1. Combine the flour and salt in a large bowl.

2. Cut in the butter, then the lard, until the mixture resembles bread crumbs.

3. Add the water, mixing just to bring the dough together.

4. Transfer the dough to a lightly floured surface and knead until smooth and elastic, about 3 to 5 minutes.

5. Divide the dough into three pieces and form each piece into a disk.

6. Wrap the disks in plastic wrap and chill for at least 1 hour.

FILLING

1. In a large bowl, combine the beef, potato, rutabaga, and onion.

2. Season with the salt and pepper. Refrigerate the filling until ready to use.

ASSEMBLY

1. Preheat the oven to 350°F. Line a baking sheet with parchment paper.

2. On a lightly floured surface, roll each piece of dough into an 8″ round.

3. Divide the filling evenly among the three rounds of dough, placing the filling on just half of each round and leaving a narrow border for sealing the pasty.

4. Lightly brush one edge of each round with the egg wash, then fold the dough over the filling. Seal and crimp the edges.

5. Vent the pasties, then brush the tops with additional egg wash.

6. Bake the pasties for 50 to 55 minutes, until the pastry is golden brown and the filling is bubbling.

Scottish Meat Pies

Yield: eight 3¾˝ pies

These British classics come in the most counterintuitive of packages: the hot water crust. Like the Cornish pasty crust, it seems to break every rule of pie-making, but it works, as you'll see from the first tender bite. While the pasty crust incorporates kneading, here we take the rule-breaking one step further, melting the fat entirely before adding it to the dough. Because the fat is liquid, it combines uniformly with the flour, unlike fat that's cold and distributed in chunks. The resulting crust has less small, tilelike flakes but is still quite tender and crispy with an incredible sturdiness; you can understand why the technique was created to be used for traditional meat pie fillings like this one, which is heavy and substantial. We use English muffin rings to shape the pies but not to bake them: We find that removing the rings before baking yields a crispier and better browned exterior.

GRAVY

28 grams (2 tablespoons) unsalted butter

14 grams (2 tablespoons) unbleached all-purpose flour

296 grams (1¼ cups) beef broth

¼ teaspoon salt

¼ teaspoon freshly ground black pepper

FILLING

500 grams (about 1 pound) ground lamb or beef

½ teaspoon mace

½ teaspoon nutmeg

¼ teaspoon salt

¼ teaspoon freshly ground black pepper

2 teaspoons Worcestershire sauce

148 grams (½ cup + 2 tablespoons) gravy, from left

CRUST

500 grams (4 cups + 2 tablespoons) unbleached all-purpose flour, plus more for dusting

¼ teaspoon salt

170 grams (¾ cup) lard

178 grams (¾ cup) water

egg wash

GRAVY

1. In a medium saucepan, melt the butter over medium heat. If it starts to spatter, remove it from the heat and stir to melt.

2. Add the flour, whisking to combine.

3. Whisk in the broth, salt, and pepper.

4. Increase the heat to medium-high. Whisking constantly, bring the mixture to a boil. Lower the heat and simmer for 1 to 2 minutes, stirring occasionally, until the gravy thickens. Remove from the heat and set aside to cool. Refrigerate the gravy until ready to use.

(Continued)

FILLING

1. Combine the meat, mace, nutmeg, salt, pepper, Worcestershire sauce, and gravy in a bowl. Cover and refrigerate the filling until ready to use.

CRUST

1. Combine the flour and salt in a large bowl. Set aside.
2. In a medium saucepan, bring the lard and water to a boil over medium-high heat.
3. When the lard is completely melted, pour it into the flour mixture, stirring until the dough comes together.
4. Transfer the dough to a lightly floured surface and knead it for about 3 to 5 minutes; this develops the gluten and strengthens the dough.

ASSEMBLY

1. Roll the dough into a log, cutting off one-third for the tops of the pies.

2. Cut the remaining two-thirds of the dough into eight pieces; these will be the bottom crusts. Place these pieces back in the warm saucepan to keep warm; the dough will become harder to handle as it cools.

3. On a lightly floured surface, roll the reserved dough for the top crusts into a circle about ⅛″ thick. Using an English muffin ring or a 3″ to 3½″ cutter, cut out eight rounds.

4. Next, roll one of the eight bottom crusts into a 5″ to 6″ circle. Place the circle in the ring, pressing it against the sides to form the base of the pie.

5. Place about 3 tablespoons of the filling in the center of the base.

6. Place one of the rolled-out top crusts over the filling and use your fingers or a fork to press its edge onto the sides of the bottom crust.

7. Cut a vent into the top crust.

8. Gently remove the ring and place the pie on a parchment-lined baking sheet.

9. Repeat this process to form the remaining pies.

10. Lightly brush the egg wash over the tops of the pies.

11. Bake the pies in a preheated 350°F oven until the crust is a pale golden and the filling is bubbling, about 35 to 45 minutes. Remove the pies from the oven. Reheat the remaining gravy and serve with the warm pies.

I Want More Hand Pies!

Don't we all? The sturdy yet tender quality of these meat pie crusts make them ideal for sweet applications, too. The pasty crust could serve as the case for fruit-filled hand pies, while the Scottish crust would make a wonderful case for a toaster tart filled with something a bit thicker, along the lines of apple butter or cinnamon sugar made with brown sugar.

Master Class
S'mores Tart

Yield: one 9˝ round tart, plus extra marshmallows

THE BAKER

Wilhelm Wanders is an eighth-generation Master Pastry Chef who grew up working in his family's pastry shop in Kleve, Germany. After completing his apprenticeship in Europe, he moved to America to continue his training, eventually opening Chocolaterie Wanders with his wife, Melanie (the mastermind behind the Sticky Toffee Pudding, page 316). He and Melanie moved with their family to New England in 2011 to work for King Arthur Baking Company. It's an incredible asset for students to be exposed to—and inspired by—a pastry chef of his caliber with such a depth of experience.

THE TART

This tart elevates the classic s'mores to an elegant showstopper, building upon the pie techniques we've covered so far. Instead of a press-in cookie crust, Wilhelm rolls out a dough made with whole wheat flour, cinnamon, and molasses that evokes the taste of a graham cracker in a neater, more precise form. A hint of cinnamon in the chocolate ganache filling is a nod to the crust's flavor, and the entire tart is topped off with a pile of pillowy home-made marshmallows, torched briefly with a handheld kitchen torch to give that campfire feeling and to create a beautifully dark golden char.

I tasted my first s'mores under a clear evening sky in Vermont; we didn't have them growing up in Germany. Now we often enjoy them with our kids, and I wanted to find a way to enjoy the taste and the campfire nostalgia, but with a bit more sophistication. My sister features this tart seasonally at her café in Germany as a way to introduce this sweet treat to other Germans who have never had the pleasure.

—WILHELM WANDERS

CRUST

43 grams (⅓ cup) all-purpose flour

142 grams (1¼ cups) whole wheat flour

52 grams (¼ cup) granulated sugar

2 grams (½ teaspoon) baking powder

1 gram (¼ teaspoon) baking soda

2 grams (⅓ teaspoon) salt

1 gram (¼ teaspoon) cinnamon

66 grams (9 tablespoons) unsalted butter, cold, cut in ½" cubes

8 grams (½ teaspoon) honey

16 grams (¾ teaspoon) molasses

32 grams (2 tablespoons) water, cold

1 gram (¼ teaspoon) vanilla extract

GANACHE

332 grams (2 cups) milk chocolate (chips or chopped)

50 grams (⅓ cup) dark chocolate (chips or chopped)

200 grams (¾ cup + 2 tablespoons) heavy cream

2 grams (¾ teaspoon) cinnamon

½ cinnamon stick

MARSHMALLOWS

340 grams (1 cup + 6 tablespoons) cold water

30 grams (3 tablespoons + 1 teaspoon) powdered gelatin

540 grams (2¾ cups) granulated sugar

215 grams (⅝ cup) light corn syrup

18 grams (1 tablespoon + 1 teaspoon) vanilla extract

confectioners' sugar, for dusting

Tip: Professional bakers, like our guest instructors, use weight—not volume—for best results (see page xvi for more on why).

CRUST

1. In the bowl of a stand mixer, combine the flours, sugar, baking powder, baking soda, salt, and cinnamon.

2. Add the butter, mixing on low speed until the dough is the consistency of cornmeal.

3. Whisk together the honey, molasses, water, and vanilla in a small bowl. Add to the dough and mix until just combined. Form the dough into a disk, wrap well, and chill for at least 1 hour.

4. Once chilled, preheat the oven to 375°F. Roll the dough out to an 11" round about 3.5 mm thick (about the thickness of a quarter).

5. Transfer the dough carefully to the pan, taking care to gently but firmly press the dough into a 9" round tart pan, and trim the edges. Dock the crust, then chill for at least 1 hour (or as long as overnight).

6. Bake for 11 to 12 minutes. Remove from the oven and let cool.

Tip: Be sure to use couverture chocolate (see sidebar).

GANACHE

1. Place the chocolates in a large, heatproof bowl.

2. Place the cream and cinnamon in a saucepan. Roughly break the cinnamon stick into a few pieces and add it to the cream. Bring the mixture to a boil—as soon as it reaches a boil, remove the cinnamon stick pieces from the cream and pour the hot cream carefully over the chocolate.

3. Let it sit for a minute, then stir gently until smooth. Pour the ganache into the cooled tart shell and refrigerate until set.

MARSHMALLOWS

1. Line a half-sheet pan (13″ × 18″) with parchment, then spray the sides of the pan and the parchment with baking spray (or grease with oil lightly but thoroughly). Set aside.

2. Combine 170 grams of the cold water with the gelatin in the bowl of a stand mixer fitted with the whisk attachment.

3. In a small saucepan, bring the remaining water, sugar, and corn syrup to a boil and cook until it registers 238°F.

4. Remove from the heat and carefully pour into the gelatin mixture; immediately start whipping at medium-high speed for 8 minutes.

5. Add the vanilla and whip for another minute to incorporate.

6. Pour the mixture evenly onto the prepared sheet pan. Spray an offset spatula with baking spray, then use it to level the top of the marshmallows. Lightly spray the top with baking spray and cover with parchment paper.

7. Let the marshmallows cool for at least 3 hours at room temperature.

8. Once cooled, peel the parchment off and dust the top with confectioners' sugar before cutting them into ½″ squares—as you cut, you can continue to dust and toss them with confectioners' sugar to help keep them separated and from sticking.

9. To assemble the tart, pile the marshmallow cubes onto the top of the tart and carefully toast the tops using a handheld kitchen torch.

Tip: Keep a close eye on the temperature of the marshmallow mixture. The gelatin stabilizes the foam structure, but only when warm. Once the marshmallow temperature drops to just slightly warmer than room temperature, quickly deposit it onto the pan to firm up.

TIPS FOR GANACHE

Ganache is an emulsion of fats + solids + liquids. For chocolate ganache, the chocolate adds cocoa butter and cocoa solids, and the liquid is typically cream, although other liquids can be used. When perfectly executed, those elements are in balance, yielding a smooth mouthfeel and a certain sturdiness. Additional flavorings in ganache can be added by infusing the liquid (coffee beans, tea leaves, etc.) or as a finishing step (liqueurs, cordials, extracts, etc.).

When making a ganache, you're looking for a smooth texture and shiny appearance. Here, we use a classic chocolate + cream formula. First, hot cream is poured over chopped chocolate. Gently stirring with a spatula melts the chocolate and drops the temperature. As you stir, you're forming an emulsion, so take care not to blend it too much—the texture can become pasty if it gets overemulsified.

What if the ganache doesn't come together? If you're not seeing a smooth, shiny consistency as you stir, it's likely that the balance between fat and liquid is off. To fix it, introduce a little bit of milk (1 tablespoon at a time) until the texture is shiny and the ganache appears thicker and stronger.

Aim to keep the temperature around 88° to 90°F: Cooler or warmer temperatures will affect the ganache consistency greatly.

What Makes Good Chocolate Good?

For ganache, Wilhelm likes to use the Caoba and Gran Saman varieties from Chocolates El Rey, but other high-quality chocolates will work, too, if you know what to look for. Chocolate comes in many different types, from baking chocolate to fine couverture; milk, dark or white; and with different percentages. Dark chocolate consists of only a few ingredients: cocoa beans (solids and butter), sugar, and sometimes flavorings (e.g., vanilla) and lecithin (an emulsifier). Milk chocolate adds dry milk powder to the mix, and white chocolate eliminates the cocoa solids, deriving its "chocolate" primarily from cocoa butter.

The percentage listed on chocolate refers to the overall cocoa content. A 70% chocolate contains 70% cocoa (cocoa solids and cocoa butter) and roughly 30% sugar. The higher the percentage of cocoa, the more bitter the chocolate tastes, as it contains less sugar. But not all high-percentage chocolate tastes bitter! Origin affects the flavor, too, through its soil and climate. Single-origin and vintage bars have distinct flavor characteristics, which become important when pairing the chocolate with other flavors in your confections.

When working with chocolate to create confections and pastries, it pays to use higher-quality couverture chocolate rather than baking chocolate. Couverture chocolate has a higher cocoa butter content than baking chocolate (it must have a minimum of 35% cocoa butter compared to cocoa solids), which allows it to melt more smoothly, with a better shine and snap when firm. It's ideal for tempering and for creating a silky ganache.

chapter 5.

COOKIES

The Classroom

Every year like clockwork, right around the end of November, our cookie classes take off, filling up and overflowing onto long waitlists. In response to the demand, we added a 3-day intensive cookie camp to our December schedule, and students clamor to join. Although the December class recipes are largely holiday related, we're careful to teach techniques that are applicable for any time of year. One of the students in our very first cookie camp wrote us a few months later to share what a difference it had made in her life. She'd realized while in the classroom that baking cookies is what she loved most, and she was empowered enough by what she learned to believe that she could make a career of it. Her note ended by telling us that she had quit her job and begun a baking career!

Most of the time, students arrive in the classroom with their own ideas of favorite cookies and plenty of experience making them. They generally feel confident and comfortable—rarely are they approaching the class as an entirely new subject. Instead, they're looking to expand their repertoire, refine their techniques with tips and advice, and have some fun baking in a community atmosphere. And yet, almost everyone is surprised by how much they wind up learning in the process of baking alongside our instructors.

As we walk through the lessons and break down simple cookie recipes, it's so rewarding to see students begin to understand *why* they're using a particular ingredient or technique. This aligns precisely with our overall philosophy in the school: We're not just telling you *how* to put together a recipe but showing you why it's done that way and the impact of every choice, from ingredient to method.

The collection of recipes we've selected for this chapter includes some of our very favorites, each of which illustrates the principles that underlie baking cookies. Because our cookie classes are most popular around the holidays, you'll see more festive recipes represented here than in other chapters, but the cookie genre includes such a diversity of styles, shapes, flavors, and textures.

We begin the chapter with lemon shortbread, a simple yet versatile cookie that can be shaped and adapted to your personal tastes. From there we move to drop cookies, rolled cookies, and formed cookies, as well as bars (and even layered bars). As you work your way through the recipes, you'll see different techniques for creaming; try your hand at a variety of flavors, from coconut to toasted almond to saffron; and pick up our tips and advice for success with a range of cookies.

The Lessons

The lessons in our cookie classes are universal to the craft of cookie-baking and will serve you well in any cookie recipe, from assessing doneness to practicing various ways to shape and form cookie dough. We think it's most educational for you to:

- See the importance of the temperature of ingredients, specifically fats and eggs

- Try techniques for four types of cookies: rolled, drop, formed, and bar

- Practice the creaming method and determine the difference between creaming to combine and creaming to aerate

- Practice rolling out cookie dough to the proper thickness

- Learn how to store cookie doughs and baked cookies

- Observe visual cues to assess when cookies are properly baked

KEY INGREDIENTS

Cookies aren't universal in shape, size, or flavor—the ingredients will vary quite a bit depending on the type of cookie you're baking. The real lesson we focus on in our cookie classes is understanding *why* ingredients work within a recipe so you're empowered to know when and how you can swap them, if at all.

These are the functional ingredients we focus on as teaching points during our cookie classes—and what students find waiting at the bench. For more on our ingredient philosophy, please see page xix.

FAT

Cookie recipes can call for a range of fats, from butter to shortening to coconut oil. The type of fat affects both flavor and texture; in particular, the type and temperature of fat is often the main factor in how much the cookie spreads (or doesn't spread) as it bakes. For example, melted butter is absorbed by flour, whereas softened butter coats it. This affects gluten formation, which is what helps hold the cookie together and affects spread. Cookie doughs tend not to contain much liquid, so the flour doesn't get as hydrated. As we saw in the bread chapter, hydration is one way to develop gluten, so cookie recipes tend to not have much gluten structure, making them more tender.

FLOUR

Most cookies call for all-purpose flour, but they tend to be very flexible, as many of these recipes were developed over time in people's homes, and bakers would use whatever they had on hand. They can usually tolerate experimentation with other types of flour, such as whole wheat, rye, or spelt. Just bear in mind that changing the flour will change the texture (and the flavor, of course)—it could make it more dense or more crumbly or crispy, and you may need to adjust the quantity of the flour or of any liquid in the recipe.

SUGAR

A cookie essential—from granulated to brown to confectioners', although some recipes will use alternative sweeteners. In any recipe that calls for brown sugar, we use light brown sugar. Using dark brown sugar will work, though it'll yield a more caramelized, robust flavor and may sometimes slightly affect the texture of your cookie.

ADD-INS

If your cookie recipe already calls for add-ins, you can substitute your own favorites up to the weight called for in the recipe. Adding more than that can affect the final product. So, if a recipe calls for 340 grams of chopped nuts, you can substitute up to 340 grams of other nuts, chips, or dried fruit.

If you're adding rather than substituting ingredients, start with a smaller amount. Sturdy cookie doughs can handle extra ingredients, but it really depends on the recipe. We recommend starting with no more than 20% of the flour—too many add-ins and the cookie won't hold together. Give it a try to see how the dough tolerates the extras. You can mix and match with flavors and add-ins, letting your own palate guide you. Have fun with it!

This is how exceptional creations, like pecan sandies, are born—you start with a great shortbread recipe, you add a nut you like, and voilà.

EQUIPMENT

BAKING SHEETS

If you bake a lot of cookies, it's worth investing in quality baking sheets. We like a heavy-gauge sheet that won't warp in the high heat of the oven. They also hold and distribute the heat evenly for a uniform bake. One-sided sheets (sheets with a rim only along one side) are handy for removing cookies quickly, but they're often thinner—try to find a heavier sheet if you're going this route.

COOKIE SCOOPS

We love cookie scoops for so many reasons! They're a wonderful time-saver and great for even portioning to ensure more uniform baking—and you can use them for fillings, too. They're an obvious choice for drop cookie recipes, where the recipe instructs you to scoop out the dough, but you can also use them to portion out dough for formed or rolled cookies, as using the scoop is a better gauge than eyeballing dough when you're trying to get equal pieces.

PARCHMENT PAPER

We always use parchment paper when baking cookies: Nothing sticks to it, and cleanup is so much easier. But there are other options. Silicone baking mats are a great, reusable alternative. You can also lightly grease your baking sheets: Spritz them with a nonstick baking spray or brush them with neutral vegetable oil, melted coconut oil, or shortening. We don't recommend butter, as the milk solids can caramelize and brown in the heat of the oven, increasing the chance your cookies will stick to the baking sheet.

Some recipes call for rolling or cutting out your cookies on a piece of parchment—and sometimes chilling them—before transferring them to a baking sheet. In these cases, we use a clean sheet of parchment for baking rather than reusing the one you had your dough on originally. If you don't use a clean sheet, keep in mind there can be a bit of residual dough left on the parchment from rolling that might overbrown or burn in the oven, and if you've chilled the dough, parchment that has been chilled tends to absorb some moisture and won't stay completely flat.

STAND MIXER

Many cookie recipes call for making the dough in a stand mixer, usually fitted with the paddle attachment (in our recipes, always use the paddle [flat beater] attachment unless the instructions specifically state otherwise). A stand mixer is useful for creaming together butter and sugar, which requires a lot of work. Can you make cookies successfully by hand? Yes! But be prepared to use some muscle to achieve the right consistency in the creaming step. Electric hand mixers are an option as well—in power, they rank somewhere in between your own hands and a stand mixer. They can usually handle the creaming step pretty well but won't be as useful in mixing the final dough (you may have to use a spoon to work in the flour, as the motor of a hand mixer tends to struggle with thicker doughs).

Temperature

The temperature of ingredients plays a huge role in cookie-making. If your recipe calls for creaming butter, the butter should always be at room temperature before you begin. Eggs and any liquids, too, should be at room temperature so they don't cool the soft butter and reduce aeration. To warm refrigerated eggs, place them in a bowl of warm water for a few minutes before cracking and adding to your dough.

Remember, room temperature varies, so we use a visual cue to know whether your butter is at the proper temperature. It should be pliable, and you can test it by pressing your finger onto the surface—it should leave an indentation. If it doesn't, the butter is too cold; if your finger goes right in and the butter is glossy, it's a little too warm.

IF YOUR BUTTER IS SLIGHTLY TOO COLD AT ROOM TEMPERATURE

Cut the butter into ½″ cubes, then pound down on the cubes with your fist. The combination of force and slight heat from your hand flattens the butter. Gather the flattened butter pieces together and continue this process until the butter is smooth and properly softened. Don't want to use your hands? Try a rolling pin and bench knife with uncubed butter instead.

IF YOUR BUTTER IS SLIGHTLY TOO WARM AT ROOM TEMPERATURE

Place it in the fridge for a few minutes, checking it frequently to make sure it doesn't chill too much; you want it to be pliable but not completely firm. If you choose to mix it without chilling, either use a cold egg to balance out the butter temperature or flatten the mixed dough into a 1″-thick disk and chill until it's pliable but not firm (about 20 minutes) before proceeding.

The Bake

Our cookie recipes all include a time range for baking as well as a visual indicator of doneness. Oven temperatures can vary, and even within your own oven, there can be hotter and cooler spots. The best way to ensure that your cookies are properly baked is to keep a close eye on them and remove them when they've reached the specified color (pale golden, golden brown, and so on). Let your cookies cool for about 5 minutes on the pan before transferring to a wire rack to finish cooling. If you move them too quickly, they can fall apart.

Commonly Asked Questions

CAN I REDUCE THE SUGAR OR FAT?

There are guidelines for successfully reducing the sugar or fat in cookie recipes, but the best way to know if something works is to try it, since it'll likely change the flavor or appearance of the cookie to some degree. In general, you can reduce the sugar in a cookie recipe by 10% and not see a big difference in the final result, but more than that will affect the spread and texture of the cookie.

Reducing fat is more challenging, as it plays a crucial role in the texture and flavor of the cookie. The safest route is to find a recipe that already calls for less fat or uses a different ingredient (such as fruit purée) to substitute.

CAN I USE WHOLE GRAINS?

If a recipe calls for all-purpose flour and you'd like to add whole grains, start by replacing 25% of the all-purpose with a whole-grain flour. Whole-grain flours absorb more moisture but at a slower rate than all-purpose, so for every 120 grams of all-purpose flour you replace, add an additional 15 grams of any liquid called for to the recipe. If the recipe doesn't call for liquid, reduce the amount of flour by 5%. In either case, let your dough sit for 20 minutes after mixing to allow the flour to hydrate. You can continue to experiment by increasing the amount of whole-grain flour in small increments. Try one-third of the flour next time, then half, and so on until you get the result you want.

CAN I CHANGE THE FLAVOR?

Many cookies are excellent candidates for customization. If you start with a simple base cookie recipe, it's easy to create your own unique, delicious cookies by adding spices, extracts, or even some larger add-ins. Cookies that already have very distinctive defining flavors aren't as easy to customize, but you can try substituting spices or nuts.

Plain doughs like shortbread or traditional sugar cookies can be transformed by adding spices, herbs, or other flavorings to the creamed mixture. Add more for milder flavors and add less for more intensely flavored additions. Bake one cookie first to test and adjust the flavors before baking the entire batch.

Lemon Shortbread Cookies

Yield: 3 dozen cookies

This is such a simple yet versatile cookie recipe, and over the years we've made it as a drop cookie, a rolled sandwich variation, and even a hand-formed tartlet—which is why we start with it and keep it separate from the other categories of cookies that follow. The butter here is fully creamed (as it would be for a cake batter) to provide leavening for the cookie, so you'll notice there's no baking soda or powder. The confectioners' sugar makes for an incredibly tender, melt-in-your-mouth texture rather than the sandy texture you often find with shortbread. This cookie is butter-rich but not too sweet. If you like a sweeter cookie, dredge in granulated sugar before baking or confectioners' sugar after—or sandwich them together with sweet icing. Shortbread lends itself to any number of variations—you can change or omit the lemon zest, add different spices or extracts, or just leave it plain. Feel free to play with some of your own favorite flavor combinations. (*See photo on page 249.*)

---

227 grams (16 tablespoons) unsalted butter, room temperature

¼ teaspoon salt

57 grams (½ cup) confectioners' sugar, plus more for garnish (optional)

zest of **1 medium** lemon, or **⅛ teaspoon** lemon oil

240 grams (2 cups) unbleached all-purpose flour, plus more for dusting

1. Line two baking sheets with parchment.

2. Combine the butter and salt in the bowl of a stand mixer and cream together until soft and fluffy.

3. Mix in the confectioners' sugar and lemon zest.

4. Add the flour and mix until well combined.

5. Transfer the dough to a lightly floured surface and pat it into a disk about 1˝ thick. Wrap the disk and chill for about 15 minutes, or until cool but not firm.

6. Preheat the oven to 350°F.

7. On a lightly floured surface, roll the dough to about ¼˝ thick.

8. Using a 2˝ round cutter, cut shapes from the dough. Gather the scraps and continue to roll out and cut until you've used all the dough.

9. Place the shapes on the prepared baking sheets.

10. Bake the cookies for about 10 minutes, or until just golden around the edges.

11. After cooling, dust the cookies with confectioners' sugar, if desired.

➤ VARIATION: DROP COOKIES

Using a cookie scoop (teaspoon or tablespoon), drop the dough directly on the prepared baking sheets. Bake the cookies at 350°F for 8 to 10 minutes for teaspoon-scoop size or 15 minutes for tablespoon-scoop size, or until the edges are lightly golden. Allow the cookies to cool a few minutes on the baking sheets before transferring them to a wire rack to cool completely.

➤ VARIATION: THUMBPRINT COOKIES

Scoop the dough as above, then roll each scoop of dough in your hands to form a smooth ball. Using the back of a wooden spoon or your thumb, make a deep indentation into each ball. Fill each indentation with your favorite filling (jam, lemon curd, peanut butter, chocolate hazelnut spread, etc.). Bake as directed above.

➤ VARIATION: SLICE-AND-BAKE COOKIES

Divide the dough in half. On a lightly floured surface, form each piece of dough into a log about 1½˝ in diameter and 6˝ long. Wrap the logs tightly and refrigerate until firm. Once firm, cut into ¼˝ slices. Place the slices on a parchment-lined baking sheet and bake in a preheated 350°F oven for 8 to 10 minutes, until set and just starting to brown around the edges.

A Finishing Touch

You can dress up the outside of your cookies. For slice-and-bake cookies, brush the outside of the log with egg white, then roll it in finely chopped nuts, sparkling sugar, flavored sugar, or something creative, like sesame seeds. You'll end up with a ring of flavor and texture around the outside edge of each cookie. Dipping one cut side of the cookie in a topping before baking is also an option.

COOKIE CREAMING

Creaming is an essential step in many cookie doughs. By beating together fat and sugar, the sugar aerates the butter and fills it with bubbles that can capture the gases released by your leavener, usually baking soda and/or baking powder. The more bubbles you create, the lighter and crisper your cookies will be.

But not all cookies are light—some are meant to be dense or chewy or firm. Cookies that need to be lighter will require more creaming (to aerate) rather than simply creaming to combine.

When creaming to combine, mix the ingredients on a lower speed for a shorter amount of time until they come together smoothly. Here, you're looking for the mixture to be homogenous but not to increase considerably in volume—it will often look sandy (see photo 1, below). When creaming to aerate, beat ingredients at a higher rate of speed for a longer amount of time. You'll see the mixture lighten in color and increase in volume, becoming fluffy (see photo 2, below).

Benne Wafers

Yield: about 56 cookies

Benne wafers have been a favorite of Southern bakers for more than a century, and once you make them, you'll see why. We like teaching them because they illustrate the effect of sugar on spread and what happens when you dramatically increase the amount of sugar in the recipe. They come together quickly and are dropped onto cookie sheets to bake without extended chilling. The butter is mixed to combine, and there's a low ratio of flour to sugar in this recipe, so the cookies spread significantly and bake up crisp yet chewy. If you want to increase the nutty quality, toast the sesame seeds lightly before using.

113 grams (8 tablespoons) unsalted butter, room temperature

213 grams (1 cup) brown sugar

¼ teaspoon salt

¼ teaspoon baking soda

1 teaspoon vanilla extract

1 large egg

120 grams (1 cup) unbleached all-purpose flour

142 grams (1 cup) sesame seeds

1. Line two baking sheets with parchment paper.
2. Place the butter, brown sugar, salt, baking soda, and vanilla in the bowl of a stand mixer and mix on medium speed until combined.
3. Add the egg and mix until combined.
4. Add the flour and mix until a soft dough forms.
5. Stir in the sesame seeds.
6. Drop the dough by teaspoonfuls onto the prepared baking sheets, leaving at least 2″ between the cookies, as they'll spread.
7. Chill the pans for 10 to 15 minutes.
8. Preheat the oven to 350°F.
9. Bake the cookies for 8 to 10 minutes, until the edges are set and they're golden brown and fragrant.

Oat Chocolate Chip Cookies

Yield: about 3 dozen cookies

These beloved cookies eschew butter for a different fat: coconut oil. We began to explore different fats in traditional cookie applications and appreciated the flavor and texture it adds to this classic cookie, so we brought it to the classroom. The creaming method is more complex here, with melted oil whipped with cold water and a cold egg to emulate the creaming action of butter.

142 grams (½ cup + 2 table-spoons) melted coconut oil

213 grams (1 cup) light brown sugar

1 teaspoon baking powder

¼ teaspoon baking soda

¾ teaspoon salt

1 large egg, cold

30 grams (2 tablespoons) water, cold

1 teaspoon vanilla extract

180 grams (1½ cups) unbleached all-purpose flour

149 grams (1½ cups) old-fashioned rolled oats

170 grams (1 cup) semisweet chocolate chips

1. Preheat the oven to 375°F. Line baking sheets with parchment.

2. Combine the melted coconut oil, brown sugar, baking powder, baking soda, and salt in the bowl of a stand mixer and cream together on medium-high speed until well combined.

3. Add the egg, water, and vanilla and beat until creamy, scraping the bowl as needed.

4. Add the flour and oats and mix on low speed until combined.

5. Stir in the chocolate chips.

6. If necessary, chill the dough for about 15 to 20 minutes, until firm enough to scoop. Keep in mind that if the dough chills too long, the coconut oil will become very firm and the cookies will be hard to scoop.

7. Drop the dough by tablespoonfuls onto the prepared baking sheets, leaving about 1½˝ between them.

8. Bake the cookies for 10 to 13 minutes, until the edges are set and the cookies are lightly golden.

Coconut Oil

Butter is the traditional fat of choice for chocolate chip cookie and oatmeal cookie recipes. Here, we wanted to experiment with coconut oil, so we developed this recipe by converting a recipe that called for room-temperature butter. This isn't as simple as swapping in one fat for the other because it's difficult to find the "sweet spot" of temperature for coconut oil. It's fluid at warmer temperatures and very hard at cooler temperatures. When the coconut oil is firm, it's almost impossible to measure since you can't slice it like butter and it usually comes in a jar, so we decided to use melted coconut oil. To approximate the texture of creamed room-temperature butter, we added a cold egg and cold water to the coconut oil. The cold ingredients help set the oil to a softened butter consistency. The dough should be stiff enough to scoop: If it's too soft, refrigerate it for 10 or 20 minutes, until just stiff enough to scoop and hold shape. If it's chilled too long, the dough will be too hard to scoop easily.

Water may seem like an unusual ingredient in a cookie recipe, but it plays an important role: Butter contains 80% fat and 20% water, but coconut oil is 100% fat, so adding water allows us to better mimic the composition and performance of butter and match the texture we all expect in a classic oatmeal cookie.

We talk through this recipe development process in class as a good example of the importance of thinking through the role of each ingredient and why you can't always easily swap in one for the other.

Coconut Macaroons

Yield: about 2 dozen cookies

Here's a traditional grain-free favorite. Our Vermont bakery makes these in the shape of pyramids, but here we opt for the simplicity of a simple drop cookie. This version is based on making a meringue from the egg whites and cream of tartar before adding the rest of the ingredients. We use sweetened coconut here for a wonderfully moist cookie. You can dress up the presentation and flavor of these baked cookies by dipping them in or drizzling them with tempered chocolate once they've cooled.

---

2 large egg whites

⅛ **teaspoon** salt

¼ **teaspoon** cream of tartar

149 grams (¾ cup) granulated sugar

½ **teaspoon** vanilla extract

255 grams (3 cups) sweetened shredded coconut

1. Preheat the oven to 325°F. Line a baking sheet with parchment.

2. Combine the egg whites, salt, and cream of tartar in the bowl of a mixer fitted with the whisk attachment.

3. Whisk the mixture on medium speed until frothy.

4. Gradually add the sugar, whisking until the meringue is glossy and firm (see below).

5. Stir in the vanilla and coconut.

6. Drop the dough by tablespoonfuls onto the prepared baking sheet.

7. Bake the cookies for 18 to 22 minutes, until they're lightly golden and set.

Why Whisk?

Many classic coconut macaroon recipes take the fast approach of simply mixing together all the ingredients rather than whisking the whites and sugar into a meringue. Why the extra step? Our method creates a macaroon that's lighter and less dense than most; whipping the egg whites into a meringue also stabilizes them, making them less apt to "pool" or get a "foot" of liquid that sets around the bottom. Whipping also whitens the egg mixture and creates more contrast between the golden, caramelized outer shell of the macaroon and the creamy, sweet, almost white center. When you beat the egg whites, be sure that you've *very* carefully separated the yolks out first—you don't want to have any speck of fat in your bowl because it can prevent the whites from whipping up properly.

Sugar Cookie Cutouts

Yield: about 2 dozen 3" cookies

This is the base recipe for most of our cookie decorating classes. It's delicious, simple to make, and yields a perfect blank canvas with a crisp, snappy texture for any decorations you like. We roll and cut directly on parchment paper, which helps minimize the flour dust around the kitchen. Be sure to bake these only until the cookies just begin to color, then let them cool completely before decorating.

---

170 grams (24 tablespoons) unsalted butter, room temperature

112 grams (½ cup + 1 tablespoon) granulated sugar

1 teaspoon baking powder

½ teaspoon salt

1 teaspoon vanilla extract

1 large egg

300 grams (2½ cups) unbleached all-purpose flour, plus more for dusting

Classic Royal Icing (recipe follows)

Tip: Be sure the reused baking sheets are fully cooled between batches.

1. Place the butter, sugar, baking powder, salt, and vanilla in the bowl of a stand mixer and mix on medium speed until combined.

2. Add the egg and mix to combine. Scrape down the paddle, sides, and bottom of the bowl.

3. Add the flour and mix on medium-low speed until a cohesive dough forms.

4. Divide the dough in half.

5. Roll out each piece of dough to ¼" thick on its own lightly floured sheet of parchment paper and refrigerate until firm to the touch, about 30 minutes.

6. When you're ready to bake the cookies, preheat the oven to 375°F. Line two baking sheets with parchment.

7. Cut out shapes, using a floured cutter. Reroll scraps as necessary. If the dough becomes too soft, refrigerate again until firm.

8. Place the cutouts about 1" apart on the prepared baking sheets. Refrigerate until firm (about 20 to 30 minutes); this will prevent the cookies from spreading.

9. Bake the cookies for 10 to 12 minutes, until their edges just begin to brown.

10. Let the cookies cool for 5 minutes on the pans, then transfer them to a rack to cool completely.

11. Once cool, decorate the cookies as desired with Classic Royal Icing.

ROLLING TIPS

Rolling on a lightly floured surface is our go-to method for rolling out dough for cutout cookies; if you choose this option, don't use more than a dusting of flour, which is all you need to prevent sticking. Parchment is another good option for rolling dough and preventing sticking: you can roll your dough directly on top of a single piece of parchment, or—if you find your dough is sticking to the rolling pin—you can roll it between two sheets of parchment. Another smart tip is to flour your cutter before cutting out shapes: This helps the cutter release cleanly.

Classic Royal Icing

Yield: about 986 grams (4½ cups)

Meringue powder is the secret to no-fuss royal icing. It stands in for fresh egg whites and speeds up the process because you don't have to separate eggs (plus, it eliminates any concern consuming about raw eggs). Once you've made the icing, you can adjust the consistency as needed for outlining or flooding. Divide it into smaller batches to tint with food coloring if you like. Royal icing dries to a hard consistency, so be sure to cover the bowl tightly if you're not using it right away. We like to fill pastry bags and seal them tightly so they're prepped and ready whenever it comes time to decorate.

43 grams (⅓ cup) meringue powder

178 grams (¾ cup) water, cold

765 grams (6¾ cups) confectioners' sugar, sifted

food coloring (optional)

1. Place the meringue powder and water in the bowl of a mixer fitted with the whisk attachment and mix on medium speed until combined. Increase the speed to high and beat the meringue to medium-stiff peaks.

2. Add the confectioners' sugar all at once, then mix at medium-low speed until smooth. The icing should be on the thicker side (aim for the consistency of toothpaste), which is ideal for outlining and decorative work.

3. Tint with food coloring, if desired.

4. Adjust with water as needed to create different icing consistencies.

Icing Consistency

When decorating with royal icing, there are two basic techniques: outlining and flooding. *Outlining* is just what it sounds like: creating an outline around the edge of the cookie or around certain areas. *Flooding* means filling in larger areas with icing (doing an outline first creates a barrier for flooding). You'll want a different consistency depending on which technique you're using.

To check for the proper consistency, scoop up a bit of icing onto a spatula or spoon and then drizzle it in lines back and forth over the surface of the icing in the mixing bowl. After a few seconds, the icing will "dissolve" back in, such that you can barely see the lines you made. If the lines dissolve after 7 seconds, that's the right consistency for outlining. For flooding, add just enough water so the lines dissolve in 5 seconds.

Brown Sugar Snaps

Yield: about thirty-two 3˝ cookies

We teach many variations of this cookie in the school, changing the flavors to suit the season. Our base version is a simple brown sugar cookie, and you can spice it up by adding citrus zest or flavoring oils, or even seeds or finely chopped nuts. The sparkling sugar is optional but adds a glitzy, professional-looking touch.

---

170 grams (12 tablespoons) unsalted butter, room temperature

266 grams (1¼ cups) light brown sugar

½ teaspoon salt

½ teaspoon baking soda

1 large egg

360 grams (3 cups) unbleached all-purpose flour, plus more for dusting

72 grams (¼ cup) sparkling sugar (optional)

1. Place the butter, brown sugar, salt, and baking soda in the bowl of a stand mixer and mix on medium speed until thoroughly combined.

2. Beat in the egg, then add the flour, mixing until a cohesive, soft dough forms.

3. Transfer the dough to a lightly floured surface and divide it in half. Shape each piece into a disk about 1˝ thick.

4. Wrap the dough and chill for about 20 minutes, until it's cool but still pliable.

5. Preheat the oven to 350°F and line two baking sheets with parchment.

6. Place the dough on a lightly floured surface and tap it gently with a rolling pin to soften and flatten slightly.

7. Roll out the dough to about ⅛˝ thick. Using a floured 3˝ fluted round cutter, cut out as many cookies as you can. Reroll the scraps as necessary.

8. Place the cutouts about 1˝ apart on the prepared baking sheets. Sprinkle them with sparkling sugar, if desired.

9. Bake the cookies for 10 to 12 minutes, until they're fragrant, the edges are lightly golden, and the centers are set.

FREEZING AND STORING DOUGH AND COOKIES

Most cookie doughs can be stored in the refrigerator for 2 to 3 days, or you can freeze your dough for longer storage (up to 3 months, well wrapped). Once baked, cookies can be stored in airtight containers at room temperature for up to 2 weeks, or frozen for longer storage. Some cookies that are crunchier and snappier (such as brown sugar snaps) might lose some of their crisp texture if stored at room temperature, especially in humid conditions; if you're worried about maintaining the texture, opt for the freezer. To prevent baked cookies from breaking apart while frozen, first freeze them in a single layer on a parchment-lined baking sheet for about an hour. Once chilled, place the cookies into a resealable plastic bag or a sealed container and return to the freezer.

Follow these best practices for freezing dough:

DROP COOKIES: Scoop the dough onto a parchment-lined baking sheet, leaving about ½″ of space between each ball. Freeze the dough until the balls are solid (at least an hour). Once frozen, put them into a resealable plastic bag or a sealed container before returning to the freezer. When you're ready to bake, take out the number of cookies that you want to make and place them on a parchment-lined baking sheet while the oven preheats. Frozen dough often needs a little longer to bake, so add a few minutes to the bake time and keep a close eye on them.

ROLLED COOKIES: You can form the dough into a disk, wrap tightly, and freeze it for up to 3 months. Thaw the dough overnight in the refrigerator before allowing it to soften slightly at room temperature. Before you roll it out, tap down on the dough with your rolling pin; it should yield to gentle pressure. If it cracks when you try to roll it, the dough is most likely too cold: Let it sit at room temperature for a few minutes before trying again.

You can also roll your dough *before* freezing: Roll it out between layers of parchment paper, wrap tightly, and freeze. When you're ready to cut and bake, remove the sheets of dough from the freezer and set them out at room temperature while you preheat the oven, which gives the dough just enough time to soften so you can cut shapes and bake immediately.

Best of all, you can roll *and* cut your cookies, then freeze the cut shapes. This is a good way to front-load the work and get ahead on prep. For this option, roll and cut the shapes, place them on a parchment-lined sheet, and freeze until solid (at least 1 hour). Once solid, you can stack or consolidate the shapes. Bake the shapes directly from the freezer (no need to bring them to room temperature), but add a few minutes to the bake time and keep a close eye on them.

Snickerdoodles

Yield: About 16 cookies

Snickerdoodles are universally popular and a great introduction to hand-formed cookies. Our version uses baking powder instead of the more traditional cream of tartar and baking soda since most households already have baking powder. This change gives them a cakier texture and reduces the spread a bit. The only difference between the method used here and the drop cookie method is that you roll these into balls by hand before dredging them in spiced sugar. It's fun to mix up the spices in the sugar mixture—we've done chai-spiced sugar, and an instructor favorite is sugar with Chinese five-spice powder.

DOUGH

113 grams (½ cup, 1 stick) unsalted butter, room temperature

106 grams (½ cup) brown sugar

½ teaspoon salt

½ teaspoon baking powder

1 teaspoon vanilla extract

1 large egg

180 grams (1½ cups) unbleached all-purpose flour

FINISHING

25 grams (2 tablespoons) granulated sugar

1 teaspoon cinnamon

DOUGH

1. Preheat oven to 350°F.

2. Line a baking sheet with parchment paper. Set aside.

3. In a large bowl, mix together the butter, brown sugar, salt, baking powder, and vanilla until well combined.

4. Add the egg and mix to combine. Scrape the sides of the bowl to make sure everything is well incorporated.

5. Stir in the flour, mixing until a soft dough forms.

FINISHING

1. In a small bowl, combine the granulated sugar and cinnamon.

2. Scoop the dough using a tablespoon scoop, roll the cookies into a ball, then coat them in the cinnamon sugar mixture.

3. Place the cookies about 2″ apart on the prepared pan.

4. For flatter, wider cookies, flatten the dough with the back of a measuring cup or glass. For thicker, rounder cookies, do not flatten the balls of dough, but bake as is.

5. Bake the cookies for about 10 to 12 minutes, until fragrant and set and just starting to brown around the edges.

6. Allow the cookies to cool for a few minutes on the baking sheets, then transfer to a wire rack to cool completely.

Toasted Almond Crescents

Yield: about 30 cookies

Like the brown sugar snaps, this is another very versatile dough, this time made with ground nuts. Different versions of the base recipe are all wonderful, from cherry (see variation below) to spiced chocolate to orange cranberry. We used to teach this recipe in its classic form—coated in a snowy dusting of confectioners' sugar—in our holiday cookie class, but here we've given the recipe a little twist by using coconut milk powder and granulated sugar for a subtle flavor that enhances the toasty nuttiness of the almonds.

DOUGH

60 grams (¾ cup) almond flour, toasted

99 grams (½ cup) granulated sugar

156 grams (⅔ cup) unsalted butter, room temperature

¼ teaspoon salt

1 teaspoon vanilla extract

210 grams (1¾ cups) unbleached all-purpose flour

GARNISH

75 grams (¼ cup + 2 tablespoons) granulated sugar

42 grams (¼ cup + 2 tablespoons) coconut milk powder

DOUGH

1. Preheat the oven to 350°F. Line two baking sheets with parchment paper.

2. Place the almond flour, sugar, butter, salt, and vanilla in the bowl of a stand mixer and mix on medium speed until well combined.

3. Stir in the flour, mixing until a crumbly dough forms. Remove the dough from the bowl and knead it a few times by hand on an unfloured surface to bring it together.

4. Scoop the dough in generous teaspoonfuls; shape each piece into a smooth ball.

5. Roll each ball on an unfloured surface to about 1″ at the center and tapered on both ends, then shape into a crescent.

6. Space the cookies about 1″ apart; they won't spread.

7. Bake the cookies for 10 to 12 minutes, until they're set and just starting to turn golden.

8. Let the cookies cool for 5 minutes on the pans before coating with their garnish.

GARNISH

1. In a small bowl, whisk together the sugar and coconut milk powder.

2. Dredge the slightly warm cookies in the sugar mixture. If desired, let the cookies cool completely and then dredge them again.

(Continued) —

Pulse 50 grams (¼ cup plus 2 tablespoons) of dried cherries in a food processor with 25 grams of the granulated sugar from the dough recipe until they're finely chopped. Let them hydrate in 30 grams (2 tablespoons) of tart cherry concentrate or cherry liqueur for at least 20 minutes, or overnight. Because cherries and almond pair so well, replace the vanilla with almond extract and proceed with the recipe, using untoasted almond flour in place of the toasted almond flour. Add the cherry mixture after beating the butter but before the flours are added. Shape into teaspoon-size balls and place about 1″ apart on prepared baking sheets. Bake the cookies for 8 to 10 minutes, until set and starting to brown on the bottom. Let cool slightly, then dredge in confectioners' sugar. Let cool completely, then dredge a second time.

How to Toast Almond Flour

Toasting almond flour is a simple way to amplify its naturally nutty flavor. Preheat the oven to 350°F. Place the almond flour in an even layer on a parchment-lined or ungreased baking sheet. Bake for 5 minutes, then use a spatula to stir and redistribute the flour on the pan. Continue to bake until lightly golden and fragrant, 2 to 5 minutes more. Pay very close attention, as this will happen quickly and the flour can easily scorch. Transfer the almond flour to a bowl and allow to cool to room temperature before using.

Chocolate-Hazelnut Biscotti

Yield: about 40 biscotti

This nutty chocolate version of biscotti more closely resembles a modern cookie than a traditional Italian biscotti—the addition of butter makes it more tender and less crunchy. We don't toast the nuts before baking because once you cut the slices, the chopped nuts are exposed and will toast during the second bake.

---

57 grams (4 tablespoons) unsalted butter, room temperature

111 grams (½ cup plus 1 table-spoon) granulated sugar

¾ teaspoon baking powder

⅛ teaspoon salt

½ teaspoon vanilla extract

1 large egg yolk

1 large egg

128 grams (1 cup + 1 tablespoon) unbleached all-purpose flour, plus more for dusting

14 grams (about 2½ tablespoons) cocoa powder

107 grams (¾ cup) hazelnuts, coarsely chopped

1. Place the butter, sugar, baking powder, and salt in the bowl of a stand mixer and mix on medium speed until combined.

2. Add the vanilla, then the yolk and whole egg, one at a time, mixing well after each addition.

3. Add the flour and cocoa powder, stirring until almost all the flour is incorporated, then add the hazelnuts and continue to mix until just combined.

4. On a well-floured surface, form the dough into a log, then divide it into quarters.

5. Form each piece of dough into a log about 6″ long. Place the logs about 3″ apart on parchment-lined baking sheets.

6. Chill the logs for at least 20 minutes (or until firm) before baking.

7. Preheat the oven to 375°F.

8. Bake the logs for 10 to 15 minutes, until they spring back slightly when lightly pressed in the center.

9. Remove the logs from the oven (but leave the oven on) and allow them to cool for a few minutes on the baking sheet.

10. Transfer the logs to a cutting board. Using a serrated knife, carefully cut the logs on the diagonal into ½″-thick slices.

11. Return the biscotti to the baking sheets (cut side down, flat) and continue to bake for an additional 10 minutes, or until the centers feel dry and they're very fragrant.

Biscotti di Prato

Yield: about 40 biscotti

We include two biscotti recipes in this chapter to illustrate the range of the cookie. This one, Biscotti di Prato, is made in the traditional Italian-style without any added fat, which yields a quite hard, crunchy texture. It must be dunked in liquid to be eaten, which is how biscotti were traditionally consumed. Here we use the method known as *la fontana* ("the well"), which is similar to making pasta. You mix the dry ingredients together before making a well and adding the eggs. In the classroom, we use a large fork to mix in the eggs right on the countertop. You can do this in a bowl with a regular fork or a bowl scraper, but we find it romantic and comfortingly old-fashioned to use an oversize pasta-style fork.

⅛ **teaspoon** saffron threads

30 grams (2 tablespoons) hot water

198 grams (1⅔ cups) unbleached all-purpose flour, plus more for dusting

198 grams (1 cup) granulated sugar

½ **teaspoon** baking powder

⅛ **teaspoon** salt

2 large eggs

71 grams (½ cup) almonds, toasted and coarsely chopped

Tip: If your slices are too thick, the biscotti will not crisp properly. If they are thicker than 1/2", flip them over halfway through the bake.

1. In a small bowl, steep the saffron threads in the hot water for 5 to 10 minutes. Meanwhile, start the dough.

2. In a medium bowl, combine the flour, sugar, baking powder, and salt.

3. Make a well in the center and add 1 whole egg, 1 egg yolk (reserve the white for later), and the steeped saffron (including its water).

4. Gradually work the flour into the ingredients in the well.

5. When the flour is almost worked in, add the almonds and continue to mix to distribute them evenly throughout the dough.

6. Preheat the oven to 350°F. Line a baking sheet with parchment paper.

7. Divide the dough in half. On a lightly floured surface, roll each piece of dough into a 1¼″-diameter log about 12″ long.

8. Place the logs about 2″ apart on the prepared baking sheet.

9. Brush the reserved egg white over the tops of the logs.

10. Bake the logs until they spring back to the touch and are golden brown on top, about 25 to 30 minutes.

11. Remove the logs from the oven and allow them to cool for a few minutes on the baking sheet.

12. Transfer the logs to a cutting board. Using a serrated knife, carefully cut the logs on the diagonal into ½″-thick slices.

13. Place the biscotti back on the baking sheet (cut side down, flat) and continue to bake until pale brown and completely dry, about 15 minutes.

Mahmoul

Yield: about 46 cookies

This version of mahmoul was brought to us by one of our instructors, Karen Ogrinc, whose family has made them for generations. If you're lucky enough to own a mahmoul mold, you'll be able to make incredibly beautiful cookies that are like little works of art. If you don't have a mold, don't be deterred; you can make a delicious version using just your hands.

FILLING

50 grams (¼ cup) granulated sugar

85 grams (¼ cup + 2 tablespoons) water

450 grams (3 cups) chopped pitted dates

57 grams (4 tablespoons) unsalted butter, room temperature

¼ teaspoon salt

1 teaspoon cinnamon

½ teaspoon cardamom

15 grams (1 tablespoon) orange blossom water, or the zest of 1 large orange

DOUGH

454 grams (1 pound) unsalted butter, room temperature

113 grams (1 cup) confectioners' sugar, plus more for dusting

½ teaspoon salt

1 large egg

15 grams (1 tablespoon) vanilla extract

135 grams (¾ cup) dry farina

570 grams (4¾ cups) unbleached all-purpose flour, plus more for dusting

FILLING

1. Combine the granulated sugar and water in a small saucepan and bring to a boil, stirring until the sugar dissolves. Remove from the heat.

2. Place the dates, butter, salt, cinnamon, cardamom, and orange blossom water in the bowl of a food processor fitted with the metal blade. With the machine running, pour in the hot sugar water, processing until the mixture is smooth.

3. Transfer the filling to a heatproof bowl and let cool to room temperature. Once cool, portion the filling into teaspoonfuls, then roll them into balls. Cover and set aside or refrigerate (see sidebar).

DOUGH

1. Mix together the butter, confectioners' sugar, and salt in a large bowl.

2. Add the egg and vanilla and mix to combine.

3. Stir in the farina and flour, mixing to make a smooth, soft dough.

4. Preheat the oven to 350°F. Line two baking sheets with parchment.

Getting Ahead

For success with mahmoul cookies, it's important that the filling is cooled to at least room temperature so that it doesn't warm or melt the butter in the dough as you shape the cookies. To save time on bake day, make the filling ahead and keep it in a covered bowl or scooped on a tray and covered, then refrigerated. If you're making the filling and using it right away, just make sure it cools to room temperature—no need to refrigerate it.

ASSEMBLY

1. Portion the dough with a tablespoon-size scoop, then roll them into balls (about the size of a walnut if you don't have a scoop).

2. Press the portioned balls of dough into 3″ diameter disks with your fingers. Press a disk into a lightly floured mahmoul mold, then place a ball of filling in the center. Bring the dough's edges up around the filling and pinch to close. Gently press the dough into the mold to set the pattern on the surface, then tip over and tap the shaped dough out of the mold. Place the shaped dough on the prepared baking sheets, leaving 1″ of space between the cookies.

3. Alternatively, you can place a portion of dough in your palm and use your thumb to make an indentation. Place a ball of filling in the center of the dough and wrap the dough to completely seal the filling. Place the shaped dough on the prepared baking sheets, leaving 1″ of space between each.

4. Bake the cookies for 18 to 20 minutes, until golden brown.

5. Let the cookies cool for 5 minutes on the baking sheets, then transfer them to a rack to cool completely.

6. Just before serving, dust the cookies with additional confectioners' sugar.

Chocolate Coconut Blondies

Yield: one 9″ × 13″ pan or two 8″ square pans

Brownies get all the attention, but blondies are where added flavors—such as coconut—really shine. The butter and brown sugar yield a very rich and chewy bar. The combination of coconut and chocolate with the blondie dough is delicious, but you can vary the additions to feature whatever you have on hand or whatever flavors you like most. Dried fruit (we like cranberries) is delicious, as are toasted nuts, citrus zest, cacao nibs, candied ginger—use your imagination here!

---

170 grams (¾ cup) unsalted butter, melted

320 grams (1½ cups) brown sugar

1 teaspoon baking powder

½ teaspoon salt

2 large eggs

1 teaspoon vanilla extract

180 grams (1½ cups) unbleached all-purpose flour

113 grams (1 cup) unsweetened shredded coconut, toasted

113 grams (1 cup) pecans, chopped

85 grams (½ cup) semisweet chocolate chips

85 grams (½ cup) white chocolate chunks

1. Preheat the oven to 350°F. Lightly grease one 9″ × 13″ pan or two 8″ square pans.

2. Combine the butter, brown sugar, baking powder, and salt in a large bowl.

3. Stir in the eggs and vanilla, then the flour, coconut, pecans, and chocolate chips and chunks.

4. Spread the batter evenly into the prepared pan(s).

5. Bake the bars for 23 to 28 minutes (for the 8″ pans), or about 30 minutes (for the 9″ × 13″ pan), until a toothpick inserted into the center comes out clean.

6. Remove from the oven and allow the bars to cool in their pan(s) for at least 30 minutes before slicing. They're easiest to cut when completely cool.

Florentine Bars

Yield: one 9″ × 13″ pan or two 8″ square pans

Don't be fooled by the simplicity of this shortbread base. The chewy, caramelized topping makes these bars impossible to resist. We love the flavor and texture contrast of tart cranberries with toasty sliced almonds, but in keeping with the common theme of so many of these cookie recipes, you can substitute any fruit and nut combination you like (chop any larger fruits or nuts into smaller pieces).

CRUST

113 grams (8 tablespoons) unsalted butter, room temperature

50 grams (¼ cup) granulated sugar

⅛ teaspoon salt

¼ teaspoon vanilla extract

1 large egg yolk

150 grams (1¼ cups) unbleached all-purpose flour

TOPPING

42 grams (2 tablespoons) honey

42 grams (3 tablespoons) unsalted butter

132 grams (⅔ cup) granulated sugar

119 grams (½ cup) heavy cream

108 grams (1¼ cups) sliced almonds

57 grams (½ cup) dried cranberries

8 grams (1 tablespoon) unbleached all-purpose flour

CRUST

1. Preheat the oven to 375°F. Lightly grease (or line with parchment) a 9″ × 13″ pan or two 8″ square pans.

2. Combine the butter, sugar, salt, and vanilla in the bowl of a stand mixer and beat until smooth.

3. Beat in the egg yolk.

4. Add the flour and stir until a soft, cohesive dough forms.

5. Press the dough in an even layer in the prepared pan(s).

6. Prick (dock) the bottom of the crust with a fork and refrigerate for 30 minutes before baking.

7. Bake the crust about 10 to 12 minutes, until it's set and starting to take on color.

8. Remove the crust from the oven and set it aside. Lower the oven temperature to 325°F.

TOPPING

1. Bring the honey, butter, sugar, and cream to a boil in a small (1- to 2-quart) heavy saucepan over medium-high heat. Cook until lightly golden brown (it should read about 240°F on a digital thermometer).

2. Remove the topping from the heat, then quickly stir in the almonds, cranberries, and flour.

3. Using a silicone spatula, evenly spread the topping over the partially baked crust.

4. Bake the bars until the nuts are toasted and the topping is bubbling, about 10 to 15 minutes.

Master Class
Macarons

THE BAKER

En-Ming Hsu holds degrees in baking and pastry from the Culinary Institute of America and specialized in studio arts as an undergraduate at Skidmore College, which has influenced the design and presentation of her pastry creations. En-Ming served as team captain for the winning US team at the World Pastry Cup in 2001, won the Paris Gourmet Pastry One Competition in 1997, and has been recognized with numerous awards. She has taught cake, cookie, and pastry classes at King Arthur for over a decade to both employees and students and currently works as a pastry consultant in Las Vegas.

THE COOKIE

With their delicate shell and almost chewy interior, macarons are the holy grail for many bakers—and are notoriously finicky. En-Ming has long used these two recipes to train bakers because they're more forgiving than most. They use different methods, but both yield a stable batter, which helps prevent such common pitfalls as uneven feet (the term for the ruffled base of the cookie), cracked shells, or gummy interiors. Taken side by side, these two recipes are excellent examples of how two different methods for the meringue can create different results. The almond macaron uses an Italian meringue to create a lighter, more ethereal cookie, whereas the chocolate macaron uses a French meringue to make a denser and more fudgelike texture, though in return you get an easier batter to work with. Mix and match the cookies and fillings as you like.

Every kitchen is different; conditions are always different, from humidity to temperature, and this changes a lot about how the recipe behaves. But there's a tremendous amount of satisfaction that comes from making a macaron recipe and having success.

—EN-MING HSU

Almond Macarons

Yield: 50 filled 1″ macarons

95 grams (1 cup) almond flour

95 grams (6 tablespoons + 2 teaspoons) confectioners' sugar

0.5 gram (scant ⅛ teaspoon) fine sea salt

75 grams (⅓ cup) aged egg whites (see page 282), divided

95 grams (½ cup) granulated sugar

25 grams (1 tablespoon + 2 teaspoons) water

5 grams (¾ teaspoon) light corn syrup

Tip: Professional bakers, like our guest instructors, use weight—not volume—for best results (see page xvi for more on why).

1. Place the almond flour, confectioners' sugar, and salt in a food processor and process until the almond flour is finely ground. Be careful not to overprocess—you don't want it as finely textured as flour.

2. Spread the almond flour mixture on a baking sheet and let it sit at room temperature overnight to dry out.

3. Combine the almond flour mixture with 30 grams of egg whites. Mix to form a smooth paste. Cover the paste and set aside.

4. Place the remaining 45 grams of egg whites in the bowl of a stand mixer fitted with the whisk attachment.

5. In a small saucepot, combine the sugar, water, and corn syrup.

6. Bring the mixture slowly to a boil, stirring if needed, over medium heat. Increase the heat to high once the syrup comes to a boil.

7. Meanwhile, begin to beat the egg white mixture in the mixer on medium speed.

8. Cook the syrup until it reaches 248°F. Remove from the heat and, working carefully, slowly pour the hot syrup into the egg white mixture (don't turn off the mixer as you add the syrup). Continue to beat the meringue until it's shiny and peaked. The meringue will be almost completely cooled by this time.

9. Using a stiff spatula, gradually fold the meringue into the almond paste mixture. Use a rubber spatula to complete the folding.

10. Continue to fold the macaron mixture to deflate it somewhat. The batter should fall slowly in a ribbon when lifted with the spatula.

11. Have four baking sheets ready, lined with silicone mats or parchment paper.

12. Using a pastry bag fitted with a 13 mm (½″) plain tip, pipe the batter into 1″ rounds.

13. Firmly tap the pans on the table four or five times to help the rounds spread evenly.

14. Allow the trays to sit at room temperature for about 20 minutes, or until the surfaces of the rounds feel slightly dry to the touch.

15. Bake the cookies at 300°F for about 10 minutes. The cookies will have formed feet and will feel firm when lightly tapped.

16. Remove from the oven and let the macarons cool fully on the baking sheets before filling. Store in the freezer or refrigerator until ready to serve.

THE TAP

This almond macaron recipe uses the traditional Italian meringue method. The extra step of cooking the syrup (which removes some of the water) makes the batter more stable, allowing it to handle a little overworking—which is easy to do when you're learning to make macarons. Since this batter is so stable, the cookies can sometimes be a bit too high after piping. Tap the pan a few times to smooth out the surface slightly and settle the batter a bit, encouraging the macarons to take on a uniform height.

MACARONAGE

"Macaronage" is the term pastry chefs use to describe the step in which the batter is folded to create a flowing, smooth consistency before piping. You're looking for different visual cues for the macaronage stage in these two recipes: The chocolate batter is a bit thicker, so you'll want to fold the batter until it seems close to ready, then stop folding and take a look at the edge of the batter at the sides of the bowl. The batter should look shiny—let it settle for a minute and watch how it moves. It should flow slowly, leaving a clean, rounded edge. If you overmix it, the batter will run very quickly and will look flat instead of rounded at the edge. If you undermix it, it will be too thick and will hold a peak, which is too stiff. You're aiming for the sweet spot where the mixture holds its shape and isn't runny. Finding that perfect consistency is a matter of practice.

For the almond batter, students often think they've made a mistake when mixing, thinking it looks too thick or that there isn't enough meringue. Don't panic in this case! You simply need to carry on mixing and folding enough to achieve the right consistency: The Italian meringue can handle this.

Aging Egg Whites

When egg whites are fresh, they have more water content. "Aging" them dries them out—as you lose water, you're concentrating the proteins in the egg whites, making them stronger, more stable, and easier to whip. To age egg whites, crack them into a bowl and leave them loosely covered (allowing plenty of air exchange so that water can evaporate) at room temperature for 2 days or longer if it's very humid. This isn't an absolutely critical step, but it's one of the simplest ways to improve your macarons.

Almond Paste

For both the cinnamon almond and coconut fillings, it's important to use an almond paste that's made up of at least 50% almonds. Some brands will list the percentage of almonds on the label—for those that don't, check the ingredient list. If it lists simply "almonds, sugar," you can assume almonds make up more than 50% of the paste. If there's a third ingredient listed (such as glucose or water), it's likely less than 50% almonds.

Chocolate Macarons

Yield: 50 filled 1˝ macarons

200 grams (1¾ cups) confectioners' sugar

130 grams (1⅓ cups) almond flour

18 grams (1 tablespoon + 2 teaspoons) cocoa powder

0.5 grams (scant ⅛ teaspoon) fine sea salt

100 grams (7 tablespoons) aged egg whites

25 grams (2 tablespoons) granulated sugar

Tip: Dutch-process cocoa powder will yield a fudgier, stronger flavor. If you're struggling with the batter, try switching to a cocoa powder with a lower fat percentage, as fat can sometimes interfere with the batter's texture.

1. Combine the confectioners' sugar, almond flour, cocoa powder, and salt in a medium bowl. Allow the mixture to sit at room temperature overnight to dry out. Sift and set aside.

2. Combine the egg whites and sugar in a stand mixer fitted with the whisk attachment and whisk together until shiny and peaked. Gently fold the almond flour mixture into the meringue. The batter will be stiffer than the almond macaron batter.

3. Line baking sheets with silicon mats or parchment paper and pipe 1˝ rounds onto them.

4. Let sit at room temperature for about 20 minutes to dry out.

5. Bake at 300° for 12 to 15 minutes. The cookies will have formed feet and will feel firm when lightly tapped.

6. Remove from the oven and let the macarons cool fully on the baking sheets. Fill and store in the freezer or refrigerator until ready to serve.

Freezer Storage

For the best results with chocolate macarons, store them in the freezer for at least a few hours after filling and before serving. The freezer rest gives the macarons time to absorb moisture from both the atmosphere and the filling. This particular recipe is denser and richer in mouthfeel, unlike the almond macarons, which are lighter and airier—the absorption of moisture helps to amplify their fudgelike quality. Another bonus to the freezer rest is that it will help correct any overbaking (even 1 minute of overbaking can make these too chewy or crisp, and the freezer rest will soften the macarons into the perfect texture).

Cinnamon Almond Filling

Yield: enough to fill approximately fifty 1″ macarons

125 grams (½ cup) almond paste

43 grams (3 tablespoons) heavy cream, plus more as needed

1 gram (¼ teaspoon) cinnamon

13 grams (1 scant tablespoon) amaretto liqueur

1. Combine all the ingredients in a food processor. Mix until smooth and adjust the consistency by adding cream as needed.

2. Refrigerate until ready to use.

Coconut Filling

Yield: enough to fill approximately fifty 1″ macarons

50 grams (3 tablespoons + 1 teaspoon) coconut milk, plus more as needed

5 grams (1 tablespoon) dried coconut, toasted

88 grams (⅓ cup) almond paste

5 grams (1 teaspoon) coconut-flavored rum, such as Malibu

1. Combine the coconut milk and dried coconut in a small bowl. Let sit for 20 minutes to hydrate.

2. Combine all the ingredients in a food processor. Mix until smooth and adjust consistency by adding coconut milk as needed.

3. Refrigerate until ready to use.

Chocolate Ganache Filling

Yield: enough to fill approximately fifty 1″ macarons

150 grams (¾ cup + 2 tablespoons) dark chocolate, chopped

185 grams (¾ cup + 1 tablespoon) heavy cream

10 grams (¾ teaspoon) wildflower honey

15 grams (1 tablespoon) unsalted butter

1. Place the chocolate in a medium heatproof bowl.

2. Heat the cream with the honey in a small saucepan (or in a microwave-safe bowl in a microwave) until it just begins to simmer.

3. Remove from the heat and pour the hot cream mixture over the chocolate; let stand for 1 minute, then whisk until smooth. Whisk in the butter.

4. Let the ganache rest overnight at room temperature before using.

chapter 6.

QUICK BREADS

The Classroom

Quick breads are so much fun to teach! Our quick bread classes cover biscuits and scones, muffins and sweet loaves, and even include simple cakes, such as coffeecakes and gingerbread. The first quick bread we had class requests for was scones. They were becoming popular in bakeries, and not many people knew exactly how to make them, so we offered instruction in scones in our basic breads class to highlight the difference in handling between quick and yeast breads. Then we began to get more requests for help baking biscuits, and our first quick bread class, Biscuits and Scones, was born.

The very first session we taught was on a Thursday evening. We had rolled biscuits and patted scones on the agenda, but by 7:45 p.m. we were done with both recipes, and the instructor had to think fast. Should she dismiss the class early? Instead, she demonstrated a favorite recipe for maple corn biscuits that she knew by heart. The students were enthusiastic, and we kept it on the curriculum permanently!

Quick breads use chemical leaveners, such as baking powder or baking soda, as opposed to yeast. These ingredients start their rise as soon as they're moistened. That's why the breads are called "quick"—you'll see the contrast to the slow process you find with yeast breads.

In class, we emphasize the "quick" aspect for mixing techniques, too. Here, we're looking for a moist, tender crumb. You want to use a light hand when working with these doughs and batters to keep from overmixing, which can overdevelop the gluten and result in a tough, dense product. (This is *such* an important point that we used to hold up actual STOP sign to remind students to stop mixing their muffin batter, often before they thought it was time.) It's not that you need to obsess about precision here—quick breads are forgiving—but these recipes need less handling than you might think.

Quick breads might not boast the sophistication of laminated doughs or pastry, but they do have an endearing quality. Imagine the deliciously sumptuous texture of a buttery biscuit or the crumbly, craggy top of a cream scone studded with currants. Muffins and tea breads, which have a more refined, cakelike texture, still possess a certain cozy homeyness that's hard to resist.

In class, we focus on the *how* and *why* of technique and ingredients. Instead of trying to define the precise line between a biscuit and a scone, we teach the basics in each genre and leave the quibbling to others. We run into the same question of boundaries with many recipes in our quick bread classes: Why is a coffeecake a quick bread? Or gingerbread? We include them here because they're simpler to make and less sweet than most cake recipes, and they nicely bridge the gap between our quick bread and cake classes.

The Lessons

Quick breads are simple to mix and quick to bake, offering as close to instant gratification as you get in the baking world. Although these are humble recipes made in home kitchens for decades, students enjoy hearing how they can be shifted to accommodate their own tastes. Our goal for each of you is to:

- Understand the function of ingredients in biscuits and scones and the effect of variations in ingredients and techniques

- Observe the effect of different leaveners in a range of baked goods

- Practice different methods for incorporating fats into batters and doughs: cutting and creaming with butter and emulsifying with oil

- Practice techniques for mixing and baking a variety of quick breads

- See how to switch shapes and flavors by turning muffins into loaves, and sweets into savories

KEY INGREDIENTS

The ingredients for quick breads are relatively commonplace and usually have multiple substitutions available for them. Here we list those ingredients that play unique roles in the production of successful quick breads.

These are the functional ingredients we focus on as teaching points during our quick bread classes—and what students find waiting at the bench. For more on our ingredient philosophy, please see page xix.

BAKING SODA

Baking soda is an alkaline leavener that reacts with acidic ingredients, such as buttermilk, molasses, or cocoa powder, to create carbon dioxide gas in the form of bubbles (think of your grade school volcano experiment here). Baking soda is used in smaller quantities than baking powder, and if your recipe uses soda without an acid to activate it, you'll notice a soapy flavor. Baking soda also requires liquid to react, and it releases most of its gas immediately. If your recipe is leavened only by baking soda, it's critical to get the recipe into the oven as quickly as possible since the leavening power begins to diminish shortly after it's combined with liquid.

BAKING POWDER

Baking powder is a complete leavener made up of alkaline baking soda and acidic cream of tartar. When baking powder gets wet it produces carbon dioxide, which leavens your baked good. Baking powder comes in two forms: single-acting (which is activated once, by liquid) and double-acting (which is activated twice: first by liquid and second by the heat of the oven). Double-acting is far more commonly used and is what we call for in our recipes. Because it's activated in part by heat, double-acting baking powder buys you a bit more flexibility with timing the bake. Single-acting baking powder starts working the moment that you add the liquid to your recipe, so just as with baking soda, you need to get the batter or dough into the oven quickly.

BUTTERMILK

Buttermilk is a fermented milk product, high in acid and low in fat. It's popular in many quick bread recipes because its acid reacts with baking soda to provide leavening. If you substitute it for regular milk in a recipe that uses baking powder for leavening, you'll taste the tang since there's no soda to counteract the acidity.

FATS

The fats most commonly used in quick breads include oil, cream, and butter, though substitutes can be used successfully. Biscuits and scones rely on butter for the flakiest results. The butter is cut into the flour, as you would for pie crust, coating some of the flour to add tenderness but retaining small pieces to release steam in the oven, creating flake. Recipes made with cream indicate a biscuit or scone that will have a very tender mouthfeel but virtually no flake. The most basic muffins and quick loaves use oil or melted butter as their fat. You mix the fat with the wet ingredients, then mix in the dry ingredients with a few quick strokes for a tender, somewhat coarse crumb. Those breads and muffins that call for creamed butter and alternating addition of dry and wet ingredients will give you a cakier, more delicate structure.

SPARKLING SUGAR

This coarse white sugar stays intact through the heat of baking, leaving a nice glittery finishing touch to the tops of muffins and scones. It's an entirely optional addition, and you can substitute a bit of turbinado or granulated sugar: They won't add quite the same sparkle, but they'll give you a sweet crunch and a shinier look.

Freshness Matters

Because leaveners play such an essential role in quick bread recipes, be sure your baking soda and powder are fresh. Often those ingredients sit in your pantry for months or even years before the package is emptied. Over time they lose their efficacy, so it's important to check their potency if you're in doubt. For baking soda, mix a small spoonful with a spoonful of vinegar or lemon juice. It should react quickly (and audibly), bubbling fizzily in the bowl. If not, it's time to get a new box for baking purposes. For baking powder, mix a small spoonful with ¼ cup hot water. It should bubble vigorously. If it doesn't, it's time to replace it.

EQUIPMENT

BISCUIT CUTTERS

These sharp-edged cutters are ideal for slicing through biscuit dough; they come in all kinds of shapes and sizes, from square to round to scalloped. You can also use a knife to cut out your biscuits, but whatever you use, be sure it's something with sharp edges rather than, say, a dull-edged drinking glass. A clean, sharp cut will ensure that the flaky layers separate fully for the highest rise (see page 296).

LOAF PANS

Quick breads are often baked in loaf pans. Most recipes call for either an 8½″ × 4½″ pan or a 9″ × 5″ pan—the key is to make sure that the batter doesn't fill the pan up too high (you want a few inches of space) or there won't be enough space to accommodate it as it rises in the oven.

MUFFIN TINS

Have on hand a standard-sized muffin tin with 12 wells. You can also use jumbo or miniature muffin tins if you like; just adjust the bake time accordingly (a few more minutes for jumbo muffins and less time for minis). Muffin liners come in all shapes and sizes, from the classic fluted paper liners to pretty bakery-style tulip papers. You can easily make your own tulip papers by cutting out a square of parchment paper and folding up the edges. If you prefer to forgo liners altogether, be sure to grease the pan well.

PARCHMENT AND PAN SPRAY

We love parchment—it's nonstick, helps greatly with cleanup, and can be reused repeatedly for baking biscuits and scones. You can also give your pans a quick spray with a pan spray or grease them lightly with a neutral oil. The most important thing is to prep your pans in some way to prevent your baked goods from sticking.

PASTRY BLENDER

We find a pastry blender to be an invaluable tool for cutting in butter, whether for biscuits, scones, or pie crusts. A pastry blender makes quick work of the task while avoiding any contact between the warmth of your hands and the cold fat. If you don't have one, you can use a fork or your fingertips (see page 177 for more) for successful results.

Commonly Asked Questions

WHY DIDN'T MY BISCUITS RISE?

First, check your baking powder to be sure it's fresh (see page 293 for testing). Next, think about your technique. Did you add enough liquid? A dry dough will yield less rise. Did you overhandle the dough when mixing? Overworking the dough will make for a tough, tight biscuit. Did you handle the dough enough? A few light kneads help your biscuits achieve their highest rise. Did you pat or roll it out too thin? Biscuits will only rise by about half again their height when rolled, so if you've rolled to ¼″, your baked biscuits will only be about ⅜″ high. Last but not least, did you use a sharp enough cutter and press straight down when cutting? A dull cutter or twisting as you cut will compress the edges of the biscuit, preventing a full rise (see facing page for an illustration of the difference).

CAN I CUSTOMIZE QUICK BREADS?

Biscuits, scones, and muffins are simple to customize. It's easy to vary the add-ins already called for in your recipe. Just be sure to use the same relative quantity of ingredients, or you'll weigh down the dough. Some recipes, such as our Buttermilk Biscuits, don't call for any add-ins, but you can choose to include them. Grated cheese, ground spices, dried or fresh herbs, and seeds are all good ideas to experiment with here. When you don't have an existing add-in to use as a guideline, aim for no more than 30% of the flour weight. Biscuits and scones also benefit from a finishing touch that matches the ingredients inside the dough: For cheese biscuits, sprinkle a little grated cheese on top. For apple cinnamon scones, finish the tops with a bit of cinnamon sugar.

WHAT IF I DON'T HAVE BUTTERMILK?

Buttermilk plays a few different roles in quick bread recipes. It adds a slightly tangy flavor to recipes like Buttermilk Biscuits where other flavors don't dominate. It also helps quick breads rise in combination with baking soda. If you don't have it, you can make your own by combining 1 tablespoon of of an acid like vinegar or lemon juice with enough milk to measure 1 cup. Let it sit for about 5 minutes before adding to your recipe.

CAN I USE MORE WHOLE GRAINS?

Absolutely, try it! In many ways, quick breads are the easiest products to experiment with when it comes to whole grains since you don't want as much gluten development. There are some useful rules of thumb to help guide you (see page 31 for details), but we encourage students to play with alternative flours in this category.

Cream Drop Biscuits

Yield: 14 to 16 (2″) biscuits

These drop biscuits are the fastest, simplest biscuit recipe, coming together in less time than it takes to preheat the oven. This is your go-to recipe for last-minute strawberry shortcake (double or triple the sugar for a sweeter biscuit) or for a quick breakfast. You can vary the recipe by snipping in such fresh herbs as chives or rosemary, or stirring in such add-ins as chopped jalapeño or candied ginger, but remember less is more with biscuits—they'll rise higher if you don't weigh them down with add-ins.

---

227 grams (2 cups) unbleached all-purpose flour

12 grams (1 tablespoon) baking powder

½ teaspoon salt

8 grams (2 teaspoons) granulated sugar

283 grams (1¼ cups) heavy cream, or more as needed

1. Preheat the oven to 425°F. Lightly grease a baking sheet or line it with parchment.

2. In a medium bowl, combine the flour, baking powder, salt, and sugar.

3. Stir in the cream, adding additional cream as necessary to make a soft dough.

4. Using a scoop or spoon, drop the dough by heaping tablespoon-fuls, about 2″ apart, onto the prepared baking sheet.

5. Bake the biscuits for 10 to 12 minutes, until they're golden brown.

Biscuit Go-Withs

Some of our happiest school memories are of tastings at the end of Biscuits and Scones classes, where we pull out all the jams, Devon creams, honeys, and butter we can find, and everyone gathers around the bench to taste and discuss what they learned. Not only are toppings on biscuits delicious, but they're a smart way to vary the flavor. We love butter and honey, of course, but feel free to serve with your favorite toppings, from blueberry jam to olive tapenade.

Biscuit Business

Biscuits are probably the most challenging quick bread for students, partly because the characteristics of a great biscuit depend on the eye of the beholder. Everyone knows you want them to be tender (melt in your mouth) and flaky (lots of light layers), but those descriptions can vary from person to person. Another stumbling block is the term "high-rising": Students imagine the biscuits will quadruple or more in the oven. They roll the dough out thin, thinking they'll cut more biscuits that way, only to find the biscuits come out of the oven a disappointing ½" tall. When we talk about focusing on light handling and rolling thicker, it's a revelation.

Buttermilk Biscuits

Yield: six 3˝ biscuits

To create an even flakier biscuit, we borrow the same "cutting-in" technique we use when adding butter to a pie crust. For the highest rise, be sure your biscuit cutter is sharp enough that it doesn't compress the dough as you cut. And remember, a biscuit will only rise about half its height, so be sure you're not patting or rolling too thin if you want flaky, high-rising biscuits. A light hand is key here, but a few folds in the bowl will help the biscuits achieve their highest rise.

---

240 grams (2 cups) unbleached all-purpose flour

10 grams (2½ teaspoons) baking powder

½ teaspoon salt

8 grams (2 teaspoons) granulated sugar

85 grams (6 tablespoons) unsalted butter, cold

177 grams (¾ cup) buttermilk

1. Preheat the oven to 425°F. Lightly grease a baking sheet or line it with parchment.

2. In a medium bowl, combine the flour, baking powder, salt, and sugar.

3. Cut in the butter with a pastry blender until the mixture is unevenly crumbly, with some larger bits of butter (between pea- and currant-size) remaining. You're aiming for pieces of butter that are slightly smaller than what you'd have in Extra-Flaky All-Butter Crust (page 186).

4. Add the buttermilk and stir to make a cohesive dough.

5. While it's still in the bowl, fold the dough over on itself a few times to pick up any dry bits.

6. Turn the dough out onto a very lightly floured surface and pat it to ¾˝ thick.

7. Cut rounds or squares with a biscuit cutter or sharp knife.

8. Place the dough cutouts about 2˝ apart on the prepared baking sheet.

9. Bake the biscuits for 15 to 18 minutes, until they're golden brown.

Tip: Press down instead of twisting to ensure the flakiest biscuits (see page 296).

Maple Corn Drop Biscuits

Yield: 20 mini biscuits

These tender drop biscuits get a little crunch from the cornmeal. We borrowed the recipe from Elizabeth Alston's charming book *Biscuits and Scones*, and we've tweaked it over the years to fit it into the abbreviated time frame of our classes, pulling them out of the oven in just 10 minutes. Our version has even more maple syrup than the original (we're Vermonters—we can't help ourselves!). For a softer biscuit, you can form them in larger scoops and extend the baking time.

---

150 grams (1¼ cups) unbleached all-purpose flour

140 grams (1 cup) whole-grain cornmeal

25 grams (2 tablespoons) granulated sugar

12 grams (1 tablespoon) baking powder

½ teaspoon salt

70 grams (5 tablespoons) unsalted butter, cold

100 grams (scant ½ cup) milk

100 grams (⅓ cup) pure maple syrup

1. Preheat the oven to 425°F.

2. Combine the flour, cornmeal, sugar, baking powder, and salt in a large bowl.

3. Cut in the butter until the mixture resembles coarse crumbs.

4. Stir the milk and maple syrup into the dry ingredients just until the mixture is combined. Add additional milk, if needed, to create a soft batter that can be scooped.

5. Drop the batter by the spoonful (or portion using a tablespoon scoop) about 1″ apart onto a parchment-lined baking sheet.

6. Bake the biscuits for 10 to 12 minutes, until golden brown.

Oven Racks

Students often ask which rack to use when baking, but what works best in one oven will be different in another. The best advice for any baker is to practice and observe: The more you bake in your own oven, the more you'll become familiar with its hot spots. Start with the middle rack as your default, but you might need to adjust placement or rotate your pans to get the best result in your oven.

Savory Breakfast Buttermilk Biscuits

Yield: six 3″ biscuits

Here's our version of a breakfast sandwich, with our favorite ingredients rolled right into the biscuit—bacon, cheddar, paprika, and even a hint of maple to amplify the bacon flavor. The weight of the extra add-ins means the biscuits don't rise quite as high, but the flavor punch matches the texture perfectly. If you're not a fan of the spice, you can omit the paprika, but we recommend giving it a try first: It's not strong but adds a richness and depth to the biscuits that really makes them stand out.

---

200 grams (1⅔ cups) unbleached all-purpose flour

40 grams (⅓ cup) whole wheat flour

10 grams (2½ teaspoons) baking powder

½ teaspoon salt

1 teaspoon smoked paprika (optional)

85 grams (6 tablespoons) cold unsalted butter, cut into ½″ cubes

115 grams (½ cup) sharp cheddar, grated

30 grams (2 strips) bacon, cooked and chopped

6 grams (2 tablespoons) fresh chives, chopped

177 grams (¾ cup) buttermilk

12 grams (2 teaspoons) pure maple syrup

1. Preheat the oven to 425°F. Lightly grease a baking sheet or line it with parchment.

2. In a medium bowl, combine the flours, baking powder, salt, and paprika.

3. Cut in the butter until it is worked down to very small pieces, between pea- and currant-size.

4. Stir in the cheddar, bacon, and chives.

5. Add the buttermilk and maple syrup, stirring to make a cohesive dough.

6. While it's still in the bowl, fold the dough over on itself a few times to pick up any dry bits.

7. Turn the dough out onto a very lightly floured surface and pat it ¾″ thick.

8. Cut rounds or squares with a biscuit cutter or sharp knife.

9. Place the dough cutouts about 2″ apart on the prepared baking sheet.

10. Bake the biscuits for 15 to 18 minutes, until they're golden brown.

BISCUITS OR SCONES?

At first glance, a biscuit and a scone look very similar. Biscuits (the American kind—a British "biscuit" is what we'd call a cookie) are often savory, although they can be sweet, and tend to be fluffy and flaky, relying on fat (usually butter) for tender, well-defined layers. Scones are often sweeter, with a denser, more crumbly texture—thanks to the addition of richer ingredients, such as cream and eggs. As with so many quick breads, though, the definitions are loose at best! Some biscuits (e.g., a drop biscuit) are firmer and denser, edging closer into scone territory, while some scones can be less dense and more delicate than others.

The definition gets even less distinct when you consider the provenance of the recipe. For example, the British have a very long and beloved tradition of making cream scones. A traditional British scone is much more specific, and British bakers tend to hold more tightly to the classic formula that yields a tender yet denser crumb. When the scone came to America, bakers didn't have such a cultural instinct to stick so closely to the traditional recipe, so it began to morph into something different: American scones are often sweeter and feature many more add-ins, almost like the way we treat muffins.

Cream Scones

Yield: 8 scones

As we shift from biscuits to scones, we start off with the most traditional approach: the denser, more tender British-style scone. This scone is quite different from our Buttermilk Biscuits recipe (page 300) but very similar to the Cream Drop Biscuits (page 298); in both, we use cream instead of butter to achieve tenderness without flake, but here we get a denser texture by cutting back on the proportion of baking powder. When you first add the cream to the dry ingredients, you'll be surprised by how loose the batter seems—don't worry! As you stir, the cream gets absorbed quickly, forming a thick dough that's easy to shape into a round. For the shaping step, remember to use a light hand and just a whisper of flour on your work surface.

WHOLE WHEAT SCONES, PAGE 306

CREAM SCONES

300 grams (2½ cups) unbleached all-purpose flour

8 grams (2 teaspoons) baking powder

½ teaspoon salt

12 grams (1 tablespoon) granulated sugar

85 grams (½ cup) dried currants or other add-ins

354 grams (1½ cups) heavy cream, cold; plus more for brushing

sparkling sugar (optional)

1. Preheat the oven to 400°F. Lightly grease a baking sheet or line it with parchment.

2. In a large bowl, combine the flour, baking powder, salt, and sugar.

3. Stir in the currants or other add-ins.

4. Stir in the cream; it will look wet.

5. While it's still in the bowl, fold the dough over on itself a few times to pick up any dry bits. There should be no visible flour left in the bowl.

6. Shape the dough into a disk about 6˝ in diameter and place it on the prepared baking sheet.

7. Cut the dough into eight equal wedges. Separate the wedges by pulling them apart about 1˝ at their outer edge, but leave them in a circle.

8. Brush the tops of the scones lightly with cream and sprinkle with sparkling sugar, if desired.

9. Bake the scones for 15 to 18 minutes, until they're lightly browned.

> **VARIATION: QUICK MAPLE STICKY BUNS**

Try this variation with any of the rolled or patted biscuit and scone recipes (minus any add-ins). If you don't have maple syrup on hand, simply substitute honey or corn syrup.

Prepare the biscuit dough, adding 1 teaspoon vanilla extract with the liquid in the recipe. Prepare the topping by combining 50 grams (¼ cup) light brown sugar with 28 grams (2 tablespoons) melted unsalted butter and 78 grams (¼ cup) pure maple syrup. Spread this topping mixture evenly into a lightly greased 9˝ round pan, then sprinkle with 40 grams (¼ cup) chopped pecans or walnuts. Roll the dough out to a 9˝ × 12˝ rectangle. Brush the dough with water, then sprinkle with 70 grams (⅓ cup) brown sugar, leaving a ½˝ margin free of filling along one short side. Starting with the filling-covered short side, roll the dough into a log, pinching the seam to seal. Using unflavored dental floss, a bench knife, or a serrated knife, cut the dough into nine buns about 1˝ wide. Arrange the buns atop the topping in the pan. Bake the buns at 350°F until the edges are golden brown, about 33 to 38 minutes. Let the buns cool in the pan for about 5 minutes before inverting them onto a rack. Scrape any topping stuck to the pan back onto the buns, then let them finish cooling on the rack.

Whole Wheat Scones

Yield: 8 scones

These whole wheat scones are what we consider "American style," with a more crumbly texture than the cream-based British scones and the added leavening of baking soda. We encourage students to invent their own favorites by varying the flavors. Cherry chocolate chip is one of our go-to combinations, along with orange cranberry, but you can experiment. If you want a savory scone, eliminate the sugar and add any savory mix-ins you like. Try white whole wheat flour for a lighter flavor and color or traditional red whole wheat flour for a more pronounced whole-grain taste. If you don't have whole wheat flour, use all-purpose flour but increase the weight by about 25%, or 56 grams.

---

226 grams (2 cups) whole wheat flour

25 grams (2 tablespoons) granulated sugar

8 grams (2 teaspoons) baking powder

½ teaspoon baking soda

½ teaspoon salt

113 grams (8 tablespoons) unsalted butter, cold

71 grams (½ cup) dried currants or other add-ins

177 grams (¾ cup) buttermilk

1 large egg, separated

sparkling sugar (optional)

1. Preheat the oven to 375°F. Lightly grease a baking sheet or line it with parchment.

2. Combine the flour, granulated sugar, baking powder, baking soda, and salt in a large bowl.

3. Cut in the butter until it's in very small pieces; the mixture will have the texture of coarse sand.

4. Stir in the add-ins.

5. Whisk together the buttermilk and egg yolk. Add to the dry ingredients, stirring to make a soft dough.

6. While it's still in the bowl, fold the dough over on itself a few times to pick up any dry bits.

7. Pat the dough into a flat disk about 7″ in diameter.

8. Transfer the disk to the prepared baking sheet and slice into eight equal wedges. For scones with crispier, firmer edges, separate the wedges; for softer, higher-rising scones, leave them in a circle.

9. Brush the tops of the scones with beaten egg white and sprinkle with sparkling sugar, if desired.

10. Bake the scones for 18 to 25 minutes, until they're light golden brown.

BREADS, MUFFINS, BOTH?

Quick breads can be shaped in loaf or muffin form, and the two aren't as different as they appear. In general, any muffin can become a quick bread loaf and any quick bread loaf can be transformed into a muffin simply by changing the pans. A recipe that yields a standard-size batch of muffins (12 muffins) will fit nicely into an 8½″ × 4½″ or 9″ × 5″ loaf pan, and vice versa. Aim to have the batter fill the pan about two-thirds to three-fourths full. For quick breads, it's a safe bet to bake your loaves at 350°F, whereas we use 375°F or 400°F for muffins—a higher temperature can create more rise (and consequently, a higher domed top). In either case, you'll need to keep an eye on your baked goods and rely on visual cues to know when they're fully baked. Quick breads will usually bake for 45 to 75 minutes (moister and larger loaves will need more time); muffins will take anywhere from 18 to 30 minutes.

CREAMING VS. WHISKING

Some quick bread recipes call for creaming butter with sugar—a method similar to baking a cake. Others call for whisking oil or melted butter into the batter. Why use one over the other? First, let's understand what's happening in both scenarios: Whether you're creaming or whisking in the fat, your goal is to emulsify, which means forcing together two ingredients (in this case liquid and fat) that don't naturally want to mix. When creaming, as in our Blueberry Muffins recipe (page 309), you're aerating the butter and sugar mixture by trapping small pockets of air inside the mixture, which contributes to the light texture of the final baked good. After creaming, you add eggs, which act as an emulsifier, binding together the liquid and fat that otherwise don't want to combine: Think of it as a classic "opposites attract" love story! If you find that the batter starts to separate as you add the eggs, you can try adding a tablespoon or two of the flour from the recipe and beat that in before adding more egg—this can help to stabilize the emulsion and bring it back together.

Other quick breads rely on an even faster method of combining the fats and liquids: These recipes simply have you whisk together the oil (or sometimes melted butter) into the wet ingredients. Here, it's important to whisk thoroughly: As you whisk, you're forcing the fat to disperse evenly throughout the liquid, creating a stable emulsion. You don't need to worry about overmixing at this stage, because you haven't added the flour yet. This yields a baked good with a good rise and uniform texture; if the fat isn't stable in the liquid, it can yield a flat or dense baked good with a greasy texture.

Blueberry Muffins

Yield: 1 dozen muffins

To yield the ultimate blueberry muffin, we borrow some techniques from our cake classes—creaming the butter and alternating the addition of flour and liquids. The result? A muffin with the tender texture of a cupcake, perfect for those of us who crave cake for breakfast but want to call it something else! Muffins are best when they combine a light interior with a beautifully domed top. To achieve that, we rely on baking powder for leavening and a higher oven temperature than many cakes. Be sure your baking soda is fresh and your oven temperature is accurate. If you want to switch the blueberries for another ingredient, keep the quantity the same to keep your muffins light.

---

113 grams (8 tablespoons) unsalted butter, room temperature

149 grams (¾ cup) granulated sugar

8 grams (2 teaspoons) baking powder

½ teaspoon salt

5 grams (1 teaspoon) vanilla extract

2 large eggs, room temperature

240 grams (2 cups) unbleached all-purpose flour

119 grams (½ cup) milk, room temperature

425 grams (2½ cups) blueberries, fresh or frozen

36 grams (2 tablespoons) sparkling sugar or Demerara sugar (optional)

Tip: If using frozen berries, don't thaw; this will help prevent any juice from streaking the batter.

1. Preheat the oven to 375°F. Lightly grease the wells of a standard 12-cup muffin tin or line the pan with papers and grease the papers.

2. Combine the butter, granulated sugar, baking powder, salt, and vanilla in the bowl of a stand mixer and beat together on medium speed for about 2 minutes, or until the mixture is light and fluffy.

3. Add the eggs, one at a time, scraping the sides and bottom of the bowl between each addition as necessary.

4. On low speed, stir in one-third of the flour, then half of the milk.

5. Mix in another third of the flour, the remaining milk, then the final third of the flour. Scrape down the bottom and sides of the bowl and mix briefly.

6. Gently fold in the berries.

7. Scoop the batter into the prepared pan, filling each well between two-thirds and three-fourths full. Sprinkle the tops of the muffins with sparkling or Demerara sugar, if desired.

8. Bake the muffins for 18 to 20 minutes, until a tester inserted into the center comes out clean and the muffins spring back when lightly touched.

Lemon Poppy Seed Bread

Yield: one 8½″ × 4½″ loaf

This recipe is a beloved example of a classic quick bread, made with oil and swiftly combined for a tender, cakelike texture (the speed of the recipe is a true illustration of the quick bread method). We find it improves the bread to whisk the wet ingredients with the sugar, rather than adding the sugar with the dry ingredients. This creates a smooth, emulsified batter that makes for a slightly less oily texture. You can easily modify this recipe to make an equally delicious orange or grapefruit poppy seed loaf by switching out the citrus.

---

240 grams (2 cups) unbleached all-purpose flour

2 teaspoons baking powder

¼ teaspoon salt

28 grams (3 tablespoons) poppy seeds

132 grams (⅔ cup) vegetable oil

198 grams (1 cup) granulated sugar

2 large eggs

119 grams (½ cup) milk

1 teaspoon lemon zest

59 grams (¼ cup) lemon juice

1 teaspoon vanilla extract

1. Preheat the oven to 325°F. Lightly grease an 8½″ × 4½″ loaf pan.

2. In a medium bowl, combine the flour, baking powder, salt, and poppy seeds.

3. In a separate bowl, whisk together the oil, sugar, and eggs.

4. Whisk the milk, lemon zest, lemon juice, and vanilla into the egg mixture.

5. Whisk the wet ingredients into the dry ingredients.

6. Pour the batter into the prepared pan.

7. Bake for 40 to 50 minutes, until a tester or toothpick inserted into the center comes out clean.

Tip: Don't worry about curdling—there's enough sugar and fat here to smoothly emulsify the batter.

Pumpkin Quick Bread

Yield: two 8½″ × 4½″ loaves

This simple quick bread is popular in the colder months, and the enticing scent of it as it bakes is good enough reason in its own right to include it in our classes! It serves as a nice counterpart to the Lemon Poppy Seed Bread (page 310), as it shows how beating the butter and sugar together makes for a cakier bread. If you like, you can vary the spices, of course, and we wouldn't say no to adding a generous handful of chocolate chips or toasted walnuts!

---

170 grams (¾ cup) unsalted butter, room temperature

280 grams (1⅓ cups) brown sugar

8 grams (2 teaspoons) baking powder

½ teaspoon baking soda

5 grams (2 teaspoons) cinnamon

1 teaspoon ginger

¼ teaspoon allspice

¾ teaspoon salt

360 grams (3 cups) unbleached all-purpose flour

3 large eggs, room temperature

425 grams (one 15-ounce can) pure pumpkin purée

1. Preheat the oven to 350°F and grease two 8½ x 4½″ loaf pans.

2. Combine the butter and brown sugar in the bowl of a stand mixer and beat on medium speed until well blended.

3. Beat in the baking powder, baking soda, cinnamon, ginger, allspice, and salt.

4. Add the flour and blend on low speed. The mixture will look crumbly.

5. Add the eggs, one at a time, scraping the bowl between additions.

6. Stir in the pumpkin and mix until the batter is smooth.

7. Pour the batter evenly into the prepared pans.

8. Bake for about 45 to 50 minutes, until a toothpick inserted into the center comes out clean.

9. Remove from the oven, allow to cool in the pans for 10 minutes, then remove and let cool completely on a wire rack.

Fresh Ginger Gingerbread

Yield: one 8˝ cake

The double punch of fresh and candied ginger in this recipe elevates the flavor beyond a traditional gingerbread. The butter here is melted, so it behaves like oil in the way it tenderizes but still brings the butter flavor we love. The moisture of this quick bread makes it a perfect host for rye flour, as you see in the variation. When adding a whole grain, we increase the proportion of liquid by decreasing the overall flour weight. The result is a gingerbread that remains light and tender while adding a great depth of flavor from the rye.

---

186 grams (¾ cup + 2 table-spoons) light brown sugar

85 grams (¼ cup) molasses

178 grams (¾ cup) water, boiling

57 grams (¼ cup) unsalted butter, softened

1 teaspoon baking soda

½ teaspoon salt

½ teaspoon cinnamon

¼ teaspoon cloves

1 large egg

210 grams (1¾ cups) unbleached all-purpose flour

29 grams (2 tablespoons) grated fresh ginger

46 grams (¼ cup) diced crystal-lized ginger

1. Preheat the oven to 350°F. Lightly grease an 8˝ square pan.

2. Whisk together the brown sugar, molasses, water, and butter in a large, heatproof bowl, stirring until the butter melts.

3. When the mixture has cooled to lukewarm, stir in the baking soda, salt, cinnamon, cloves, and egg.

4. Stir in the flour, then the fresh ginger and crystallized ginger.

5. Pour the batter into the prepared pan.

6. Bake the gingerbread for 25 to 30 minutes, until a toothpick inserted into the center comes out clean.

> **VARIATION: RYE GINGERBREAD**

To make a rye gingerbread, use 90 grams (¾ cup) unbleached all-purpose flour and 106 grams (1 cup) medium rye flour instead of 210 grams (1¾ cups) unbleached all-purpose flour.

Cocoa Streusel Coffeecake

Yield: 1 coffeecake

We love coffeecakes, both yeasted and chemically leavened. This example is the perfect bridge to the world of cakes. We cream the butter just to combine it with the sugar and the eggs rather than creaming to aerate as cake recipes often do, and the result is a somewhat denser crumb. The cake itself is rich with sour cream and vanilla, and the streusel adds both flavor and texture to make this a classic example of the genre. The baking soda reacts with the acidity of the sour cream to leaven the cake, but we also add baking powder to help lift the butter and streusel. This cake is spectacular baked in a Bundt or tube cake pan, but in a pinch you could bake it in a 9″ × 5″ loaf or a 9″ square baking pan.

CAKE

113 grams (½ cup) unsalted butter, room temperature

198 grams (1 cup) granulated sugar

2 teaspoons baking powder

¼ teaspoon baking soda

¼ teaspoon salt

1 teaspoon vanilla extract

2 large eggs

240 grams (2 cups) unbleached all-purpose flour

300 grams (1⅓ cups) sour cream, room temperature

FILLING

106 grams (½ cup) light brown sugar

6 grams (1 tablespoon) cocoa powder

2 teaspoons cinnamon

19 grams (2 tablespoons) dried currants

71 grams (⅔ cup) walnuts or pecans, chopped

CAKE

1. Preheat the oven to 375°F.

2. Place the butter, granulated sugar, baking powder, baking soda, salt, and vanilla in the bowl of a mixer and beat together on medium speed until well combined.

3. Add the eggs, one at a time, beating until thoroughly combined after each addition.

4. Add the flour in three portions, alternating with the sour cream and mixing until well combined after each addition. Set aside.

5. Thoroughly grease an 8-cup Bundt pan.

FILLING AND ASSEMBLY

1. Combine all the filling ingredients.

2. Spoon half of the batter into the prepared pan, smoothing the top.

3. Sprinkle the filling evenly over the batter, then top with the remaining batter. Lightly and briefly swirl together the batter and filling with a small spatula or knife.

4. Bake the cake for 45 minutes, or until a tester inserted into the center comes out clean. If the cake is browning too quickly, cover it loosely with foil for the last 15 minutes of baking.

No Bundt?

If you don't have an 8-cup Bundt pan, you can use another pan of a similar capacity: A 9″ square pan will work nicely. If you're unsure about the size of any pan, you can test it out first with water; an 8-cup Bundt pan holds 8 cups of water when filled to the brim. The batter, on the other hand, comes only about two-thirds of the way up the pan, or it would spill out as it rose in the oven. To find a pan that will accommodate your batter, you'll want to look for a pan that holds about 8 cups of water when filled, meaning the batter will fill it to the proper level for optimum rise, whatever the shape.

Master Class
Sticky Toffee Pudding

Yield: eight 3¾″ × 3½ cakes or one 10-cup Bundt cake

THE BAKER
Melanie Wanders has worked at King Arthur since 2011, focusing on developing and teaching the Baking School's pastry curriculum for 10 years before moving to the test kitchen to continue her pursuit of product development and all things sweet. She interned at the famed Chez Panisse and—along with her husband, Wilhelm (the mastermind behind the S'mores Tart, page 232)—owned Chocolaterie Wanders, an artisan chocolate shop and bakery in Virginia, before moving to Vermont.

THE PUDDING
On a trip to Scotland, Melanie set out to enjoy a slice of sticky toffee pudding in every village she visited. Ever the pastry chef, her mind was on how to re-create her perfect version, which you'll find here. Her take on this homestyle dessert consists of a dark, moist cake drizzled with a rich, brandy-spiked caramel sauce and served with a large dollop of unsweetened whipped cream. The line that separates a quick bread from cake is a blurry one, as all the recipes in this chapter illustrate. It could be defined by the amount of sugar, the choice of baking pan, or the chemical leaveners used for rise. Here, Melanie labels her own simple pudding as a quick bread. Compared to other cakes, it has much less fat—and though you have the option of baking it in a Bundt pan here to dress it up a bit, it's often made in a square baking pan or loaf pan and cut into squares rather than slices for a more rustic approach than many other cakes.

66

The final texture of the pudding should be moist and tender with a fine, somewhat dense crumb. The sauce should be satiny smooth, and if you prefer not to use brandy, just omit it from the recipe. Because the cake and sauce are very sweet (just the way I like it), I prefer to serve this with unsweetened whipped cream to balance the sweetness, though it's equally delicious with a scoop of vanilla ice cream. While I think it's best served warm, I wouldn't turn it away cold, either!

Melanie Wanders

—MELANIE WANDERS

CAKE

225 grams (1½ cups) pitted dates, chopped

296 grams (1¼ cups) water

1 teaspoon baking soda

57 grams (¼ cup) unsalted butter, room temperature

198 grams (1 cup) granulated sugar

½ teaspoon salt

1 teaspoon baking powder

1 teaspoon vanilla extract

2 large eggs

180 grams (1½ cups) unbleached all-purpose flour, sifted

SAUCE

500 grams (2½ cups) brown sugar

½ teaspoon salt

237 grams (1 cup) heavy cream

113 grams (½ cup) unsalted butter, room temperature

30 grams (2 tablespoons) brandy

1 teaspoon vanilla extract

GARNISH

unsweetened whipped cream (optional)

Tip: Professional bakers, like our guest instructors, use weight—not volume—for best results (see page xvi for more on why).

CAKE

1. Preheat the oven to 350°F.

2. In a medium saucepan, combine the dates and water, then bring the mixture to a boil over medium-high heat.

3. Remove from the heat, then stir in the baking soda. Set aside to cool to room temperature before moving on. If the date mixture is still hot, it can melt the butter in the next step, which will yield a dense, greasy texture in the cake.

4. Combine the butter, sugar, salt, baking powder, and vanilla in the bowl of a stand mixer and mix on medium speed until well combined.

5. Add the eggs, one at a time, mixing well to combine.

6. Add half of the flour, then half of the date mixture, then mix well.

7. Repeat with the remaining flour and remaining date mixture. Scrape the bottom and sides of the bowl.

8. Grease eight miniature (3¾″ × 3″ × 3″) loaf pans or one 10-cup Bundt pan and pour the batter evenly into the pan(s).

9. Bake miniature loaves for 20 minutes or Bundt cake for 40 to 45 minutes—the cake is ready when a tester inserted into the center comes out clean.

10. Allow the cake to cool in the pan(s) for 10 to 20 minutes, then invert onto a wire rack and allow to cool completely. At this point, the cake may be stored covered at room temperature for up to 2 days, refrigerated for up to 4 days, or frozen for up to 3 months.

SAUCE AND GARNISH

1. Combine the brown sugar, salt, cream, and butter in a medium saucepan and cook over medium-low heat, stirring just until the sugar is dissolved, then increase the heat to medium and bring the mixture to a boil. Lower the heat and allow the mixture to simmer, without stirring, for 3 minutes to reduce.

2. Remove from the heat, then stir in the brandy and vanilla. Store the sauce covered at room temperature for up to 4 hours, or refrigerate for up to 1 week. Reheat the sauce gently before using.

3. When ready to serve, slice the cake into pieces and drizzle the sauce over the top. Serve with a dollop of whipped cream, if desired.

Why Sift?

Sifting your flour does take time—and adds an extra step. We don't call for it in our recipes unless it makes a noticeable difference: Here, sifting ensures that the cake stays tender and as light as possible. This pudding contains a lot of water, and when water is mixed with flour, gluten begins to form. You need *some* gluten formation to hold baked goods together, but the more we stir or agitate the batter, the more gluten forms, making the texture chewier and less tender. Sifting lightens the flour and removes any lumps, which means you need to do less mixing to get a smooth batter.

Your Ideal Caramel

Caramel can be made wet (with sugar and a liquid) or dry (with just sugar). When making a wet caramel such as this, be sure to heat the mixture on medium-low, stirring to ensure that all the sugar crystals are dissolved before the mixture comes to a boil. If the mixture starts to bubble but the sugar crystals are not yet dissolved, lower the heat and continue to stir until the mixture is smooth and the sugar crystals are fully dissolved (undissolved crystals can make the caramel grainy upon cooling). Once the sugar is completely dissolved, increase the heat and refrain from stirring. Continue cooking the caramel, swirling the pot as necessary until it is reduced and caramelized to your liking. This can take up to 3 minutes or more, depending on how dark you like your caramel. If necessary, you can gently scrape the bottom of the pot during caramelization and reduction. Be sure to stir slowly and gently (as if using a paintbrush to slowly move back and forth on the bottom of the pot). If you stir the mixture vigorously, it can splash onto the sides of the pan, cooling the sugar mixture and causing it to recrystallize, which will make the sauce grainy. As far as doneness, remove the caramel from the heat when it's one shade lighter than you want it—it'll continue to cook after it's taken off the heat. After stirring in the brandy (optional though delicious) and vanilla, both of which will slightly cool the mixture and halt the cooking process, transfer the sauce to a separate container to cool completely at room temperature.

Date Success

Melanie uses Medjool dates in the classroom because they're easy to find in most grocery stores, but feel free to use any date you like—just make sure it's plump and on the softer side rather than shriveled and hard.

Adding baking soda to the water when you're soaking dates breaks down their firm skin. Because baking soda is alkali (caustic), it softens the date skins and frees up amino acids and sugars, allowing them to brown during the bake. This is similar to the idea of using a lye or baking soda bath for pretzels. When you first mix the batter, it will turn a light cream color with darker flecks of dates. As the pudding bakes, it takes on a dark, caramelized, coffeelike brown color.

chapter 7.

CAKES

The Classroom

Everyone loves cake . . . and cake classes! Both the cake decorating and traditional cake classes on our calendar sell out quickly. This comes as no surprise: Cakes are the centerpieces of so many of life's most memorable occasions. They signify pleasure and celebration; they remind us of beloved birthday traditions and favorite moments; and they encompass every possible flavor anyone could love or want. It brings us great joy that so many people choose to come to us to elevate their own celebrations. We always wrap up cake classes full of smiles, feeling like we're able to be a tiny part of the significant merriment that lies ahead.

Students arrive in the classroom eager to master the foundational techniques to make delicious *and* beautiful cakes. We teach more than traditional tiered layer cakes swathed in buttercream and topped with piped frosting; we also teach more "humble" cakes, such as cupcakes, upside-down fruit cakes, Bundts (gorgeous in their own right), and more. We offer guidance on different components of cakes, from the layers themselves to the fillings and frostings, and we finish with instructions for some of our favorite assembled cakes, such as an intricate opera torte with layers of coffee syrup-soaked sponge cake and a shiny chocolate ganache topping.

We've honed our curriculum over the years to focus on lessons that will equip you to make your very best cakes regardless of the style. Learning how to combine ingredients to yield different results, from a fine-grained, tender crumb to a sturdier, more moist texture, means that life's happiest moments can be accompanied by cakes that shine at center stage.

The Lessons

Just as cakes vary greatly in type and style and flavor, the techniques needed for cake success range widely. In our classes, we cover the basic skills and then illustrate all the ways to use them on your cake journey, so you will:

- See the difference between creamed and blended cakes

- Prepare a simple white cake, using the paste method

- Gain tips for prepping pans and assessing a proper bake

- Observe the effect of various flours in different types of cakes

- Make and troubleshoot basic buttercream frostings

- Use a pastry bag to pipe fillings and frostings

- Learn to assemble and store finished cakes and cake components

- Customize cakes, from the layers to the frostings and fillings

KEY INGREDIENTS

The ingredient list for our cake classes doesn't differ drastically from the rest of our classes, but we emphasize different functions and characteristics for each. Here, we focus on how basic ingredients, such as cocoa powder, baking powder, and all-purpose flour, affect texture, crumb, and rise.

These are the functional ingredients we focus on as teaching points during our cake classes—and what students find waiting at the bench. For more on our ingredient philosophy, please see page xix.

CHEMICAL LEAVENERS

Most American-style cakes rely on chemical leaveners (baking soda or baking powder) to rise; some recipes rely entirely on mechanical leavening (such as creaming butter and sugar or beating egg whites) to produce loft. Some recipes use a combination of chemical and mechanical leavening to get the most volume.

Baking soda requires an acid to spark its chemical reaction. Often this is an obvious ingredient, such as buttermilk, vinegar, or citrus juice. Other ingredients found in cake recipes—for instance, brown sugar, molasses, or pumpkin purée—are also acidic enough to activate baking soda.

Baking powder is a shelf-stable version of the chemical reaction discussed above. It's used for leavening in recipes that don't call for acidic ingredients or alongside baking soda when additional leavening is needed. When labeled "double-acting," baking powder gives two punches of leavening power: first, when liquid is added, and second, in the heat of the oven. Imagining pancake batter gives a good visual of this: Bubbles rise to the surface once you make the batter, then you get a second rise when the batter hits the hot griddle.

COCOA POWDER

For cakes (such as our Dark Chocolate Cake, page 335), we prefer to use dark cocoa powder rather than natural cocoa powder, as it yields a deeper, richer chocolate flavor and a wonderfully dark color.

Some cakes may call specifically for natural or Dutch-process cocoa. Natural cocoa powder is lighter in color, with a slightly acidic, milder chocolate flavor. Recipes using natural cocoa powder often call for baking soda, which neutralizes the acidity of the natural cocoa. Dutch-process cocoa powder is alkalized to neutralize the acidity, giving it a smoother, more intense chocolate flavor. Without the added acidity, cakes made with Dutch-process cocoa powder are often leavened with baking powder. If your recipe doesn't specify a particular type of cocoa powder, use what you have on hand.

If you're using cocoa powder in a frosting (such as our American-Style Chocolate Buttercream, page 357), stick with natural or Dutch-process cocoa powder, both of which will impart a warm, milk chocolate hue to the frosting, rather than dark cocoa powder, which tends to produce frostings with a slightly grayish hue.

EGGS

The two components of eggs—whites and yolks—each affect cakes in different ways. Egg whites are roughly 90% water and 10% protein. Their protein provides structure and helps the cake hold its shape. Egg yolks contain fats and emulsifiers (lecithin). The fat from yolks gives cakes a tender crumb and adds a delicate, golden hue to the crumb color. The lecithin helps emulsify the fats and liquids in the batter, bringing them together smoothly in harmony, which ultimately affects the texture of the final crumb.

FATS

Butter and oil contribute to the flavor, tenderness, and moistness of cakes. Unless otherwise specified, choose unsalted butter and neutral oils. The temperature of ingredients in cakes also plays a role in its crumb structure (see page 340 for more on temperature and fats).

It's useful to remember here how the structure of butter and oil differs: On the one hand, butter is made of water and fat, so it's also contributing some hydration to your batter. Oil, on the other hand, is 100% fat. Both add tenderness and moisture to cakes but in different amounts. In any cake calling for oil, any neutral oil will work well (such as vegetable, grapeseed, refined coconut, or canola), unless otherwise specified.

FLOUR

Most cake recipes call for all-purpose flour or cake flour. The mixing method, type of fat, and any other non-wheat dry ingredients (such as cocoa powder or nut flour) in the recipe all play a part in determining the type of flour used.

All-purpose flour provides crumb structure and stability in blended, oil-based cakes. Butter-based cakes tend to utilize unbleached or bleached cake flour (both of which contain less gluten-forming protein than all-purpose) to produce a lighter, finer, more tender crumb. King Arthur cake flour is unbleached, but you'll find that many brands of cake flour are bleached. Bleached cake flour has been treated with chlorine to give it an ultrawhite appearance. Bleaching also affects the flour's flavor, pH, and absorbency, which changes how it performs in a recipe. For this reason, it's best to stick with the flour called for in your cake recipe. If you find you're out of cake flour, visit our website to learn how to make your own, or call our Baker's Hotline (855-371-2253) to talk through the best flour substitution for your recipe.

LIQUID

In the classroom, we use whole milk in our recipes. Milk fat contributes to flavor, moisture, and tenderness in baked goods, while milk sugars promote browning and caramelization during the bake. Most cakes have high amounts of fat and sugar in them, so using a lower-fat milk, such as skim or 1%, should not affect the outcome; use the dairy you have on hand.

SUGAR

Sugar plays three main roles in cakes: flavor, color, and texture. Flavorwise, it makes our cakes taste sweet. As the cake bakes, the sugars begin to caramelize, which provides an additional depth of flavor (think notes of caramel and toasted nuts) as well as a golden brown color to the exterior of the cake. Although sugar is a dry ingredient, it's hygroscopic, which means it pulls moisture from its surroundings, and once moistened, sugar liquefies. Because of this, sugar also adds moistness and tenderness to cakes.

EQUIPMENT

CAKE PANS

A sturdy cake pan is an essential for any baker looking to make cakes. For layer cakes, we recommend having on hand at least two of each size (8″ and 9″ round being the most common)—or more if there are intricate, multitiered cakes in your future. If you can, invest in pans that are at least 2″ high, which will give you the best insurance against any overflow. Many cake batters—especially the simpler ones, such as our Tender White Cake (page 342)—can be doubled and baked in a 9″ × 13″ pan or as cupcakes. When preparing pans for baking cakes, use a nonstick spray on the bottom, or line the bottom of the pan with parchment spray.

For Bundt cakes, you'll want to use a Bundt pan, which can come in a number of stunning shapes and designs. Check the capacity called for in the recipe because Bundt pans range in size. When baking with Bundt pans, be sure to thoroughly grease them right before pouring in your batter—these kinds of cakes are notorious for sticking, and you can avoid that heartbreak with careful pan preparation (see page 347).

CAKE TURNTABLES

Cake turntables can be a great tool to help you perfect your decorating techniques. These turntables allow you to spin your cake to easily frost all sides.

CUPCAKE LINERS/PAPERS

When using paper liners for cupcakes (or muffins), always grease the liners. While silicone-coated cupcake papers tend to release cleanly from the cupcakes, most of the readily available paper liners in grocery stores will stick to the baked cupcakes and will benefit from a light spritz of nonstick spray to encourage a smooth release after baking. If you don't have liners, just be sure to thoroughly grease the wells of the pan before adding your batter.

OFFSET SPATULAS

These are useful tools for frosting cakes and leveling cake batter. Some batters are fluid enough that they'll settle evenly once poured into a pan, but others are thicker and will need a bit of encouragement. In those instances, use an offset spatula to gently smooth the top of the batter into an even surface. They're also helpful for encouraging the cake to release from the pan once it's baked because they're thinner and more flexible than most knives and easier to run around the edge of the pan.

PASTRY BAGS

An omnipresent tool in most bakeries, pastry bags are our go-to approach for everything from piping frostings to adding fillings to creating decorative touches like the gorgeous swirls on top of our Gâteau St. Honoré (page 370). You can fit a pastry bag with many different kinds of tips, depending on the result you're after—some recipes will specify the type of tip if you need a particular design. If you don't have a pastry bag, you can easily use a clean, food-safe plastic bag with the corner snipped off. For more tips on filling and using pastry bags, see page 356.

PARCHMENT

Lining your pans with parchment prevents the cake from sticking. Although it may seem like an unnecessary extra step, take the added precaution of also lightly greasing the parchment. Consider it insurance for all of your hard work!

STAND MIXER

Depending on the method called for in your recipe, a stand mixer can be a cake baker's best friend. When you need to cream to aerate, relying on a mixer for power and speed is extremely helpful. Other cake methods, such as those used for simple blended cakes, are better mixed by hand. When using a stand mixer, always use the paddle (flat beater) attachment unless the recipe specifically states otherwise.

TESTER OR TOOTHPICK

Cake testers are thin metal skewers designed to test the doneness of your cake; a toothpick or regular stainless-steel kitchen skewer (or any similar implement you have on hand) will work just as well. The idea here is that a very thin implement won't leave a mark when you insert it into the cake, allowing you to check and see whether any wet batter clings to it, which would indicate that the cake needs more time in the oven.

WHISK

Some cake batters (such as most simple blended cakes with oil) are only gently mixed together; for these, you don't want to use a stand mixer, or you risk overmixing the batter. Instead use a whisk, which allows you to incorporate all the ingredients smoothly and thoroughly by hand.

Commonly Asked Questions

WHY DO I ADD THE EGGS ONE AT A TIME?

Many cake recipes instruct you to add eggs one at a time, beating between each addition. Why not just add them all at once? Eggs contain both water and fat, so adding an egg introduces water to the batter, which can be difficult to incorporate smoothly. If you add the eggs all at once, it's too much water to emulsify. Adding the eggs one at a time keeps the light, fluffy texture of the batter without having it break. A broken emulsion results in a cake with a denser, coarser crumb structure.

DO I HAVE TO SIFT MY FLOUR?

If a recipe specifically calls for sifting the flour, there's usually a reason for it, such as thoroughly mixing dry ingredients, or making the flour lighter before measuring by volume. Many older recipes call for sifting flour for every baked good, but nowadays all flours are presifted at the mill. So unless your recipe specifically calls for it or you see that your flour is clumpy from humidity, there's no need to sift your flour for every recipe (bakers rejoice!).

Keep in mind that "1 cup of sifted cake flour" and "1 cup of cake flour, sifted" are not the same if you're working by volume. If you're working by weight, it doesn't matter whether you sift the flour before or after weighing it; the weight always stays the same. If your recipe calls for "sifted cake flour," sift the flour first, then measure. If it calls for "cake flour, sifted" and you're using volume, measure first, then sift.

CAN I MAKE MY CAKE TALLER?

You'll notice that many of the recipes in this chapter yield one 8″ round single layer cake. If you want to create a showstopper with multiple layers, you can! Just double (or triple) the recipe to yield the number of layers you want. Keep in mind that a single layer can be sliced in half horizontally and filled and frosted to yield two cake layers.

HOW DO I MIX AND MATCH FLAVORS?

Layer cakes are perfect for mixing and matching—take any frosting you like and pair it with the cake of your choosing. Our classes cover some of the most fundamental recipes, such as basic yellow, white, and chocolate cakes along with essential frostings. You can make a yellow cake with chocolate buttercream or a chocolate cake with Swiss meringue buttercream. And beyond that, there's an entire world of options once you consider flavoring your buttercreams (see page 358) or adding extra ingredients, such as a layer of chopped fresh fruit with the fillling, toasted coconut, or chocolate curls for garnish on top of the cake.

Vanilla Cupcakes

Yield: 1 dozen cupcakes

These simple cupcakes were developed for our children's classes. They're just a step away from muffins—using a similarly simple method of a quick mix of wet and dry ingredients. We've made these with a variety of flours over the years with great success. All-purpose flour yields a cupcake with a sturdier and more muffinlike crumb, while unbleached cake flour makes a more tender version. However you choose to make them, they're fast to mix, bake, and frost for spur-of-the-moment festivities. And when it comes to frostings, have at it! Almost any flavor you can dream up will pair well with these; we love a classic chocolate buttercream or a coconut frosting topped with toasted coconut.

---

225 grams (1¾ cups + 2 tablespoons) unbleached all-purpose flour

8 grams (2 teaspoons) baking powder

½ teaspoon salt

198 grams (1 cup) granulated sugar

132 grams (⅔ cup) vegetable oil

2 large eggs

177 grams (¾ cup) milk

15 grams (1 tablespoon) vanilla extract

1. Preheat the oven to 350°F. Line a 12-cup muffin tin with paper liners or grease each well thoroughly.

2. In a medium bowl, whisk together the flour, baking powder, and salt.

3. In a separate large bowl, whisk together the sugar, oil, and eggs.

4. Add the milk and vanilla to the egg mixture, whisking to combine.

5. Add the dry ingredients to the wet ingredients, whisking to combine. The batter should be smooth, with no lumps of flour remaining.

6. Scoop the batter into the prepared pan, filling each well two-thirds to three-fourths of the way full. A muffin scoop works well here.

7. Bake the cupcakes for 20 to 24 minutes, until a tester inserted into the center comes out clean.

8. Remove the cupcakes from the oven and allow to cool for 5 minutes in the pan.

9. Transfer the cupcakes to a rack to cool completely.

10. Once cooled, frost the cupcakes as desired.

Dark Chocolate Cake

Yield: one 8″ round single layer (easily doubles for two-layer cake)

Here, we move on to another blended cake, this time rich with chocolate. The classic blended cake method is very quick and easy—made by mixing wet and dry ingredients separately, then whisking them together, almost like a quick bread—and it yields a slightly coarser crumb than other cakes. In the classroom, we use very dark Dutch-process cocoa powder to give the cake a deep chocolate flavor and an intensely dark color. Buttermilk's acidity reacts with the baking soda here to help leaven the cake and adds flavor and tenderness as well. Top the cake with chocolate ganache for an added layer of chocolate flavor.

---

105 grams (¾ cup + 2 tablespoons) unbleached all-purpose flour

21 grams (¼ cup) dark Dutch-process cocoa powder

1 teaspoon baking soda

¼ teaspoon salt

½ teaspoon espresso powder (optional)

120 grams (½ cup + 2 tablespoons) granulated sugar

74 grams (⅓ cup) vegetable oil

119 grams (½ cup) buttermilk

1 large egg

½ teaspoon vanilla extract

1. Preheat the oven to 350°F. Lightly grease an 8″-diameter, 2″-high round cake pan and line it with parchment.

2. In a medium bowl, whisk together the flour, cocoa powder, baking soda, salt, and espresso powder.

3. In a separate small bowl, whisk together the sugar, oil, buttermilk, egg, and vanilla.

4. Add the liquid ingredients to the dry, whisking until well combined.

5. Pour the batter into the prepared pan.

6. Bake the cake for 20 to 25 minutes, until a tester inserted into the center comes out clean and the edges pull away from the pan.

7. Remove the cake from the oven and let cool in the pan for 10 minutes before turning it out of the pan onto a rack. Let cool completely before storing or frosting.

The Blending Method

Some of our simplest cakes rely on the blending method, whereby we vigorously whisk together the wet and dry ingredients until no lumps remain in the batter. Don't use an electric mixer as it can overmix. Whisking by hand gives the batter enough structure to keep the cake slightly domed or level after baking. The temperature of ingredients, such as eggs, isn't important with oil-based blended cakes.

DO I HAVE TO SCRAPE DOWN THE BOWL?

Do not skip this step! "Scrape the bowl" is a phrase you'll hear instructors say again and again in the classroom (we joke that once students get home, they'll hear us whispering in their ear over their shoulder as they bake). Scraping the bowl is extremely important when making cakes, particularly when using the creaming method.

Scraping ensures that the cake batter is homogeneous, that the ingredients are thoroughly combined, and that there aren't unincorporated clumps of creamed butter and sugar or pockets of dry flour. Stand mixer bowls are notorious for hiding a ring of unincorporated ingredients or thicker batter around the base where the paddle doesn't quite reach. To make sure you're blending everything together, stop the mixer and give the sides and bottom of the bowl, as well as the paddle attachment, a thorough scraping with a spatula. Once the batter is completely mixed, remove the bowl from the mixer and do a few strokes by hand with a spatula just for extra insurance that no clumps or dry spots are hiding. If you've ever made cakes or cupcakes and seen a volcanic eruption on the surface of the cake, it's most likely an area of creamed butter and sugar that didn't get fully incorporated during the mixing process. (This happens because sugar and fat melt in the heat, but there's no protein from egg or flour to set the mixture, or starch to absorb the excess moisture, so it leaves a bubbled up, shiny area on the cake.)

HOW DO I KNOW WHEN MY CAKE IS DONE?

As with baking in general, rely on your senses—visual cues are some of the best ways to know if a cake is ready. Every oven will be calibrated slightly differently (which is why we strongly advocate using a thermometer to check yours!), and the times in any recipe are never entirely exact: Treat them as guidelines and use touch and sight to know exactly when a cake is ready.

Check on your cake first through the window because your oven loses heat very quickly once the door is open.

If your cake is not yet domed or "puffed" in the center, it's best to leave the oven door closed; there's no reason to lose heat when the cake is still most likely underbaked in the center.

If the cake is domed, color and aroma are the next indicators of doneness: White or yellow cakes should be golden brown; chocolate cakes should be fragrant.

Cakes should bounce back when gently pressed in the center. If your finger leaves an indentation (and the cake doesn't bounce back), the cake needs more time.

The cake will begin to pull away from the sides of the pan when fully baked.

The final test is to insert a tester or toothpick into the center. It should come out clean or with just a few moist crumbs attached. There should be no visible wet batter.

Let most 8″ to 9″ cakes cool in the pan for 10 to 15 minutes on a wire rack before unmolding them. Unmolding them any sooner can cause hot cakes to fall apart, as their structure is not yet set. Use a small offset spatula to gently go around the outside of the cake pan, then invert the cake into your hand or onto another wire rack. Remove the parchment paper from the bottom, then turn the cake right side up and allow it to cool completely before frosting or wrapping or freezing.

Classic Yellow Cake

Yield: one 8″ round single layer (easily doubles for two-layer cake)

This yellow cake recipe was formulated to use our unbleached cake flour and gives wonderfully tender results if you choose that flour—if you don't have it, all-purpose flour will work but won't yield as fine a crumb. We cream the butter and sugar mixture for a long time—up to 5 minutes—to really aerate the batter, which lightens the texture of the cake as you're beating in air and trapping it within the ingredients. This is the basic layer for a birthday cake and can be combined with any of the icings at the end of the chapter.

---

85 grams (6 tablespoons) unsalted butter, room temperature

149 grams (¾ cup) granulated sugar

¼ teaspoon salt

6 grams (1½ teaspoons) baking powder

1 teaspoon vanilla extract

2 large eggs, room temperature

150 grams (1¼ cups) unbleached cake flour, sifted

89 grams (¼ cup + 2 tablespoons) milk, room temperature

1. Preheat the oven to 350°F. Lightly grease an 8″-diameter, 2″-high round pan and line it with parchment.

2. Combine the butter, sugar, salt, baking powder, and vanilla in the bowl of a stand mixer and cream on medium-high speed until light and fluffy. This can take from 2 to 5 minutes, depending on your mixer.

3. Add the eggs, one at a time, beating well at medium-high speed and scraping the sides and bottom of the bowl after each addition.

4. Add the flour in thirds, alternating with the milk, beginning and ending with the cake flour. Scrape the bowl well after each addition.

5. Pour the batter into the prepared pan and smooth the top.

6. Bake the cake for 23 to 27 minutes, until a tester inserted into the center comes out clean and the edges pull away from the pan.

7. Remove the cake from the oven and let cool in the pan for 10 minutes before turning it out of the pan onto a rack. Let cool completely before storing or frosting.

THE CREAMING METHOD

For cakes that utilize the creaming method, butter and sugar are beaten together before you add the eggs. Then you add the flour and liquid, alternating between both, always starting and ending with the flour to emulsify the batter. There are a few tips that we teach students to ensure success with creamed cakes:

1. It's important to use room-temperature ingredients when making any creamed cake that calls for softened or room-temperature butter. The temperature of the other ingredients affects the temperature of the butter—so if you've gone through the trouble to soften the butter but the rest of your ingredients are very cold, they'll cool the butter and affect how the batter comes together. Keeping everything at room temperature will yield a finer crumb structure and a softer, "fluffier" texture. If you're taking your eggs straight from the refrigerator, warm them in a bowl of hot water for a few minutes to take the chill off.

2. Add the leavener, salt, and flavorings with the butter and sugar mixture. This ensures that the ingredients get fully distributed within the mixture.

3. Once you start adding the flour, be sure to mix just to combine. Beating the batter too much once the wet and dry ingredients have been combined can result in too much gluten formation (gluten forms when water and flour combine, and even more forms through the physical act of mixing), which can lead to a tough, chewy cake (not our ideal descriptors!).

UNDERCREAMED

PERFECTLY CREAMED

OVERCREAMED

Tender White Cake

Yield: one 8″ round single layer (easily doubles for two-layer cake)

When King Arthur shifted from making bleached cake flour to unbleached cake flour, we developed this cake to highlight its benefits. It uses the paste method of mixing to make a cake with a fine, light, tender crumb. The paste method sounds intimidating, but it's actually what you're doing when you make cake from a boxed mix. It involves beating the butter into the dry ingredients (rather than creaming the butter and sugar, adding eggs, then adding liquid and dry ingredients). By beating well after the addition of each egg, we're able to build the cake's structure. Using egg whites, not yolks, gives it a whiter appearance and lighter flavor, making it a good foil for fillings and icings with more dominant flavors, such as citrus-scented buttercream or a bold mocha frosting.

---

210 grams (1¾ cups) unbleached cake flour

198 grams (1 cup) granulated sugar

8 grams (2 teaspoons) baking powder

½ teaspoon salt

113 grams (8 tablespoons) unsalted butter, room temperature

1 large egg, room temperature

2 large egg whites, room temperature

119 grams (½ cup) milk, room temperature

1 teaspoon vanilla extract

1 teaspoon almond extract (optional)

Tip: Almond extract adds a nice depth of flavor, reminiscent of many wedding cakes or bakery sheet cakes.

1. Preheat the oven to 350°F. Lightly grease an 8″-diameter, 2″-high round cake pan and line it with parchment.

2. Combine the flour, sugar, baking powder, and salt in the bowl of a stand mixer and mix on low speed.

3. Add the butter and mix on medium-low speed until evenly crumbly, like fine, damp sand.

4. Add the whole egg and then the egg whites, one at a time, mixing on medium speed after each addition. Scrape down the paddle, sides, and bottom of the bowl after each addition.

5. Combine the milk, vanilla, and almond extract. Add this mixture in three parts, mixing the batter at medium speed for 1 minute and scraping down the paddle, sides, and bottom of the bowl after each addition. The batter should be smooth and look fluffy.

6. Transfer the batter to the prepared pan, gently smoothing the top.

7. Bake the cake for about 40 minutes, or until a tester inserted into the center comes out clean and the edges pull away from the pan.

8. Remove the cake from the oven and let cool in the pan for 10 minutes before turning it out of the pan onto a rack. Let cool completely before storing or frosting.

The Paste Method

Although there's a lot of beating with this method, it still makes for a wonderfully tender cake. Why? Mixing the butter directly into the dry ingredients coats most of the flour with butter, which reduces the amount of liquid needed and keeps the cake tender. On top of that, cake flour has less protein (thus less capacity for gluten production) than all-purpose flour, so that's another way we add tenderness. To build structure in the cake, we introduce mechanical leavening through mixing. The introduction of air helps to create a fluffy, fine-textured cake with an exceptionally tender crumb. If we just mixed the milk in to combine, without beating sufficiently, the mixture would look broken/separated and the final cake would be dense and moist instead of light and fluffy.

Maple-Pear Upside-Down Cake

Yield: one 9″ round cake

This New England twist on the classic upside-down cake is a finely textured cake that creams the butter and sugar until just combined. We use it in our classroom to introduce students to the heartiness of whole-grain flour in cakes (paired here with a hint of spice, making it a perfect dessert from early fall to late spring). Allow the cake to cool slightly before serving warm or at room temperature with a scoop of vanilla ice cream or dollop of lightly sweetened whipped cream. For a change of pace, try this with your favorite apple variety as well.

TOPPING

57 grams (4 tablespoons) unsalted butter, melted

156 grams (½ cup) pure maple syrup

1 to 2 large pears, cored and sliced ¼″ thick

CAKE

113 grams (8 tablespoons) unsalted butter, room temperature

159 grams (¾ cup) brown sugar

½ teaspoon salt

½ teaspoon cinnamon

½ teaspoon ginger

8 grams (2 teaspoons) baking powder

3 large eggs, room temperature

198 grams (1¾ cups) white whole wheat flour

178 grams (¾ cup) buttermilk, room temperature

TOPPING

1. Preheat the oven to 350°F. Lightly grease a 9″ round pan and line it with parchment.

2. In a small bowl or liquid measure, whisk together the butter and syrup and pour into the prepared pan.

3. Arrange the sliced pears in the bottom of the pan. Set aside.

CAKE

1. Place the butter, brown sugar, salt, cinnamon, ginger, and baking powder in the bowl of a stand mixer and mix on medium speed until well combined.

2. Add the eggs, one at a time, scraping the bottom and sides of the bowl between additions.

3. Add the flour and buttermilk alternately in three additions, beginning and ending with the flour. Beat gently until combined.

4. Spread the batter over the pears.

5. Bake the cake for 30 to 40 minutes, until a tester inserted in the center comes out clean.

6. Remove the cake from the oven and let it cool in the pan for 5 minutes, then invert it onto a plate. Be sure to unmold the cake while it's still warm—if the cake cools too much in the pan, it can stick to the bottom and won't unmold properly. Once you flip it, allow it cool completely before serving.

Tip: If the cake does start to stick, pop it back in a warm oven for a few minutes and try unmolding again.

Upside-Down Cake Removal

After baking, allow the cake to cool for 5 to 10 minutes in the pan before unmolding it; this reduces the fragility of the cake when inverting it. Gently run an offset spatula or knife around the edge of the pan to loosen the cake. For best success when inverting the warm cake, place your nondominant hand, covered with an oven mitt, under the warm cake pan. Then place a platter or cutting board on top of the cake, with your dominant hand opened wide on the top of the platter or board. In a careful yet swift motion, flip everything so that the platter and your dominant hand are now on the bottom and your nondominant hand is on top of the inverted cake pan. Set the platter or board down, then carefully remove the cake pan.

How Many Pears?

As we all know, fruit comes in all shapes and sizes, and you may need 1 or 2 pears to slice and cover the bottom of the 9˝ cake pan when slightly shingling (overlapping) them. The ripeness of the pear also plays a role: If the pear is very ripe, you'll want to use slightly thicker slices so that they hold their shape during baking, meaning you'll get fewer slices out of each pear. If your pear is underripe, you'll need to make thinner slices so that they bake through (so you'll get more slices out of each pear). Sometimes you end up with a small area in the center of the pan, where the tips of the slices meet, that isn't covered. When that happens, we have students fill in the gap with some diced pear, which gives the pan a pretty flowerlike pattern. In class, we usually end up using about 1½ large pears, then students snack on the extras!

Lemon Bundt Cake

Yield: one 10-cup Bundt cake

We love Maida Heatter's East 62nd Street Lemon Cake so much that we began to include it in our curriculum: We needed to spread the (delicious) word! It's a great example of a simple creamed butter cake made in a Bundt pan for a different presentation. The intensity of flavor comes from a double hit of citrus: lemon zest in the cake and fresh lemon juice in the glaze. You can switch out flavorings if you like, substituting orange for lemon or making the glaze with other flavors, but the lemon version remains our favorite. Here, the proportions of ingredients are similar to a pound cake (yielding a denser, sturdier crumb) and we cream the butter and sugar to aerate, which helps lighten the structure.

CAKE

227 grams (16 tablespoons) unsalted butter, room temperature

397 grams (2 cups) granulated sugar

1 teaspoon salt

8 grams (2 teaspoons) baking powder

zest of **1 large** lemon

4 large eggs

360 grams (3 cups) unbleached all-purpose flour

237 grams (1 cup) milk, room temperature

GLAZE

79 grams (⅓ cup) lemon juice

149 grams (¾ cup) granulated sugar

CAKE

1. Preheat the oven to 350°F.

2. Combine the butter, sugar, salt, baking powder, and lemon zest in the bowl of a stand mixer and cream on medium-high speed until light and fluffy.

3. Add the eggs, one at a time, scraping the sides and bottom of the bowl occasionally.

4. Mix one-third of the flour into the creamed mixture, then half of the milk.

5. Repeat this process with the remaining flour and milk, beginning and ending with the flour. Scrape the sides and bottom of the bowl to incorporate all the ingredients after each addition.

6. Generously spray a 10-cup Bundt pan with nonstick spray. Scoop the batter into the prepared pan.

7. Bake the cake for about 40 minutes, or until a toothpick inserted in the center comes out clean.

8. Allow the cake to cool in the pan for 10 to 20 minutes before inverting it onto a wire rack.

GLAZE

1. In a small bowl, whisk together the lemon juice and sugar.

2. Generously brush the glaze over the warm cake.

3. Allow the cake to cool completely before serving.

Unmolding Bundt Cakes

There's little more disheartening than baking an entire cake only to have it fall apart when you flip it over. This happens more commonly with Bundt cakes, since the pans tend to have all sorts of intricate nooks and crannies where batter can stick. If you've thoroughly sprayed the pan, it should release cleanly! A few tips to encourage proper unmolding:

1. In most cake recipes, we instruct you to prep your cake pan before you begin assembling the batter. This helps keep things organized, and you're all ready to go as soon as your batter is ready. We make an exception with Bundt pans because we tend to spray these pans more heavily than we'd grease other cake pans, as there are sometimes intricate designs where batter can stick. Preparing the pan just before adding the batter helps keep all that spray from pooling in the bottom of the pan (which will eventually become the top of the cake when inverted).

2. The cake should still be quite warm when you unmold it: If it cools too much, it will likely stick to the pan. The pan should be somewhat hot, but not so hot that you can't hold it in your hands for long enough to invert the cake (it should take about 20 minutes to reach this temperature). If you have to use oven mitts to grab the pan, it's still too hot. If you've waited too long and the pan is barely warm to the touch (meaning you can comfortably hold it), you might need to heat it gently in the oven to loosen the cake before unmolding it.

3. We've found the best way to unmold a Bundt is to hold it between your hands as if it were a steering wheel. With the pan at a slight angle, gently tap all the way around the edges of the pan to loosen the cake. When you can see the cake begin to separate slightly from the sides, unmold it by placing a cutting board, wire rack, or serving plate on top and quickly flipping the pan over, then firmly tapping it on a countertop. Do this in one quick, sure, and fluid motion—commit and don't second-guess yourself partway through!

Gugelhupf

Yield: one 10-cup Bundt cake

This light, tender, rich cake comes to us from longtime instructor Melanie Wanders, whose time baking at her husband's family bakery in Germany gave her a deep appreciation for European baking traditions, including this exceptional recipe. The gugelhupf is creamed with confectioners' sugar instead of granulated, adding tenderness to the crumb. The eggs are separated and the whites are whipped into a meringue for increased lightness. Half of the batter is flavored with chocolate and rum to make a marbled cake that needs no further adornment than a dusting of confectioners' sugar once it cools.

---

191 grams (about 14 tablespoons) unsalted butter, room temperature

107 grams (¾ cup + 3 tablespoons) confectioners' sugar, plus more for garnish (optional)

6 grams (1½ teaspoons) baking powder

¼ teaspoon salt

7 grams (1½ teaspoons) vanilla extract

4 large eggs, separated, at room temperature

210 grams (1¾ cups) unbleached cake flour, sifted

89 grams (¼ cup + 2 tablespoons) milk, room temperature

99 grams (½ cup) granulated sugar

107 grams (½ cup + 2 tablespoons) chopped dark chocolate, melted and slightly cooled

16 grams (3 tablespoons) cocoa powder

44 grams (3 tablespoons) rum

1. Preheat the oven to 350°F.

2. Combine the butter, confectioners' sugar, baking powder, salt, and vanilla in the bowl of a stand mixer and cream on medium-high speed until light and fluffy, about 2 to 3 minutes.

3. Add the egg yolks, one at time, mixing well after each addition. Scrape the paddle, sides, and bottom of the bowl a few times to ensure even mixing.

4. Add the flour in thirds, alternating with the milk, beginning and ending with the flour. Mix well to combine. Set aside.

5. In a separate clean bowl of the mixer fitted with the whisk attachment, beat the egg whites until foamy. Stream in the granulated sugar and continue to beat until the meringue is glossy and soft peaks form.

6. Gently stir one-third of the meringue into the batter to lighten, then fold in the remaining meringue.

7. Divide the batter in half. Leave one portion plain. Stir the melted chocolate, cocoa powder, and rum into the remaining batter.

8. Generously spray a 10-cup Bundt pan with nonstick spray. Scoop dollops of plain and chocolate batter alternately around the prepared pan.

9. Bake the cake for 35 to 45 minutes, until a toothpick inserted into the center comes out clean.

10. Remove the cake from the oven and allow it to cool in the pan for 10 minutes before turning it onto a rack to cool completely.

11. Garnish the cooled cake with a dusting of confectioners' sugar, if desired.

Tip: You can marble the cake by running a toothpick or knife through the scoops, or leave as is.

Chocolate Chiffon Cake

Yield: one 12″ × 17″ cake

This rich, moist chocolate sponge was formulated specifically for our Bûche de Noël (page 362), with the added moisture making it easy to roll. A combination of mechanical leavening (beating egg yolks until thick and pale, and egg whites to medium peaks) and chemical leavening (adding both baking powder and baking soda) creates a light, airy cake. This cake utilizes all-purpose flour for stability to offset the addition of cocoa powder, which contains no structure-forming gluten.

---

60 grams (½ cup) unbleached all-purpose flour

32 grams (⅜ cup) cocoa powder

1 teaspoon baking powder

¼ teaspoon baking soda

⅛ teaspoon salt

148 grams (¾ cup) granulated sugar, divided

28 grams (2 large) egg yolks

75 grams (⅜ cup) vegetable oil

60 grams (¼ cup) water

½ teaspoon vanilla extract

105 grams (3 large) egg whites

1. Preheat the oven to 350°F. Line a half-sheet pan (13″ x 18″) with parchment, folding the parchment so it fits evenly into the bottom of the pan (see page 353). Spray the parchment and sides of the pan with nonstick spray. Set aside.

2. Sift the flour, cocoa powder, baking powder, baking soda, and salt into a medium bowl. Whisk to thoroughly combine and set aside.

3. Combine 99 grams (½ cup) of the sugar and the egg yolks in the bowl of a stand mixer fitted with the whisk attachment and beat on medium-high speed until thickened and pale in color.

4. Add the oil, water, and vanilla, mixing until well combined.

5. Add the dry flour mixture, mixing on medium speed until well combined. Scrape the bottom and sides of the bowl thoroughly and mix briefly.

6. In a separate clean mixer bowl, use a clean whisk attachment to whip the egg whites on medium speed until foamy.

7. Stream in the remaining 50 grams (¼ cup) of sugar and continue to whip on medium to medium-high speed until the whites are glossy and hold medium peaks.

8. Using a spatula, stir one-third of the egg whites into the chocolate mixture to lighten, then gently fold in the remaining whites, mixing just until incorporated.

9. Pour the batter into the prepared pan. Use an offset spatula to smooth and level the batter; it'll be a thin layer.

10. Bake until the edges of the cake pull away from the pan and the cake springs back when lightly pressed, about 10 to 15 minutes. Remove from the oven and let cool completely.

Keep It Light

The success of a chiffon cake largely depends upon avoiding deflating the egg whites once you've beaten them into a beautiful, shiny meringue cloud. To avoid this, use a careful hand when folding the egg whites into the flour mixture. Start with a smaller amount of egg white to lighten the heavier flour mixture, then add more once you've folded in the first amount. Aim to use an "up and over" motion rather than a circular stirring motion to keep as much air as possible in the mixture. Once your batter is ready, use a silicone (or rubber) spatula or a small offset spatula to spread it evenly in the prepared pan: A gentle touch, using as few strokes as possible, will reduce any unnecessary deflation.

This same method applies when folding other ingredients—melted butter, nut flour, cocoa powder, melted chocolate—into your batter. Whenever a cake recipe calls for folding, the goal is to avoid deflating the air you've carefully beaten into your batter.

Joconde

Yield: one 12″ × 17″ cake

Joconde is the cake component of the multilayered Opera Torte (page 367). A thin sponge cake made with almond flour, it's also used as a patterned cake layer to wrap around mousse cakes (joconde imprimé). Joconde has no chemical leavener, relying solely on the beating and folding in of egg whites to make a light, airy cake. Spread the batter in an even layer and be sure not to overbake to yield a moist, delicate cake. Brush with simple syrup and layer with your favorite filling.

---

95 grams (1 cup) almond flour

95 grams (¾ cup + 1 tablespoon) confectioners' sugar, sifted

118 grams (2 large) eggs

81 grams (2 large) egg whites

13 grams (1 tablespoon) granulated sugar

29 grams (¼ cup) unbleached all-purpose flour, sifted

22 grams (1½ tablespoons) unsalted butter, melted

1. Preheat the oven to 400°F. Line a half-sheet pan (13″ × 18″) with parchment and spray generously with nonstick spray.

2. Place the almond flour and confectioners' sugar in the bowl of a mixer fitted with the whisk attachment and mix until combined.

3. Add the whole eggs, mixing on medium-low speed until well combined.

4. In a separate clean bowl, whip the egg whites until foamy, then stream in the granulated sugar and continue to beat until the meringue is glossy and holds a medium peak.

5. Fold one-third of the meringue into the almond flour mixture to lighten, then fold in the remaining two-thirds.

6. Fold in the flour, then the melted butter.

7. Use an offset spatula to spread the batter evenly in the prepared pan; the layer will be very thin.

8. Bake the joconde for 5 to 7 minutes, until it's pale golden in color and springs back when touched.

Tip: Be mindful not to overbake—the edges can get hard and brittle if you do.

Parchment Precision

Some of the more delicate cakes have loose batters that conform to the shape of your pan. These recipes call for parchment-lined pans, and if your parchment isn't neatly folded and has crinkles, the batter will flow into them and the edges of the cake won't be neat. Fold the parchment carefully, creasing it firmly so it keeps its shape and gives your cakes uniform, precise edges.

MAKING CAKES AHEAD

We recommend baking any cakes that you'll layer or decorate at least 1 day ahead of time. That way, the starches in the cake will have a chance to set up, making the crumb less fragile when splitting the cake into layers. It also ensures the cake is completely cool—if you try to decorate a still-warm cake, you run the risk of the frosting melting as you spread it.

If you plan to assemble and decorate your cake the day you bake it, you'll want to chill the layers in the refrigerator until they're completely cooled. You can do this without wrapping them since they'll be in the fridge for a relatively short time. If you plan to decorate the next day, wrap your cake layers well or store them in an airtight container overnight.

If you're baking your cake more than a day or two before assembling, let it cool completely, wrap it well in plastic wrap, then wrap it again in plastic wrap, foil, or a resealable plastic bag before freezing. This double wrapping prevents any aromas from leaching into your cake and reduces the risk of condensation when thawing. You can do this up to 1 month ahead of time.

Buttercreams, including American-style and meringue-based, can also be made ahead. If you're using the buttercream within 24 hours of making it, cover it and leave it at room temperature so it remains soft and spreadable. You can make buttercream up to a week ahead of time and store it in an airtight container in the refrigerator or freeze it for up to 1 month. (See buttercream troubleshooting, page 359, for more on using frozen or refrigerated buttercream.)

While baking your cake and preparing your buttercream ahead of time will save you time on the day of assembly, you can also assemble the entire cake ahead, then freeze it. This is helpful if you're planning intricate decorations or garnishes for the day you serve it.

Freezing won't harm the cake at all, so don't worry about it being less delicious than a freshly baked cake. To freeze an iced cake: Once you've applied your final layer of buttercream, chill your cake for at least 30 minutes, or until the buttercream feels cold and firm to the touch. Meringue-based buttercreams don't need to be covered for this step, but American buttercreams should be lightly covered or placed in an airtight container before chilling. This extra step of chilling and setting the buttercream will allow you to wrap the cake for freezing without blemishing the frosted surface of your cake.

Double-wrap the cake with plastic wrap or foil to prevent freezer burn and freeze for up to 1 month. The day before you plan to serve the cake, transfer it from the freezer to the refrigerator, allowing it to thaw slowly overnight. The next day, remove the wrapping. Note that it's helpful to make any finishing touches on a cold-from-the-refrigerator cake, so you can easily make small changes while piping or adding decorations without damaging the base frosting.

Serve meringue-based buttercreams at room temperature. Because they contain a high amount of butter, serving them at room temperature ensures the texture will be light and creamy instead of hard and buttery. American-style buttercreams can be served chilled (giving them a bit of "resistance" when you bite into the frosting) or at room temperature (making them soft and creamy). Allow enough time for the finished cake to come to room temperature before serving. Depending on the ambient temperature of your kitchen and size of your cake, that can take up to an entire day.

Vanilla Buttercream

Yield: enough to frost and fill one 8″ round double-layer cake

This is the frosting many of us grew up with—quite sweet with a thick, luscious, easy-to-spread consistency. We make ours entirely with butter, though you may be familiar with versions made with shortening. It's so simple to make that we even teach it to first-graders in our kids' camps, and they're so proud of the cupcakes they decorate to take home and share.

---

170 grams (12 tablespoons) unsalted butter, room temperature

⅛ teaspoon salt

9 grams (2 teaspoons) vanilla extract

340 grams (3 cups) confectioners' sugar

30 grams (2 tablespoons) milk, or more as needed, room temperature

1. Combine the butter, salt, and vanilla in the bowl of a stand mixer and cream on medium-high speed until light and fluffy.

2. Add the confectioners' sugar, then mix on low speed until combined.

3. Add 15 grams (1 tablespoon) of milk, mixing to combine. If needed, add additional milk to make the frosting spreadable.

4. Buttercream may be used right away, stored in an airtight container in the refrigerator up to 1 week, or frozen up to 3 months. Thaw the buttercream overnight in the refrigerator, then bring to room temperature. Stir the buttercream thoroughly before using.

Tip: Aim for the consistency of peanut butter.

The Smoothest Frostings

For a perfectly smooth texture, do two things. First, sift your confectioners' sugar. Second, have your milk at room temperature or close to it. If you're using it straight from the refrigerator, heat it slightly in the microwave to take off the chill.

FILLING A PASTRY BAG

You can always frost a cake with an offset spatula, creating a smooth or rustic appearance depending on your technique. If, however, you want to do any sort of piping work or decorative frosting design, use a pastry bag. Although it takes a bit of practice to get the hang of filling the bag with frosting and piping neatly, it's not complicated—here are the steps we use:

1. If you're using a piping tip, cut a small piece off the bottom of the bag and place the tip in the bag, pushing it taut against the bottom of the bag. If you are not using a pastry tip, wait to cut the bag until you are ready to pipe.

2. Fold the top third of the bag back over itself. Cup your nondominant hand like a C underneath the fold of the bag, so that the bag is resting on the C of your hand. Scoop the batter or buttercream with a spatula into the bag, using the hand "covered" with the piping bag to scrape off the spatula. Continue to fill until the buttercream reaches just below the C of your hand. Unfold the top of the bag and lay it flat. Using the flat end of a spatula or bowl scraper, force the buttercream down into the bottom of the bag. This should leave you with a few inches of unfilled pastry bag at the top.

3. Twist the bag to seal it, then pinch the twist of the bag right above the buttercream between your thumb and forefinger. Gently wrap your other fingers around the filled pastry bag.

4. Imagine holding your hand as if you were arm wrestling: Insert the bag between your thumb and forefinger. To exert pressure, gently squeeze your fist. All pressure should come from the top of the bag as you clench your fist. You can use your nondominant hand to guide or steady the pastry bag, but refrain from squeezing from the bottom with your nondominant hand (this forces the buttercream up and out of the top of the bag, and you'll end up with more buttercream on your hand than where you want to pipe it!). Keeping the fingers of your nondominant hand open flat or steadying the bag with just the tips of your fingers can help fight the urge to squeeze from the bottom.

5. Before piping, squeeze a bit of "test" buttercream out to release any air bubbles in the bag. (If you're piping without a tip, now's the time to cut the bag, then squeeze a bit back into the bowl.)

6. Two things to avoid: Overfilling the bag and putting pressure on the bottom of the bag to force the contents upward—both are the most common mistakes that cause bags to overflow.

American-Style Chocolate Buttercream

Yield: enough to fill and frost one 8″ round double-layer cake

Everyone needs a go-to chocolate frosting! This is a chocolate version of our vanilla buttercream, and the same lessons on technique apply (including having the liquid at room temperature). We like to use Dutch-process cocoa here, which yields a warm, reddish-brown color reminiscent of milk chocolate. (Avoid black cocoa powder, which will make the buttercream appear gray.) To prevent showers of cocoa powder or confectioners' sugar across your kitchen, start by mixing in the dry ingredients at low speed, then increase the speed as they're incorporated.

---

170 grams (12 tablespoons) unsalted butter, room temperature

¼ teaspoon salt

1 teaspoon vanilla extract

43 grams (⅓ cup) cocoa powder

79 grams (⅓ cup) heavy cream, or more as needed, room temperature

340 grams (3 cups) confectioners' sugar, sifted

1. Place the butter, salt, and vanilla in the bowl of a stand mixer and beat until smooth.

2. Add the cocoa powder, mixing on low speed.

3. Stream in the heavy cream, then increase the speed, beating to combine. If the mixture looks curdled, continue to beat until it smooths out.

4. Add the confectioners' sugar and mix to combine.

5. Adjust the consistency with more cream if necessary. The frosting should be thick but spreadable.

Swiss Meringue Buttercream

Yield: enough to fill and frost one 8″ round double-layer cake

This buttercream is like a cloud of sweetness to top your cakes. It's certainly more challenging to make than American-style buttercream, but the silky-smooth texture makes it worth the effort. There are so many ways to flavor this base recipe, and we recommend you try some of the suggestions listed here.

---

148 grams (about 4 large) egg whites

198 grams (1 cup) granulated sugar

⅛ teaspoon salt

340 grams (24 tablespoons) unsalted butter, softened

15 grams (1 tablespoon) vanilla extract (see variations below)

1. Place the egg whites, sugar, and salt in the bowl of a mixer and place the bowl over a pan of simmering water.

2. Whisk gently and constantly until the egg whites are hot (about 161°F) and the sugar is dissolved, about 3 to 5 minutes.

3. Remove the bowl from the heat and transfer to the mixer fitted with a whisk attachment. Beat until thick and glossy, about 5 minutes. The mixture should feel just warm to the touch, have considerably more volume, and look glossy like shaving cream.

4. Add the butter a little at a time while mixing on medium speed; continue to mix until the buttercream is smooth and spreadable. Stir in the vanilla.

Buttercream Variations

In place of the vanilla extract, you can use other flavoring options.

Chocolate: Add 170 grams (1 cup) dark or white chocolate, melted and slightly cooled.

Almond: Add 2 teaspoons almond extract and 1 teaspoon vanilla extract.

Spirited: Add 30 to 45 grams (2 to 3 tablespoons) of any type of liqueur.

Citrus: Add the zest of 3 to 4 small lemons or limes, 2 large oranges, or 1 large grapefruit; or 59 grams (¼ cup) freshly squeezed citrus juice; or 1 teaspoon citrus oil.

Coffee: Add 7 grams (1 tablespoon) espresso powder dissolved in 15 grams (1 tablespoon) vanilla extract.

BUTTERCREAM TROUBLESHOOTING TIPS

If you've beaten the buttercream for 5 minutes after the last addition of butter and it's still too soft and runny: The meringue may have been too warm when incorporating the butter. Try chilling the bowl in the refrigerator or freezer for 5 to 10 minutes and then beat again. Repeat this process until the buttercream is smooth and the correct consistency.

If you've beaten the buttercream for 5 minutes after the last addition of butter and it resembles cottage cheese: The butter or the meringue may have been too cold when incorporating the butter. With the mixer running, gently heat the bottom and sides of the bowl with a hair dryer until the buttercream around the edges just starts to melt. Continue to mix until the buttercream is smooth and creamy. Alternatively, remove the bowl from the mixer, place it over a pot of simmering water for a few seconds, then return it to the mixer, mixing until it is smooth and the correct consistency. Repeat as necessary until you obtain the correct consistency.

If you've refrigerated or frozen the buttercream and it's still solid: Allow the buttercream to sit out at room temperature a few hours or overnight, until it reaches room temperature. Place the buttercream in the bowl of a stand mixer. Proceed with heating and beating as described above.

Using a Bain-Marie

The terms bain-marie, double boiler, and water bath are often used interchangeably, but we're looking for a specific method for the Swiss Meringue Buttercream. You don't need to buy a special piece of equipment for this; all you need is a medium saucepan and a heatproof, preferably metal, bowl. When cooking ingredients, such as the egg whites and sugar, over a bain-marie, as we do for the Swiss meringue buttercream, there should be about 2″ of water in the pot. The bottom of the bowl should *not* touch the water: It's the steam coming up from the water that heats the ingredients rather than the hot water itself. When mixing over the simmering water, you don't need to whisk fast (you're not trying to incorporate volume into the mixture): Just aim to keep the mixture in motion so that the egg whites don't start to coagulate and cook. During this process, we're melting the sugar *and* pasteurizing the egg whites. Keep a thermometer handy, or carefully use your knuckle to test the temperature of the egg whites. The mixture should feel like a very hot bath (think "I've-had-a-very-long-tough-day" hot bath). If you start to smell sulfur, remove the egg white mixture as soon as possible from the heat and continue to whisk until you can start whipping the mixture. If you see white flecks of coagulated egg white, start over.

Italian Meringue Buttercream

Yield: enough to fill and frost one 8˝ round double-layer cake

This is the buttercream we use in our cake decorating classes (where we make it in quadruple batches in a 20-quart mixer!). Italian meringue offers more stability to the icing, making it perfect for decorating, but it's a little trickier to make than the Swiss meringue. The biggest challenge is getting the hot syrup into the meringue while you're whipping—it can help to try to pour close to the edge of the bowl. Otherwise, you can find the syrup flung around the edges of the bowl. There may come a moment when adding the butter when you think the buttercream has failed, but persevere, keep beating, and you'll wind up with a wonderfully stable, billowy buttercream, perfect for decorating.

---

57 grams (¼ cup) water

198 grams (1 cup) granulated sugar, divided

21 grams (1 tablespoon) honey

113 grams (about 3 large) egg whites

340 grams (1½ cups) unsalted butter, room temperature

7 grams (1½ teaspoons) vanilla extract

1. Place the water in a small saucepot with 170 grams (¾ cup plus 2 tablespoons) of the sugar and the honey. Stir to combine and bring the sugar syrup to a boil. Using a candy thermometer, keep an eye on the temperature. Should there be sugar crystallizing on the sides of the pot, wash down with a clean pastry brush dipped in water.

2. When the sugar syrup reaches about 225°F to 230°F, begin whipping the egg whites on medium speed. When foamy, turn to high speed. Add the remaining 28 grams (2 tablespoons) of sugar gradually and whip to soft peaks.

3. When the sugar syrup reaches 238°F, pour it steadily over the whites, still whipping on high speed.

4. Continue to whip until the bowl feels cooler, just warm to the touch. At that point, add the butter in small handfuls. At the last addition, continue to mix for several more minutes, or until the buttercream is smooth and workable (the consistency of mayonnaise). Add the vanilla.

Bûche de Noël

Yield: 1 Bûche de Noël

Gracing many holiday tables around the world, this festive dessert combines and builds upon many techniques you've learned in this chapter thus far. A basic Swiss meringue buttercream is adorned with a hint of espresso powder and melted chocolate to create a velvety, rich mocha buttercream. To create the garnishes, we make the same Swiss meringue base, with a pinch of cream of tartar added to strengthen and stabilize the mixture, then pipe it into stems and caps and bake them low and slow to create whimsical meringue mushrooms. Fresh cranberries are coated in a thick simple syrup, then rolled in granulated sugar to create a frosted edible garnish. An optional dusting of nonmelting sugar over the cake completes the winter scene. Remember that meringue-based buttercreams are best served at room temperature, so be sure to remove your cake from the refrigerator a few hours before serving to give the buttercream a chance to soften. If you want to take the cake to great decorative heights, add a few marzipan or fondant holly leaves.

---

one 12″ × 17″ Chocolate Chiffon Cake (page 350)

1 batch Mocha Buttercream (recipe follows)

1 batch Meringue Mushrooms (recipe follows)

1 batch Sugared Cranberries (recipe follows)

1. Place the cake on a clean work surface with a long side directly in front of you.

2. Spread about one-third of the buttercream evenly over the surface of the cake to the edge of three of the sides, leaving about a 1″ border of bare cake along the long side farthest away from you.

3. Using the parchment for assistance and starting with the filled long edge nearest you, roll the cake into a log, completely enclosing the filling. Wrap the parchment around the log and refrigerate until the filling is firm.

4. Remove the log from the refrigerator and unwrap it.

5. Transfer the log to a serving platter. Cut a 1″ to 1½″ slice off one end and place it on top of the cake as a small "knothole."

6. Slice two 2″ diagonal pieces and place one on each side (with the diagonal cut pressed against the log). Or place one on the side, one on the bottom; these are "branches."

7. Frost the log with the remaining buttercream and use a fork or small offset spatula to create a bark pattern.

8. Garnish as desired with meringue mushrooms and sugared cranberries. The cake is best served at room temperature.

(Continued)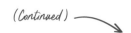

Mocha Buttercream

105 grams (3 large) egg whites

149 grams (¾ cup) granulated sugar

⅛ teaspoon salt

255 grams (1 cup + 2 table-spoons) unsalted butter, room temperature

1½ teaspoons espresso powder

8 grams (1½ teaspoons) vanilla extract

107 grams (½ cup + 2 table-spoons) dark chocolate, melted

1. Place the egg whites, sugar, and salt in the bowl of a stand mixer and set the bowl over a pan of simmering water.

2. Whisk the mixture gently and constantly until the egg whites are hot (about 161°F) and the sugar is dissolved, about 3 to 5 minutes.

3. Remove the bowl from the heat. Using the mixer fitted with a whisk attachment, beat the mixture on medium-high speed until thick and glossy, about 3 to 5 minutes; it should feel just warm to the touch.

4. Add the butter a little at a time, mixing on medium speed until the buttercream is smooth and spreadable.

5. Dissolve the espresso powder in the vanilla, then stir it into the buttercream along with the melted chocolate.

Tip: You can use the chocolate to adjust the texture of your buttercream. If the buttercream is dense and compact, use warm chocolate, and if it's already perfectly glossy and spreadable, be sure the chocolate is room temperature.

Meringue Mushrooms

70 grams (2 large) egg whites

99 grams (½ cup) granulated sugar

pinch of cream of tartar

22 grams (2 tablespoons) dark chocolate, melted

cocoa powder, as needed, for dusting

1. Preheat the oven to 225°F. Line a baking sheet with parchment. Set aside.

2. Place the egg whites, sugar, and cream of tartar in a bowl (preferably the bowl from a stand mixer) and set over a pan of simmering water.

3. Whisk the mixture gently and constantly until the egg whites are hot (about 161°F) and the sugar is dissolved, about 2 to 3 minutes.

4. Remove the bowl from the heat. Using the mixer fitted with a whisk attachment, beat the mixture on medium-high speed until the meringue is thick and glossy.

5. Transfer the meringue to a piping bag with a medium-size straight tip. Pipe round, flat "caps" about 1½″ across and an elongated "stem," about ½″ wide and 1″ tall, for each cap.

6. Bake the meringue mushrooms for 1 to 2 hours, until dry. Remove from the oven and let cool completely.

7. Affix the mushroom caps to their stems with a bit of melted chocolate, then dust the tops with cocoa powder.

8. Store completed meringue mushrooms in an airtight container at room temperature for up to 2 weeks.

Sugared Cranberries

297 grams (1½ cups) granulated sugar, divided

60 grams (¼ cup) water

50 grams (½ cup) fresh cranberries

1. Combine 99 grams (½ cup) of the sugar and water in a small pot over medium-low heat. Gently stir the mixture until the sugar is completely dissolved. Increase the heat to medium-high, bringing the mixture to a boil. Allow the mixture to boil, without stirring, until the mixture is thickened, about 2 to 3 minutes.

2. Transfer the simple syrup to a container, then refrigerate to cool completely.

3. In a medium bowl, toss the cranberries with a tablespoon or two of the simple syrup. The cranberries should be lightly coated in the sugar syrup.

4. Place the remaining 198 grams (1 cup) of sugar on a parchment-lined baking sheet.

5. Transfer the cranberries to the prepared pan, then gently shake the pan back and forth to coat the cranberries in sugar.

6. Allow the sugared cranberries to sit in the sugar until dry, about 1 to 2 hours. Store sugared cranberries, uncovered, at room temperature up to 3 days. Any leftover simple syrup may be stored, covered, in the refrigerator for up to 1 week.

Opera Torte

Yield: one 4″ × 12″ cake

Similar to the Bûche de Noël (page 362), this torte is a delicious symphony of classic components. Espresso powder and optional coffee liqueur liven up a standard simple syrup, which we brush over layers of joconde cake. The filling is a Swiss meringue buttercream to which we add espresso powder for a rich coffee flavor. Once assembled, the cake is chilled, then finished with a thin layer of dark chocolate ganache. Be sure the cake is completely cold before slicing (for the cleanest cut, use a knife that has been dipped in hot water and dried off). Wiping the knife clean after each cut ensures each piece of torte has precise edges for presentation. As with all meringue-based buttercreams, be sure to serve the torte at room temperature. This cake tastes best after resting in the refrigerator a day or two, which allows the flavors to meld and the joconde layers to soften.

---

one 12″ × 17″ Joconde (page 353)

1 batch Coffee Simple Syrup (recipe follows)

1 batch Coffee Buttercream (recipe follows)

1 batch Chocolate Ganache Glaze (recipe follows)

melted dark chocolate, as needed, for garnish

1. Using a sharp knife, cut the joconde into four equal pieces, each roughly 4″ × 12″.

2. Place one piece of joconde on a parchment-lined baking sheet. Using a pastry brush, generously soak the layer with some of the Coffee Simple Syrup.

3. Using an offset spatula, spread a thin layer of Coffee Buttercream on the cake, about the same thickness as the cake layer.

4. Top with another piece of joconde.

5. Soak the cake with more simple syrup, then spread with buttercream.

6. Repeat this procedure one more time for the third layer.

7. Invert the final piece of joconde on top of the buttercream to ensure the top layer is flat. Refrigerate the cake until the buttercream is firm.

8. Set the cake on a cooling rack and enrobe it with the ganache by pouring the ganache over the top, allowing it to cover the sides as well.

Tip: When pouring the ganache over the cake, be sure the cake is cool so the warm chocolate doesn't melt the buttercream.

(Continued) —→

9. Refrigerate the cake, uncovered, until the ganache is set and the buttercream is firm.

10. Cut the cake into 2″-wide slices, warming and wiping the knife as needed to achieve clean cuts.

11. To garnish, place a small amount of melted chocolate in a paper cone or pastry bag and pipe a design on top of each slice—if you want to get fancy, you can pipe the word "opera" in script, which is the traditional presentation. The torte is best served at room temperature.

Coffee Simple Syrup

60 grams (¼ cup) water

55 grams (¼ cup + ½ tablespoon) granulated sugar

15 grams (1 tablespoon) coffee liqueur

¼ teaspoon espresso powder

1. Place the water and sugar in a saucepan and bring the mixture to a boil over high heat. Stir occasionally, just until the sugar is dissolved.

2. Remove from the heat and stir in the liqueur and espresso powder.

3. Cover and chill until ready to use.

Coffee Buttercream

43 grams (about 1½ large) egg whites

75 grams (¼ cup + 2 tablespoons) granulated sugar

pinch of salt

128 grams (½ cup + 1 tablespoon) unsalted butter, room temperature

¼ teaspoon espresso powder

½ teaspoon vanilla extract

1. Place the egg whites, sugar, and salt in a bowl (preferably the bowl from a stand mixer) and set over a pan of simmering water. Whisk gently and constantly until the egg whites are hot (about 161°F) and the sugar is dissolved, about 5 minutes.

2. Remove the bowl from the heat. Using the mixer fitted with a whisk attachment, beat the mixture on high speed until thick and glossy, about 3 to 5 minutes; it should feel just warm to the touch.

3. Add the butter a little at a time, mixing on medium-low speed until the buttercream is smooth and spreadable.

4. In a small bowl, dissolve the espresso powder in the vanilla, then stir it into the buttercream.

Chocolate Ganache Glaze

170 grams (1 cup) dark chocolate, chopped

16 grams (2 teaspoons) honey

119 grams (½ cup) heavy cream

1. Place the chocolate in a heatproof bowl. Set aside.

2. Place the honey and cream in a small saucepan and bring to a boil over high heat.

3. Remove the pan from the heat and pour the hot cream over the chocolate. Allow the mixture to sit, undisturbed, for 1 minute.

4. Whisk the ganache, working mainly in the center, until it comes together. You should see no white streaks from the cream, and it should be smooth.

Simple Syrup

There's a long tradition of brushing baked cakes with simple syrup to add moisture and sweetness. You can also use it to vary the flavor of your cakes by brushing with a flavored simple syrup. To make simple syrup, heat equal parts granulated sugar and water over medium-low heat in a saucepan, gently stirring until the sugar is completely dissolved. Increase the heat to medium-high and simmer for about 3 minutes, until slightly thickened. Infuse flavors into the syrup by pouring the hot syrup over an ingredient (such as fresh herbs or spices, coffee beans, ginger root, berries, or citrus). Steep the mixture overnight in the refrigerator, then strain before using. If you're slicing your cake horizontally for layers, brush the syrup onto the cut side.

Advance Prep

For cakes with a lot of assembly and components, it's helpful to make as much ahead as you can (see page 354). Here, you can make the coffee syrup, the buttercream, and the ganache ahead of time. If you do make the ganache ahead of time, warm it up to a pourable consistency before using it to enrobe the cake.

Ganache Variations

Although a straightforward chocolate ganache is traditionally used in an opera torte, ganache lends itself nicely to additions. Infuse the cream by heating it with herbs or spices, coffee or tea, or even citrus zests, then strain the flavored cream over the chocolate. You can also add flavors after the ganache is made by stirring in 1 to 2 teaspoons of extract or 1 to 2 tablespoons (15 to 30 grams) of your favorite liqueur.

Master Class
Gâteau St. Honoré

Yield: six 3½″ × 7½″ gâteaux

THE BAKER

Gesine Bullock-Prado owns Sugar Glider Kitchen, a baking school in Hartford, Vermont. She's served as a guest judge on several television baking shows hosted her own Food Network show, *Baked in Vermont*; and is a prolific author, with six cookbooks to her name. Gesine has taught classes at the Baking School for more than a decade.

THE CAKE

The Gâteau St. Honoré is often regarded as the preeminent recipe for pastry chefs: It's the sum of multiple techniques that are the backbone of pastry (choux paste, puff pastry, pastry cream, and caramel), which is why it's named after the patron saint of bakers (Saint Honoré). Modernizing each element allows the baker to put their own spin on it: You can do it in the traditional round shape, or in a rectangle or square. You can customize each element with different flavors, as Gesine does with her autumnal twist on the pastry cream, inspired by her annual tradition of teaching a November class at King Arthur. You can coat the choux puffs with something other than caramel, such as a ganache or a poured fondant. Here, she builds on classic lamination techniques by using an inverse puff pastry: dough encased in butter instead of the other way around.

"

Students often ask, 'Why bother with inverse puff pastry instead of regular puff pastry?' Inverse puff is hands-down the most refined and beautiful pastry in the puff world. It has an exceptional texture that shatters with each bite—delicate, flaky, and the true expression of the Platonic ideal of puff pastry.

—GESINE BULLOCK-PRADO

Inverse Puff Pastry

Yield: 1.3 kilos (about 3 pounds) pastry dough

DOUGH

199 grams (⅞ cup) water

12 grams (2 teaspoons) salt

360 grams (3 cups) unbleached all-purpose flour, plus more for dusting

57 grams (4 tablespoons) unsalted butter, softened

BUTTER BLOCK

510 grams (36 tablespoons) unsalted butter, at cool room temperature, cut in 1″ chunks

227 grams (scant 2 cups) unbleached cake flour

Tip: Professional bakers, like our guest instructors, use weight—not volume—for best results (see page xvi for more on why).

DOUGH

1. Combine all the dough ingredients in the bowl of a stand mixer fitted with the dough hook. Mix on low speed until the dough just comes together, which can take up to 5 minutes. It will be fairly rough-looking and chunky.

2. Transfer the dough to a parchment-lined baking sheet and shape it into a rough 8″ × 6″ rectangle. Cover tightly with plastic wrap or a reusable cover and refrigerate for at least 1 hour.

BUTTER BLOCK

1. Combine the butter and cake flour in the bowl of a stand mixer and mix until smooth and pastelike.

2. Transfer the butter mixture to a piece of parchment and place a second piece of parchment on top. Using a rolling pin, shape it into an 8½″ × 12½″ rectangle; this is your butter block. Chill it for 10 minutes to firm up, then use a bench knife or chef's knife to trim just enough from the edges to make a perfectly rectangular block.

3. Refrigerate the butter block before using for about 30 minutes. It's important to get the temperature just right here, so check on it periodically: too cold and the block will break into pieces; too warm and it'll melt. When ready, the butter block will be firm and cool but will still bend without breaking.

LAMINATION

1. Place the chilled butter block on a lightly floured work surface. Place the dough block on the lower half of the butter block. Fold the top half of the butter block over the dough, like a turnover, and press on the three open edges to "lock in" the dough.

2. Turn the dough 90 degrees and roll it into a 10″ × 16″ rectangle. Fold the dough in thirds like a letter for your first letter fold.

3. Repeat step 2 for the second letter fold.

(Continued)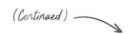

4. Wrap the dough securely and refrigerate for 1 hour. Repeat steps 2 and 3, rolling and folding twice.

5. Cover the dough and refrigerate it for at least 2 hours (or as long as overnight) before using.

6. When ready to roll the pastry, portion off a generous one-third of the pastry dough; use the remainder for something else or wrap and (freeze for later.)

Tip: The extra dough will keep, well wrapped, for up to 1 month in the freezer.

7. Preheat your oven to 375°F.

8. Roll the pastry piece into a ⅛″-thick rectangle, about 12″ × 16″. Place it in a parchment-lined half-sheet (13″ × 18″) pan.

9. Place a piece of parchment on top of the pastry, then put a second half-sheet pan on top; weigh it down with a cast-iron pan, bricks, or something else heavy and ovenproof.

10. Bake the pastry for 20 minutes, then remove the weights, top pan, and top piece of parchment. Continue to bake until the pastry is a deep golden brown, 10 to 20 minutes more. Remove the pastry from the oven and let it cool right on the pan. Trim the ragged edges before using.

11. Cut the pastry in half crosswise so you have two pieces about 11″ × 7½″. Cut each half into three equal strips lengthwise to make six approximately 3½″ × 7½″ strips.

Controlled Puff

To assemble the final gâteau properly, you don't want your puff pastry strips to be *too* puffy. It sounds counterintuitive, but here you're aiming for a nice flat surface (the pastry will still be wonderfully flaky) onto which you'll build the gâteau. This is why the recipe calls for weighing down the pastry with something heavy: It keeps the pastry flat as it bakes.

Two Flours, One Pastry

The puff pastry dough calls for all-purpose flour, but the butter block uses cake flour. Why two different flours? They're performing different functions: The all-purpose flour is forming gluten and giving structure to the dough, whereas the cake flour is acting as an absorption mechanism. For the butter block, the cake flour's function is solely to absorb some of the butter's moisture without adding gluten, as there's already enough in the dough. If you don't have cake flour, you can use all-purpose in both places, but the butter block won't have quite the same supple texture as it will with cake flour.

Choux Paste

120 **grams (1 cup)** unbleached all-purpose flour

¼ **teaspoon** salt

39 **grams (2 tablespoons)** sweetened condensed milk

113 **grams (½ cup)** whole milk

113 **grams (½ cup)** unsalted butter

5 **(or more) large** eggs

1. Preheat the oven to 425°F. Line two baking sheets with parchment paper.

2. Whisk together the flour and salt in a medium bowl.

3. Combine both milks and the butter in a medium saucepan, set over medium heat, and bring to a simmer.

4. Once simmering, pour the flour and salt mixture into the milk mixture all at once, stirring constantly with a spoon until the mixture thickens and forms a pastelike consistency while pulling away from the sides of the pan.

5. Transfer the paste to the bowl of a stand mixer and mix on medium speed for about a minute (this allows steam to evaporate).

6. Add the eggs, one at a time, mixing after each addition to make sure each egg is fully incorporated.

7. Continue to mix until a smooth, thick paste forms: It shouldn't be runny but should flow easily from a piping bag. If the mixture is still too thick to flow easily after you've added all five eggs, you may need to add one or two more eggs to achieve the proper consistency.

8. Transfer the paste to a piping bag fitted with a ½″ round tip and chill until ready to use.

9. Pipe into mounds about 1″ in diameter (the puffs will double in volume as they bake), leaving 2″ of space between them. Alternatively, if you don't have a pastry bag, drop the batter by teaspoonfuls onto the prepared sheets (a teaspoon-size cookie scoop works well here).

10. Bake the puffs for 15 minutes, then lower the oven temperature to 350°F and bake for 20 to 25 minutes more, until they're a medium golden brown. Don't open the oven door while the puffs are baking.

11. Remove the puffs from the oven and use a sharp knife to carefully cut a slit into the bottom of each for steam to escape. Return to the oven for 5 minutes, then remove from the oven and transfer to a rack to cool.

(Continued)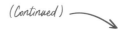

Chilling Your Choux

To encourage the choux to rise a bit more evenly, chill the choux paste overnight in the piping bag before piping it and baking. This will also deepen the flavor of the dough, and it's easier to pipe when chilled—a bonus.

Pumpkin Pastry Cream

99 grams (½ cup) granulated sugar

60 grams (¼ cup) water

⅛ teaspoon lemon juice

22 grams (1 cup) whole milk

227 grams (1 cup) heavy cream

6 large egg yolks

1 teaspoon vanilla extract, or **1 teaspoon** vanilla bean paste

pinch of salt

28 grams (¼ cup) cornstarch

113 grams (½ cup) pure pumpkin purée

1. In a large saucepan, combine the sugar, water, and lemon juice and stir over medium heat until the sugar has dissolved. Stop stirring and allow the mixture to turn a medium amber color.

2. Pour the milk and cream into the saucepan and stir over low heat until the caramel has completely melted into the dairy mixture.

3. Combine the egg yolks, vanilla, salt, and cornstarch in the bowl of a stand mixer fitted with the whisk attachment and whisk until smooth.

4. With the mixer running, slowly pour the caramel mixture into the egg yolk mixture and whisk until combined.

5. Transfer the mixture back to the saucepan and whisk over medium heat until it thickens to the consistency of mayonnaise.

6. Immediately stir in the pumpkin and mix until smooth.

7. Transfer the pastry cream to a large bowl and cover completely with plastic wrap. Refrigerate until cool.

Caramel

396 grams (2 cups) granulated sugar

120 grams (½ cup) water

1 teaspoon lemon juice

1. Combine the sugar, water, and lemon juice in a heavy saucepan set over medium heat and cook, stirring constantly, until the sugar has completely dissolved. Wash down the sides of pan to prevent any rogue sugar crystals from forming and increase the heat to medium high–high until the caramel turns a light amber color (the caramel will continue to cook and will reach a medium amber color off the stovetop).

2. Remove from the heat.

3. Carefully drop half-teaspoonfuls of caramel onto a piece of parchment; the sugar will continue to brown, and at the end you'll have a mixture of lighter and darker drops.

Whipped Cream

454 grams (2 cups) heavy cream

14 grams (2 tablespoons) confectioners' sugar

1. Whip the cream in a large bowl until soft peaks form.

2. Add the sugar and whip just until the mixture is slightly stiffer than soft peaks.

Gesine's Caramel Confidence

Caramel without added fat can crystallize easily, and Gesine teaches an unexpected trick—adding lemon juice—when she makes caramel in her classes. Adding an acid keeps sugar from recrystallizing by breaking down the sucrose molecules to fructose and glucose; similarly using an invert sugar, like corn syrup, keeps sugar from recrystallizing by diluting the sucrose molecules with glucose molecules. Using lemon juice keeps it simple and very French in style. Even with the addition of lemon juice, some sugar will crystallize on the pan as the caramel cooks. Be gentle as you stir, which will help keep the liquid from splashing up. If the crystals do form, wash down the sides of the pan by dipping a pastry brush lightly with water and brushing the inside of the pan just above where the sugar is crystallizing. Don't touch the cooked sugar; just touch right above so that the beads of water from your brush can gently encourage the errant sugar crystals back into the caramel. The caramel is ready when it reaches a color just beyond yellow (a pale amber); since it will continue to cook off the heat, you want to remove it from the heat just before it reaches the desired color of medium amber. If you find you've let it go too far and it's already reached the perfect color on the heat, stick the pan into an ice bath immediately to stop it from cooking further.

FINAL ASSEMBLY

1. Fold 2 cups of the whipped cream into the pastry cream. Fill a pastry bag with the mixture and pipe into the baked and cooled choux puffs.

2. Place the remaining whipped cream into another pastry bag fitted with a St. Honoré tip.

3. Place the puff pastry strips on a clean work surface. Use a small dollop of the caramel to affix four filled choux puffs down one side of each piece of puff pastry.

4. Pipe whipped cream in a swirl pattern to fill the other side of each piece of puff pastry.

5. Garnish with caramel.

INDEX

Bold page numbers indicate photographs.